Advance Praise

"In the early 1970s I read Tronti religio[...]

—Silvia Federici, author of *Revolution [...] Zero*

"Mario Tronti is one of the great intellectual and political figures of our age. The recognition of the importance of his work, not only as a contribution to revolutionary activism, but as a leap forward into the unknowns of specula-tion and praxis, after the 'end of history,' was long overdue. The beautiful an-thology assembled and introduced by Andrew Anastasi will make this clearly visible for a generation of new English-speaking readers, and even others."

—Étienne Balibar, coauthor of *Reading 'Capital'*

"*The Weapon of Organization* is a breakthrough in English-language schol-arship on Italian workerism, and the recovery of the history of revolutionary theory for the present. Andrew Anastasi has collected and translated pivotal texts, as well as situated them with his careful and illuminating commentary."

—Asad Haider, author of *Mistaken Identity*

"This illuminating collection provides not only an understanding of Tronti's influential anticapitalist theses but also a window into the political dynamics out of which they grew: the scene of revolutionary theory and practice in 1960s Italy. As Andrew Anastasi argues in his excellent introduction, Tronti's theses ought to be—and, in some senses, already are—central pillars of our own, contemporary political thought."

—Michael Hardt, coauthor of *Assembly* and *Commonwealth*

"Every generation of revolutionary anticapitalists has to come to terms with how to read afresh the classic formulations of Marx and Lenin in ways ap-propriate to the conditions of their times. How Tronti and some of his close colleagues did this in the 1960s is a spectacular and inspirational example of how to re-theorize class formation and the practices of class struggle from a ground-up and workerist perspective. While our contemporary world may be very different, there is much to be learned not only conceptually but also methodologically from Tronti's brilliant and incisive interventions at all levels in the politics of his era."

—David Harvey, author of *The Limits to Capital* and *Reading Marx's Capital*

The Weapon of Organization

Mario Tronti's Political Revolution in Marxism

Mario Tronti

Edited and translated by Andrew Anastasi

The Weapon of Organization: Mario Tronti's Political Revolution in Marxism
Edited and translated, with an introduction, by Andrew Anastasi

© by Andrew Anastasi (preface, introduction, translation, notes)
This edition © 2020 Common Notions

Chapters 1–14 and chapter 17 were published in Italian in *L'operaismo degli anni sessanta: da "Quaderni rossi" a "classe operaia"* © 2008 DeriveApprodi srl

ISBN: 978-1-942173-22-9
LCCN: 2020930534
10 9 8 7 6 5 4 3 2 1

Common Notions
c/o Interference Archive
314 7th St.
Brooklyn, NY 11215

Common Notions
c/o Making Worlds Books
210 S. 45th St.
Philadelphia, PA 19104

www.commonnotions.org
info@commonnotions.org

Cover design by Josh MacPhee / Antumbra Design
Layout design and typesetting by Morgan Buck / Antumbra Design
Antumbra Design www.antumbradesign.org

Printed in Canada on acid-free, recycled paper

Contents

Preface

Andrew Anastasi

Mario Tronti worked in the 1960s not to become a revered thinker but to contribute to the destruction of capitalist society. In his earliest writings he criticized how Marx had been absorbed into academic disciplines; it has been somewhat fitting, then, for Tronti to have experienced the opposite fate, remaining at the margins of Anglo-American political thought. This may now be changing as new translations ferry Tronti's work across time and space and provide entry points for a new generation of readers. As part of that larger endeavor, this book seeks to address a particular audience: those who are eager to explore Marxist theory in its rich diversity, who are rooted in the left organizations which have grown exponentially in recent years, and who have been nurtured by a thriving ecosystem of political debate online and in print.

This volume collects speeches and writings by Tronti that explore problems of Marxist theory insofar as they pertain to ongoing discussions about organization. They provide a window onto a living laboratory of thought, offering considerations and qualifications that complicate some of the claims found in *Workers and Capital*. That book contains his most important works, and it takes the reader on an exhilarating rollercoaster ride; it may also leave one with the sense that the political possibility glimpsed therein has been exhausted.[1] *The Weapon of Organization* instead returns to Tronti's work of the 1960s in pursuit of tools for struggle today. It does not approach his thought as a catechism; it seeks to learn from a process. The texts here, especially those originally spoken out loud and published without revision, provide not a snapshot of "what to think" but a framework of *how to think for revolution*.

Contributions to Marxist thought have often arrived by way of conjunctural interventions, as working-class movements provide the nourishment essential for theoretical discovery. The struggles of the 1960s inspired Tronti to

---

1. This may be especially true for the contemporary reader. Compare the exuberance of a line such as "give us the party in Italy and we will overthrow all of Europe!" to the tragic key in which Tronti reflects on this period. See Mario Tronti, "A Course of Action" [1966], in *Workers and Capital*, trans. David Broder (London: Verso, 2019), xv–xxxiv, xxxi; compare to "Our *Operaismo*," trans. Eleanor Chiari, in *Workers and Capital*, 327–48.

invert canonical readings of Marx, subject dogma of the Italian Communist Party (PCI) to withering criticism, and revisit his own output with a skeptical eye. Likewise, we should reject an uncritical Trontismo adhering to the letter of his writings without regard for the aims and needs of our movements.[2] Adapting Tronti's thought for our own times cannot mean faithfully repeating tired formulae. On the contrary, an appreciation of how his thinking developed suggests that we ought to take Tronti *beyond* Tronti.[3]

One of his most precious contributions to revolutionary thinking was his conception of the working class as an autonomous political force that struggles against capital. Rather than a blank canvass onto which ideals are projected, the class is produced and reproduced over time through struggles.[4] If in 1963 Tronti had deduced that workers must have been "all born with the same interests," he also recognized that working-class unity was a process of composition.[5]

That the working class can be composed means it can also be decomposed.[6] We see plainly today how capitalists and the state have worked to fragment and undermine formations of unity by stratifying workers in terms of gender, immigration status, and race.[7] Yet in the face of the capitalist attack, workers today continue to struggle in diverse ways to form a class.

After Tronti's interventions of the 1960s, to write "the history of the working class" in the United States, for instance, means taking stock not only of deindustrialization, tertiarization, and changes to the labor process—changes in the "technical composition" of the working class—but also the proliferation of new forms of struggle against capitalist social relations—moments

2. The earliest reference to "Trontismo" that I have found is in the work of Maria Grazia Meriggi, who used the word in the course of arguing that Tronti did not put forward a science of politics wholly opposed to "Togliattism." Several years later, the notion of Trontismo as "ideology" was in circulation. See Maria Grazia Meriggi, "Rileggendo 'Operai e capitale': dall'autonomia operaia all'autonomia del politico" [Re-reading *Workers and Capital*: from workers' autonomy to the autonomy of the political], *aut aut* 147 (May–June 1975): 47–65, 52; later collected in *Composizione di classe e teoria del partito: sul marxismo degli anni '60* [Class composition and theory of the party: on the Marxism of the 1960s] (Bari: Dedalo, 1978), 61–90, 69. See also Attilio Mangano, "Per una critica del trontismo e delle ideologie 'autonome'" [Toward a critique of Trontismo and of "autonomous" ideologies], in *Autocritica e politica di classe: diario teorico degli anni Settanta* [Self-criticism and class politics: theoretical diary of the 1970s] (Milan: Ottaviano 1978).

3. I borrow this construction from Antonio Negri, *Marx Beyond Marx: Lessons on the Grundrisse*, trans. Harry Cleaver, Michael Ryan, and Maurizio Viano, ed. Jim Fleming (South Hadley, MA: Bergin & Garvey, 1984). See also the section "Lenin beyond Lenin" in Antonio Negri, "What to Do Today with *What Is to Be Done?*, or Rather: The Body of the General Intellect," in *Lenin Reloaded: Toward a Politics of Truth*, eds. Sebastian Budgen, Stathis Kouvelakis, and Slavoj Žižek (Durham: Duke University Press, 2007), 297–307, 299.

4. Even if Tronti would seek to define "class" in a different way in his "Postscript of Problems" [1970], in *Workers and Capital*, 277–326, 325.

5. Tronti, "The Copernican Revolution (May 1963)," this volume, 92.

6. For reflections on a process of class decomposition in Italy, see Marco Revelli, "Defeat at Fiat," trans. Red Notes, *Capital & Class* 6, no. 1 (February 1982): 95–109; also available online: https://libcom.org/history/1980-defeat-fiat-marco-revelli.

7. The literature on this subject is voluminous. Some excellent starting points are: Mariarosa Dalla Costa and Selma James, *The Power of Women and the Subversion of the Community* (Bristol: Falling Wall Press, 1972); James Boggs, *The American Revolution: Pages from a Negro Worker's Notebook*, in *Pages from a Negro Worker's Notebook: A James Boggs Reader*, ed. Stephen M. Ward (Detroit: Wayne State University Press, 2011), 82–143; David R. Roediger and Elizabeth D. Esch, *The Production of Difference: Race and the Management of Labor in U.S. History* (New York: Oxford University Press, 2014).

of its "political composition."[8] We can see the enduring relevance of such a perspective if we consider the creative and persistent practices of organization developed by militant members of the Chicago Teachers Union to build citywide solidarity across neighborhoods, schools, and workplaces in support of the union's 2012 and 2019 strikes. To employ Tronti's terms, we witnessed the teachers' struggle break out of its bargaining cage and contribute to the political growth of the working class.[9]

Rather than waiting for workers of the world to become properly "conscious" of their shared lot as a class, a Trontian viewpoint today sees that antiracist, feminist, Indigenous, migrant, and tenant movements drive anticapitalist subjectivation as much as struggles over waged work.[10] This approach begins by identifying acts of refusal and seeks to build on that moving basis; it does not start from the logic of capital to fashion a plan for revolution.[11] Rather than presupposing "class consciousness" as the point to which workers must arrive, it recognizes that "people think" and, moreover, that they inquire into the world around them.[12] Rather than answers, it suggests questions: What practices are already circulating among forces refusing to collaborate with the development of capital? How might these be supported, extended, and amplified in the interests of producing a global working class, understood in political terms? Can these myriad forces constitute a unified subject which refuses to grant the demands of capital?

Preface

8. One impressive effort to extend Tronti's thinking directly onto the terrain of urban and welfare rights struggles in the United States can be found in Paolo Carpignano, "U.S. Class Composition in the Sixties," *Zerowork* 1 (December 1975): 7-31. See also Salar Mohandesi and Emma Teitelman, "Without Reserves," in *Social Reproduction Theory: Remapping Class, Recentering Oppression*, ed. Tithi Bhattacharya (London: Pluto, 2017), 37-67. For an early work that uses the analytic of class composition, see Sergio Bologna, "Class Composition and the Theory of the Party at the Origin of the Workers-Councils Movement," trans. Bruno Ramirez, *Telos* 13 (Fall 1972): 4-27. See also Salar Mohandesi, "Class Consciousness or Class Composition?" *Science & Society* 77, no. 1 (January 2013): 72-97; and Steve Wright, *Storming Heaven: Class Composition and Struggle in Italian Autonomist Marxism*, 2nd ed. (London: Pluto, 2017).

9. Another example of working-class unity built in Chicago through painstaking organizing was the original Rainbow Coalition, initiated by Fred Hampton and Bob Lee of the Black Panther Party in 1968-69 and encompassing the Puerto Rican Young Lords, the Appalachian-migrant Young Patriots Organization, and Rising Up Angry, which addressed itself to poor white Chicagoans. For a nuanced portrait of this political composition, see Patrick King, introduction to "Young Patriots at the United Front Against Fascism Conference (1969)," by William "Preacherman" Fesperman, *Viewpoint Magazine*, August 10, 2015, https://www.viewpointmag.com/2015/08/10/young-patriots-at-the-united-front-against-fascism-conference. See also Amy Sonnie and James Tracy, *Hillbilly Nationalists, Urban Race Rebels, and Black Power: Community Organizing in Radical Times* (Brooklyn: Melville House, 2011).

10. For a deeper consideration of some of these questions, see Cinzia Arruzza, "From Women's Strikes to a New Class Movement: The Third Feminist Wave," *Viewpoint Magazine*, December 3, 2018, https://www.viewpointmag.com/2018/12/03/from-womens-strikes-to-a-new-class-movement-the-third-feminist-wave; and the collectively written editorial, "The Border Crossing Us," *Viewpoint Magazine*, November 7, 2018, https://www.viewpointmag.com/2018/11/07/from-what-shore-does-socialism-arrive.

11. James Boggs, a Black revolutionary autoworker and theorist, developed a similar perspective in his work on the revolutionary potential of the "outsiders" of U.S. society. See Boggs, *The American Revolution*, and Patrick King, "Introduction to 'Black Power: A Scientific Concept Whose Time Has Come' by James Boggs," *e-flux* 79 (February 2017), https://www.e-flux.com/journal/79/94671/introduction-to-boggs.

12. See Asad Haider, "Socialists Think," *Viewpoint Magazine*, September 24, 2018, https://www.viewpointmag.com/2018/09/24/socialists-think. Haider's work here builds upon that of Sylvain Lazarus; see Lazarus's *Anthropology of the Name*, trans. Gila Walker (New York: Seagull Books, 2015), and his "Workers' Anthropology and Factory Inquiry: Inventory and Problematics (2001)," trans. Asad Haider and Patrick King, *Viewpoint Magazine*, January 9, 2019, https://www.viewpointmag.com/2019/01/09/workers-anthropology-and-factory-inquiry-inventory-and-problematics.

The strategy of refusal continues to percolate today. In the workplace, rank-and-file militants are opposing the lobby-and-compromise approach favored by union leadership and management alike, instead insisting on building antagonistic organizations to confront their bosses directly. From the home to the streets, the international women's strike—striking also from that portion of the working day which is unpaid—has inspired and embodied a "feminism for the 99 percent" that says *no* to the liberation of some women through more fulfilling work, and *no* to the notion of "leaning in" to a system that continues to attack immigrant, poor, and racialized women, as well as women in the Global South.[13] From Ferguson to Gaza, and from Paris to Hong Kong, the strategy of refusal animates those who rise up in riot rather than ask for seats at the negotiating table between representatives of state and capital.[14] Becoming ungovernable; shutting it down; launching a general, social, transnational strike: these slogans continue to be thrown up by the struggles themselves.

The heterogeneous working-class movement that in 2019 blocked Amazon's proposal to build a second headquarters ("HQ2") in the borough of Queens, New York, can also inform a Trontian framework for our times. Provoked by the prospect of mass displacement and supercharged gentrification, as well as Amazon's collaboration with U.S. Immigration and Customs Enforcement (ICE) and the Department of Homeland Security (DHS), activists rooted in diverse working-class milieus composed a powerful coalition. This formation managed to accumulate enough political force to refuse negotiation with Amazon over the terms of forthcoming exploitation. They refused to collaborate in capitalist development: precisely the kind of prospect which had so excited Tronti in his forecasts of struggles by workers at FIAT. Against a city and state administration eager to provide billions of dollars in subsidies to the world's richest man, and in defiance of the reformist perspective put forward by representatives of the official labor movement, an antagonistic class movement achieved a massive short-term victory.[15]

If we note that the working-class strategy of refusal continues to course through Queens and indeed across the globe, we must also pay attention to tactical experimentation by the political layer of activists who contributed to the success of this and other movements. These practical developments, considered

13. See Cinzia Arruzza, Tithi Bhattacharya, and Nancy Fraser, *Feminism for the 99 Percent: A Manifesto* (London: Verso, 2019).

14. For a balance sheet of accommodations and refusals in the case of Black Lives Matter, see Keeanga-Yamahtta Taylor, "Five Years Later, Do Black Lives Matter?" *Jacobin*, September 30, 2019, https://www.jacobinmag.com/2019/09/black-lives-matter-laquan-mcdonald-mike-brown-eric-garner.

15. See Andy Battle, "We Will Not Negotiate," *Commune*, February 18, 2019, https://communemag.com/we-will-not-negotiate; and Daniel A. Medina, "The grassroots coalition that took on Amazon... and won," *The Guardian*, March 24, 2019, https://www.theguardian.com/technology/2019/mar/23/the-grassroots-coalition-that-took-on-amazon-and-won.

in light of Tronti's 1967 call for action "within and against" parties and states, might offer a new framework for thinking how institutions, organizations, and personnel are implicated in collective action today. To consider one aspect of this problem, albeit at an abstract level, we can take what may be called the ideological state apparatus of nonprofit or nongovernmental organizations.[16]

There is an emergent if not absolute consensus on the anticapitalist left: nonprofit institutions reproduce capitalist social relations and channel working-class anger into forms that are manageable—productive, even—for the state and capital. From the point of view of the capitalist system's normal operation, this appraisal would appear to be correct. But, following the impulse at the heart of Tronti's research, we might consider the possibility that the existence of these institutions as articulators of contemporary capitalist society indicates not only a clever design, but a *need* the enemy has—a need that can be taken advantage of.

In a country such as the United States, which has no labor or left party and low union density, it is possible that nonprofit organizations fulfill some functions analogous to those that Tronti attributed to the "historical institutions" of the workers' movement in postwar Italy. To return to the anti-Amazon struggle, some of the organizations and personnel that contributed to that fight receive funding from philanthropies and employ paid staff. This is not to say that the struggle's endpoint was foreclosed in advance, nor, at the other extreme, to say that nonprofits contribute actively toward the struggle for working-class organization.[17] Instead, to take a cue from how Tronti read workers' relationships to trade unions, perhaps the working class relates to nonprofits in a duplicitous manner. Perhaps nonprofits are periodically plundered for the resources they offer to struggles while their strategic visions gain little traction.

What would it mean to reconstruct the history of the nonprofit state apparatus from the viewpoint of the postwar U.S. working class and its political initiatives? It would involve seeing the Civil Rights Movement and what Stanley Aronowitz has called the "unsilent fifties" as major moments in working-class struggle powerful enough to provoke political crises in the state.[18]

16. The concept "ideological state apparatus" was first developed by Louis Althusser and Nicos Poulantzas. See Louis Althusser, *On the Reproduction of Capitalism: Ideology and Ideological State Apparatuses*, trans. G.M. Goshgarian (London: Verso, 2014); and Nicos Poulantzas, "The Problem of the Capitalist State," in *The Poulantzas Reader: Marxism, Law and the State*, ed. James Martin (London: Verso, 2008), 172–85.

17. Although many nonprofits were hatched by private foundations, some began with activists trying to sustain the movements of the 1960s and 1970s, while others were established to preserve institutional memory and support fledgling campaigns during the bleak 1980s and 1990s. Today, not a few count substantial memberships of working-class people seeking a form of organization. If the distinction between grant-funded and grassroots initiatives often proves illusory (see Taylor, "Five Years Later"), the term "nonprofit," which designates tax-exempt status, may end up proving insufficient for concrete political analysis. This is only the beginning of a longer discussion that I intend to develop elsewhere.

18. Stanley Aronowitz, *False Promises: The Shaping of American Working Class Consciousness*, expanded ed. (Durham: Duke University Press, 1992 [1973]), chap. 7, 323–94.

Only then could we correctly approach community-based brokerage schemes, foundation grants, and nonprofit salaries as components of the state-managed counterattack of big capital and its scions (recalling the names of the major philanthropies). We could then hypothesize that capital and the state have come to require the active integration of not only wage struggles but citizen, immigrant, and resident struggles, and that these multitudinous social movements propel the development of the state itself as it expands its operations to administer more and more of social life. Perhaps the nonprofit state apparatus represents "not only ideological weapons of propaganda but mechanisms for the overall operation of capitalist society."[19]

Which kinds of class action might be powerful enough to combat these continual attempts of political subsumption?[20] Knowing that yesterday's struggles provoked today's institutional arrangement, what mechanisms of organization could sustain the political recomposition of the working class today? What role might the increasingly unionized layer of nonprofit staff play in this process? Is a workers' control of the nonprofit state apparatus desirable or possible? These are the types of questions that Tronti's thought can help us to ask. New slogans will also need to be identified, slogans that can be wielded as tools in the construction of a new political discourse. This discourse will need to address existing struggles within and against the nonprofit state apparatus and seek to extend their reach.

We are also haunted by our own "problem of the party," although it is quite distinct from that one confronted by Tronti. The history and structure of the U.S. Democratic Party necessitate that the tactical repertoires employed by today's socialists must differ substantially from those which informed Tronti's proposals for engaging the postwar Italian Communist Party. Tronti judged the PCI, if reconquered by the working class, to be a potentially useful tool for revolution, in no small part because it had been excluded from participation in "democratic planning" at the national level. The PCI had only ever been in the majority government during the immediate postwar period of 1944–47; the U.S. Democrats, on the other hand, have held the presidency and majorities in the Senate and House of Representatives throughout U.S. history. The machinery of this Party is run and financed by capitalists.

This qualitatively different animal requires a different analysis. Any socialist call for activity "within and against" it runs the heavy risk of autonomous organizations being liquidated. If the strategy of refusal remains operative in

19. Tronti, "Within and Against (May 1967)," this volume, 179.
20. I propose the term "political subsumption" to designate the ongoing and uneven efforts of capitalist state managers to appropriate forms of working-class organization into, and for the benefit of, the capitalist state. On this point, I am indebted to Harry Harootunian's readings of Marx on formal subsumption and Gramsci on passive revolution. See Harootunian, *Marx After Marx: History and Time in the Expansion of Capitalism* (New York: Columbia University Press, 2015).

contemporary social movements, today's tactics—as with any tactics—must be based on a "concrete analysis of a concrete situation."[21]

How can the electoral arena be used to bend the U.S. capitalist state to working-class purposes? What are the Democratic Party's mechanisms of political subsumption, and can they be outmaneuvered? Can processes of working-class subjectivation pass through it, or through the U.S. capitalist state? Which types of class action could make the Democratic Party explode? Some of these questions are already animating contemporary debates in the resurgent socialist movement in the United States. Perhaps the reader will find Tronti's thought bearing on them in surprising ways.

Finally, Tronti's contempt for catastrophism—his rejection of the notion that the inevitable collapse of the capitalist system will mark the advent of communism—may also serve our present moment, even and perhaps especially amid rising temperatures and tides. Capital, unlike the polar ice caps, will not melt away. Would it be too much to suggest that today's social capital could in fact require some measure of social struggle to secure its own future, in order, say, to prevent fossil-fuel capitalists from destroying the long-term viability of capital in general?

Fractures exist between sectors of the capitalist class, and there are rifts between companies in every industry. In the field of energy, the question has recently been posed *by capitalists* of the capitalist state's inadequate regulation of production. In 2019, Donald Trump's administration loosened environmental regulations that had restricted emissions of methane during oil and gas production. This allowed smaller and weaker firms to stay afloat, and at the same time it prompted dissent from the presidents of BP, Shell, and Exxon Mobil. In this case, if not in others, they lamented the lost regulations that drove "innovation" and capital centralization in the industry.[22]

Can climate activists exploit these kinds of fissures, hasten the division of the capitalist power bloc, and build a mass, anticapitalist environmental movement? How can processes of working-class subjectivation that have passed through Indigenous struggles, such as those at Standing Rock, be elaborated to produce not merely a Green New Deal but a Red Deal?[23] How can the experiments of Cooperation Jackson, a network in Mississippi that builds spaces of green, territorial autonomy and self-managed, sustainable production, be

Preface

21. V.I. Lenin, "Kommunismus," in *Collected Works*, vol. 31 (Moscow: Progress Publishers, 1965 [1920]), 165–67; also available online: https://www.marxists.org/archive/lenin/works/1920/jun/12.htm. See also Louis Althusser, "On the Materialist Dialectic," in *For Marx*, trans. Ben Brewster (London: Verso, 2005), 161–218, 206.

22. See, for instance, Clifford Krauss, "Trump's Methane Rule Rollback Divides Oil and Gas Industry," *New York Times*, August 29, 2019, https://www.nytimes.com/2019/08/29/business/energy-environment/methane-regulation-reaction.html.

23. This proposal has been put forward by the Red Nation; see Nick Estes, "A Red Deal," *Jacobin*, August 6, 2019, https://www.jacobinmag.com/2019/08/red-deal-green-new-deal-ecosocialism-decolonization-indigenous-resistance-environment.

circulated and scaled up?[24] To risk anticipating one possible scenario, in which some kind of Green New Deal comes to pass in the United States, we might ask: what revolutionary use can be made of environmental reformism? Could a working-class instrumentalization of the state curb climate breakdown?

The site in Queens where Amazon intended to construct its HQ2 remains home to one of New York's dirtiest power plants and the nation's largest community of tenants in public housing. What could it mean to plant a Tronti in Queensbridge, as he had proposed to bring Lenin to England? It might involve consolidating the working-class initiative against Amazon, linking it to adjacent and long-simmering fights, and working politically to multiply the anticapitalist content of these struggles. Activists are already doing this work in myriad ways, and the "productive imagination" of tactics will continue to create new possibilities for action and for theory.[25] Problems of climate, housing, and work have coevolved over the history of capitalist society; they can only be overcome by refusing their separation and by struggling against the unified obstacle they present with our own antagonistic counter-unity.[26]

The works gathered here, translated into English for the first time, shed light on the factors that shaped Tronti's thought process. All were composed between 1959 and 1967, the period during which he also wrote the essays of *Workers and Capital*, contributed to the journal *Quaderni Rossi* [Red Notebooks], and directed the newspaper *Classe Operaia* [Working Class].[27] Together, these projects heralded the birth of a new current of Marxism known as *operaismo* [workerism].[28] The present collection includes public

24. See Sarah Lazare, "We Have To Make Sure the 'Green New Deal' Doesn't Become Green Capitalism: A conversation with Kali Akuno of Cooperation Jackson," *In These Times*, December 12, 2018, http://inthesetimes.com/article/21632/green-new-deal-alexandria-ocasio-cortez-climate-cooperation-jackson-capital.

25. Tronti, "A Course of Action," xxviii.

26. For a recent political proposal for tackling climate change that considers housing, work, and other facets of social life to be interconnected, see Kate Aronoff, Alyssa Battistoni, Daniel Aldana Cohen, and Thea Riofrancos, *A Planet to Win: Why We Need a Green New Deal* (London: Verso, 2019).

27. I have elected to capitalize these and other Italian titles of journals, newspapers, and books in the body of texts and footnotes to avoid possible confusion. However, I have retained Italian-style capitalization (*Quaderni rossi; classe operaia*) in citations in the footnotes and the bibliography.

28. The first edition of *Workers and Capital*, published in 1966 by Giulio Einaudi's eponymous publishing house, collected some of Tronti's writings from *Quaderni Rossi* and *Classe Operaia*, along with a book review from 1961, a major unpublished essay on Marx written in 1965, and an introduction; see Mario Tronti, *Operai e capitale* (Turin: Einaudi Editore, 1966). The book was republished in an enlarged, second edition in 1971, with the formidable new "Postscript of Problems," written in 1970, which was then included in all subsequent editions. See *Operai e capitale*, 2nd ed. (Turin: Einaudi Editore, 1971), and subsequently *Operai e capitale* (Rome: DeriveApprodi, 2013). The most concise introduction in English to Tronti's work of the 1960s is Michele Filippini, *Leaping Forward: Mario Tronti and the History of Political Workerism* (Maastricht: Jan van Eyck Academie, 2012); see also Steve Wright, "Foreword," in Tronti, *Workers and Capital*, xii–xiv. The best work on the milieu around Tronti is Wright's *Storming Heaven*; see also David P. Palazzo, "The 'Social Factory' in Postwar Italian Radical Thought from *Operaismo* to *Autonomia*," (PhD diss., City University of New York Graduate Center, 2014). Among the many rich sources on Tronti in Italian, see: Davide Gallo Lassere, "La traiettoria teorica e politica di Mario Tronti" [The theoretical and political trajectory of Mario Tronti], *Effimera*, January 11, 2018, http://effimera.org/la-traiettoria-teorica-politica-mario-tronti-davide-gallo-lassere2; Fabio Milana and Giuseppe Trotta, eds., *L'operaismo degli anni sessanta: da "Quaderni rossi" a "classe operaia"* [The workerism of the 1960s: from *Quaderni Rossi* to *Classe Operaia*] (Rome: DeriveApprodi, 2008); and Franco Milanesi, *Nel Novecento: storia, teoria, politica nel pensiero di Mario Tronti* [In the twentieth century: history, theory, politics in the thought of Mario Tronti] (Milan: Mimesis, 2014). One can also consult Tronti's own

talks, political dispatches, organizational notes, and personal letters written by Tronti from within these collective experiences. While one cannot neatly separate his political interventions from his rereading of Marx, this volume focuses on his radical editorial and political work during the 1960s.

This collection also includes, as an appendix, a bibliography of all of Tronti's works during the period of 1958–70, from his first publication to the postscript to the second edition of *Workers and Capital*. Both English and Italian editions are listed. From this period, beyond works translated here and those available in *Workers and Capital*, Anglophones can read Tronti's first two published essays, on Gramsci and Gramscianism in the PCI, online at *Viewpoint Magazine*. Those interested in the development of his thought after 1967 may also consult the translation of the seminar "The Autonomy of the Political (1972)" via the same venue.[29] It should be recognized that this leaves a number of works still to be translated from Tronti's early period, not to mention his subsequent fifty-year career.[30]

These works are contextualized in several ways: an introductory essay surveys the period, a prefatory note precedes each text, and translator's notes are sprinkled throughout. All comments which appear bracketed in italics in the bodies of texts were inserted by Italian editors or transcribers in previous versions.[31] In the interest of allowing the flow of Tronti's argument to shine through as much as possible, I have not introduced further bracketed notes of my own into the text, nor have I highlighted translation decisions. In addition, I have taken the liberty of occasionally rearranging Tronti's syntax when it has facilitated reading in English. Any errors or misjudgments in the translation, introduction, and notes are, needless to say, my own.

reflections on this period in "Our *Operaismo*," edited and excerpted from a longer Italian essay, "Noi operaisti" [We workerists] in *L'operaismo degli anni sessanta*, 5–58. See also "Mario Tronti" [Interview], in *Gli operaisti: Autobiografie di cattivi maestri* [The workerists: Autobiographies of wicked teachers], eds. Guido Borio, Francesca Pozzi, and Gigi Roggero (Rome: DeriveApprodi, 2005), 289–307; "Intervista a Mario Tronti – 8 agosto 2000" [Interview with Mario Tronti – August 8, 2000], in CD-ROM supplement to *Futuro Anteriore: Dai "Quaderni Rossi" ai movimenti globali: richezze e limiti dell'operaismo italiano* [Future Perfect: From *Quaderni Rossi* to the global movements: the treasures and limits of Italian workerism], eds. Guido Borio, Francesco Pozzi, and Gigi Roggero, also available online: https://www.autistici.org/operaismo/tronti/index_1.htm; and "Mario Tronti" [Interview, Rome, January 12 and April 2, 1998] in *L'operaismo degli anni sessanta*, 589–612.

29. See Tronti, "Some Questions around Gramsci's Marxism (1958)" and "Between Dialectical Materialism and Philosophy of Praxis: Gramsci and Labriola (1959)," in "The Young Mario Tronti," ed. and trans. Andrew Anastasi, dossier, *Viewpoint Magazine* (October 3, 2016), https://www.viewpointmag.com/2016/10/03/between-dialectical-materialism-and-philosophy-of-praxis-gramsci-and-labriola-1959. See also Mario Tronti, "The Autonomy of the Political (1972)," trans. Andrew Anastasi, Sara R. Farris, and Peter D. Thomas, *Viewpoint Magazine*, February 26, 2020, https://www.viewpointmag.com/2020/02/26/the-autonomy-of-the-political.

30. Two early essays deserve mention: a review of several books on Marx's *Capital* for *Società*, the PCI journal in part edited by Della Volpe and Colletti, and Tronti's introduction to a collection which he edited and translated of Marx's unpublished works on political economy. It is also worth noting that Tronti's contributions to *Classe Operaia* are not exhausted by what was collected in *Workers and Capital*; the full run of the newspaper has been digitized and included as a CD-ROM accompanying Milana and Trotta, *L'operaismo degli anni sessanta*. For the early essays, see: "Studi recenti sulla logica del *Capitale*," *Società* 17, no. 6 (1961): 881–903; and introduction to *Scritti inediti di economia politica*, by Karl Marx, ed. and trans. Mario Tronti (Rome: Editori Riuniti, 1963), vii–xxxvi.

31. See the Appendix for citations of these Italian publications.

Preface

This project would not exist without the indispensable work of Fabio Milana and Giuseppe Trotta. Fabio has patiently guided my navigation of the period surveyed in this collection, and for his help I am extremely grateful. I also thank Mario Tronti for his approval of this little endeavor. I have benefited immensely from the tireless labor and kind correspondence of Michele Filippini, Matteo Mandarini, and Steve Wright. Thank you to Antonio Del Vecchio and Sandro Mezzadra for their help and hospitality in Bologna while I was preparing the manuscript. It is difficult to adequately express my appreciation for the political-theoretical laboratory of the *Viewpoint Magazine* editorial collective; thanks in particular to Cinzia Arruzza and Dave Mesing for comments on the translation, and to Asad Haider, Patrick King, and Ben Mabie for their encouragement. Thank you to Malav Kanuga for recognizing the value that Tronti's thought might have for today's students of militant history and theory, and for trusting me to steward this work to a new audience. A massive thanks to Andy Battle for his assiduous editing work and for cutting through so many tangled webs of prose. Thanks to Erika Biddle, Morgan Buck, Ash Goh, Josh MacPhee, and everyone at Common Notions for their contributions to the finished product. Thank you also to David Broder and Verso Books for sharing an advance copy of the English translation of *Workers and Capital*. Many friends and family have sustained me throughout this process. I am especially grateful to Andy and to Scott for their long-running comradeship, as well as for memes. Frank, Katy, and Miriam have been delightful interlocutors all along the way. I dedicate this book to two women who have taught me how to read, each in her own way: to Rose, who introduced me to the left, and whose eye, intellect, and patience are without rival; and to Susan, my first editor, who also first taught me the value of critique.

A concluding note of caution to the reader: this book risks the implication that operaismo emerged from the head of a Zeus rather than from a complex network of political intelligence.[32] Nothing could be further from the truth, and in Tronti's own telling, it was the "bond of political friendship" that defined the experience.[33] Names of addressees, audiences of fellow editors, and transcripts of group conversations signal that his efforts were stitches in a larger quilt. Many of his contemporaries remain to be translated; may one hundred volumes bloom. In the meantime: "Speaking right away, starting to say, giving a glimpse of what later will be—this is necessary for one to find strength, to accumulate experiences, to harvest first fruits on the terrain no longer only of ideas."[34]

---

32. See Steve Wright, *Storming Heaven*, as well as his forthcoming *The Weight of the Printed Word: Text, Context and Militancy in "Operaismo,"* on the ecosystem surrounding Tronti's thought in the 1960s.

33. Tronti, "Our *Operaismo,*" 327.

34. Mario Tronti, "Una lettera a Giulio Einaudi" [Mario Tronti to Giulio Einaudi, Rome, January 16, 1966], https://operavivamagazine.org/una-lettera-a-giulio-einaudi (my translation).

Experiments and Explosions

Tronti's Work of the 1960s

Andrew Anastasi

Fifty years ago, young radicals riding the Italian crest of an internation-al wave of struggle were reading Mario Tronti. They carried his book *Workers and Capital* as if it were their Bible.[1] These unruly subjects found Tronti's reading of Karl Marx from the perspective of their present both in-tellectually and politically exciting. His razor-sharp pen especially delighted those who were skeptical of the revolutionary potential of labor unions and the Italian Communist Party (PCI) [Partito Comunista Italiano] in the post-war era. It would be no exaggeration to say that an entire generation of Italy's extra-parliamentary left, working in the factory, the home, and the school, discovered Marx under Tronti's tutelage.

The thrust of his critique was directed at the PCI, whose theorists and pol-iticians—in the name of the whole Italian people—had developed opportu-nistic readings of Marx and Antonio Gramsci to justify the Party's accommo-dation to the capitalist state. For Tronti, the "reformist political sludge" they had produced could be cut through only by organizing the intervention of a new subjective force.[2] Italian theorists would later refer to the "Copernican revolution" Tronti wrought during the 1960s; the red-hot core of his Marxism was working-class politics.[3]

---

1. See Mario Tronti, *Workers and Capital*, trans. David Broder (London: Verso, 2019).

2. Tronti, "Letter to Raniero Panzieri (January 1963)," this volume, 80.

3. Tronti did not claim his own work had achieved a "Copernican revolution" [*rivoluzione copernicana*], but he did use the phrase in a sarcastic aside, mocking theorists who merely "pushed their desks from one corner of the room to the other." See "A Course of Action" [1966], in *Workers and Capital*, xv–xxxiv, xvii. An early use of the phrase in reference to Tronti's own contribution to Marxism can be found in an article by Maria Grazia Meriggi, where the term appears within quotation marks yet without further attribution. See Meriggi, "Rileggendo 'Operai e capitale': dall'autonomia operaia all'autonomia del politico" [Re-reading *Workers and*

His innovation was to propose that workers' struggles propelled capitalist development, and that the strength required for an anticapitalist revolution must be located in the "political development" of the working class. This political growth had to begin from the antagonism embodied in the rebellious subjectivity of industrial workers. But the accumulation of class power also required organizational labor by committed militants. Not unlike the young Gramsci who cheered on the Russian "Revolution against *Capital*," Tronti championed a "Leninist critique of Marx." He believed political actors could build the capacity to overturn the iron logic of capital.[4]

If Tronti reconceived capitalist society from the viewpoint of the working class, he did not consider capital to be inert. On the contrary, he urged his comrades to take its "disconcerting vitality" seriously.[5] For Tronti, capital's survival depended on its ability to recuperate working-class demands, via the capitalist state, for its own benefit. He illustrated how capital used the workers' fight for higher wages to spur its own innovation—investing in machinery, intensifying exploitation, and extending its domination over the whole society.

A new strategy was required if the working class was to break free from this stranglehold: what Tronti called the "strategy of refusal."[6] Beyond identifying this strategy, Tronti overturned two decades of PCI common sense by reconceiving the *relationship* between strategy and tactics. Tronti suggested, provocatively, that the Party must quit developing complex theories of capital and strategies to defeat it. The strategy of refusal already existed in embryo in the everyday struggles of a defiant working class. The Party was to limit its purview and focus on tactical actions, on elaborating the strategy in practice. This meant it would need to create new channels of communication to the factory, overhaul its organizational structure, and experiment with new political slogans.

In Tronti's estimation, for the working class to pursue the abolition of all forms of domination, it would first need to achieve a "workers' control over the party."[7] Although some of his comrades would resolve the problem of the PCI by declaring it bankrupt, once Tronti had pinpointed the need to restructure the working-class movement—the division of labor between class and party—his own thinking and practice increasingly focused on the Party. He

Capital: from workers' autonomy to the autonomy of the political], *aut aut* 147 (May-June 1975): 47-65, 58; later collected in *Composizione di classe e teoria del partito: sul marxismo degli anni '60* [Class composition and theory of the party: on the Marxism of the '60s] (Bari: Dedalo, 1978), 61-90, 79.

4. Antonio Gramsci, "The Revolution against *Capital*," in *Selections from the Political Writings (1910-1920)*, ed. Quintin Hoare, trans. John Mathews (London: Lawrence and Wishart, 1977), 34-37. Mario Tronti, "Marx, Labour-Power, Working Class" [1965], in *Workers and Capital*, 103-276, 164. I cite the latter as a single essay; the Verso edition breaks what were sections in the Italian original into chapters.

5. Tronti, "Within and Against (May 1967)," this volume, 185.

6. Tronti, "Marx, Labour-Power, Working Class," 241, 269.

7. Tronti, "The Party in the Factory (April 1965)," this volume, 139.

wagered that a reorganized PCI was the best possible vehicle for articulating and multiplying the workers' antagonism toward bosses and the state. With Marx in one hand and Lenin in the other, he proposed seizing and retooling the existing infrastructure in service of "working-class self-organization."[8]

Tronti's book *Workers and Capital* was published in Italy first in 1966, and then again in 1971 in an expanded second edition.[9] Sections were translated and circulated in Great Britain and the United States by the mid-1970s; meanwhile, a condensed version appeared in German in 1974, and the full volume was translated into French in 1977.[10] Tronti's insights from the 1960s radiated out from Italy in the decades that followed, influencing various currents of social and political theory. The Marxist feminist critiques of unwaged labor developed by Mariarosa Dalla Costa and Selma James, and their extension by Silvia Federici and other theorists of social reproduction; Stefano Harney and Fred Moten's call for a radicalism "within and against" the university and other institutions of capitalist society; Michael Hardt and Antonio Negri's proposal to invert the traditional relationships between leaders, movements, tactics, and strategy—these are only a few of the vital strains of contemporary revolutionary theory that share Tronti as a common source.[11] Trontian phrases have also found their way, through intermediaries, into the realm of parliamentary politics. In the United Kingdom, for instance, John McDonnell of the Labour Party has proposed to operate "in and against the state" to devolve central state powers to the local level.[12]

If Tronti's ideas have spread widely, his own voice has long been muffled in English. The long-awaited publication of *Workers and Capital* in a new and complete translation now offers a tremendous opportunity for Tronti's thinking to circulate to new audiences. But engaging with any text more than fifty years after its original publication presents the reader with a host

Experiments and Explosions

8. Tronti, "After the Reunion in Mestre (May 1965)," this volume, 150.

9. Verso's 2019 English translation was based on this second edition. See *Operai e capitale*, 2nd ed. (Turin: Einaudi Editore, 1971), and subsequently *Operai e capitale* (Rome: DeriveApprodi, 2013).

10. Early English translations of selections from the book have been compiled in the bibliography of Tronti's works included as the Appendix to this volume. The German translation of *Workers and Capital* omitted the introduction, the four editorials from *Classe Operaia*, and the postscript from the second Italian edition. See *Arbeiter und Kapital*, trans. Karin Monte and Wolfgang Rieland (Frankfurt: Neue Kritik, 1974); also available online: http://www.kommunismus.narod.ru/knigi/pdf/Mario_Tronti_-_Arbeiter_und_Kapital.pdf. The French translation reproduced the second Italian edition in full. See *Ouvriers et capital*, trans. Yann Moulier-Boutang and Giuseppe Bezza (Paris: Entremonde, 2016 [1977]).

11. See Mariarosa Dalla Costa, *Women and the Subversion of the Community: A Mariarosa Dalla Costa Reader*, ed. Camille Barbagallo, trans. Richard Braude (Oakland: PM Press, 2019); Selma James, *Sex, Race, and Class: The Perspective of Winning, A Selection of Writings 1952-2011* (Oakland: Common Notions/PM Press, 2012); Silvia Federici, *Revolution at Point Zero: Housework, Reproduction, and Feminist Struggle* (Oakland: PM Press/ Common Notions, 2012); Stefano Harney and Fred Moten, *The Undercommons: Fugitive Planning & Black Study* (Wivenhoe/New York/Port Watson: Minor Compositions, 2013); Michael Hardt and Antonio Negri, *Assembly* (New York: Oxford University Press, 2019).

12. McDonnell often cites a pamphlet produced in 1979 by socialists working in state and state-funded organizations. The pamphlet does not cite Tronti directly, but its authors were familiar with the *operaisti*. See London Edinburgh Weekend Return Group, *In and Against the State*, 2nd ed. (London: Pluto, 1980); also available online: https://libcom.org/library/against-state-1979.

of challenges, and although Tronti's writing is eminently quotable, it also responded dynamically to a series of political events. When one line seems to say everything, we might heed the warning given by the author in the text which begins the present collection: "an element grasped in [an] immediate way very often exists in opposition to Marxism itself."[13]

Tronti's experiments in how to think and act politically were rooted in the postwar struggle over the direction of the PCI, the largest organization of its kind in an "advanced" capitalist society, in a country in which economic planning had made it onto the national agenda just as direct workers' struggles assumed new, mass forms. His earliest essays were dedicated to injecting new life into Marxist debates in the PCI by calling for a return to the Marx of *Capital* and to the Lenin of the October Revolution. At the same time, his interventions must also be understood in the context of international developments in the global communist movement; it was the period, as Michele Filippini reminds us, "between the Soviet tanks in Budapest and the student protests at the Sorbonne."[14] These were years during which political and theoretical orthodoxies were deeply shaken, and creativity in Marxist thought reached heights not seen since the 1930s.

This introduction covers several of Tronti's key concepts and concerns: the working class and capitalist development; the capitalist state and economic planning; political intervention and the problem of organization. To introduce readers to the distinctive approach to Marxism that Tronti pioneered during this period, which he has called *operaismo politico* [political workerism],[15] it follows a recurring theme in Tronti's theorizing that first emerged in the late 1950s—the philosophical principle of the "unity of the heterogeneous," or a unity that is not an identity.[16] As his interests developed from criticizing traditions in Italian Marxism to analyzing contemporary capitalism and workers' struggles by way of a new reading of Marx's *Capital*, Tronti's specific conception of "unity" expanded from logical postulate to political conviction: the material unity of the working class was not an inert, metaphysical, or sociological unity, but rather it must be constructed, through organizational activity, to produce a political revolution. While refocusing attention on concrete questions of politics and organization, Tronti also rejected two tendencies in Marxist thinking that belied a mechanistic understanding of the relationship between history and politics: belief that the economic laws of capital will produce the system's own collapse, and faith that

---

13. Tronti, "On Marxism and Sociology (April 1959)," this volume, 48.

14. Filippini, *Leaping Forward*, 9.

15. See, for example, Tronti, "Our *Operaismo*," 346.

16. Tronti, "On Marxism and Sociology," 49. See also Lucio Colletti, "Marxism as a Sociology," in *From Rousseau to Lenin: Studies in Ideology and Society*, trans. John Merrington and Judith White (New York: Monthly Review Press, 1972), 3-44, particularly 14.

the spontaneous insurgency of the masses will inaugurate communism. His political definition of the working class and his rejection of a wait-and-see tradition in Italian Marxism would lead Tronti to begin working on a third concrete and non-identical unity: the "problem of organization," that is, the relationship between the working class and its party, or, on the opposing side, between the capitalist class and its state.[17] The harmony of each unity could not be assumed in advance. On the contrary, each required vigilant maintenance: an economic downturn, for example, might erode the existing bases of a unity; it also might provide an opportunity for militants or politicians to recompose their own side—or hasten the decomposition of the enemy. In this sense, Tronti's efforts to work through the relationship between strategy and tactics would be, in many ways, his most precious contribution to Marxism.

I begin by recapitulating the essential methodological and historical premises of Tronti's thought. I then provide a reading of his political and theoretical trajectory up until 1967, weaving together arguments from *Workers and Capital* and insights gleaned from the texts translated in the present volume, which help to clarify the stakes of Tronti's weighty and at times obscure claims. Revolutionary theory, because of its relationship to politics in movement, must always be subject to reformulation and rethinking. Tronti's willingness to experiment, to modify his own core precepts, and to strike off in new directions provides a model of dynamic theoretical practice from which we still have much to learn. It would only be fitting for the reader to abscond with these notes from his laboratory and use them for her own subversive ends.

Beginnings

To grasp the key premises of Tronti's Copernican revolution, some background is required. In late October 1956, Tronti, already a member of the PCI and directing the Communist student organization at the University of Rome, signed a letter and manifesto in solidarity with Hungarian students and workers who were rising up against the rule of the Socialist Workers' Party. Tronti and 100 other signatories questioned the PCI's alignment with Moscow—whose military would soon intervene and put an end to the revolt—and this act, an expression of international solidarity, launched from within while also directed against his own party, portended a few heresies to come.[18]

17. Tronti, "The Party in the Factory," 137.

18. Milana and Trotta, *L'operaismo degli anni sessanta*, 68. See also Emilio Carnevali, "I fatti d'Ungheria e il dissenso degli intellettuali di sinistra. Storia del manifesto dei '101' [The Hungarian events and left intellectuals' dissent. History of the manifesto of the "101"], *MicroMega*, February 9, 2010, http://temi.repubblica.it/micromega-online/i-fatti-dungheria-e-il-dissenso-allinterno-del-pci-storia-del-manifesto-dei-101. On the notion of "heresy," see Étienne Balibar, "A Point of Heresy in Western Marxism: Althusser's and Tronti's Antithetic Readings of *Capital* in the Early 1960s," in *The Concept in Crisis: "Reading Capital" Today*, ed. Nick

Later that winter Tronti would complete his studies in philosophy with a thesis on Marx. His adviser Ugo Spirito introduced him to another young Communist philosopher, Lucio Colletti. Through Colletti, Tronti learned of the work of an older Party intellectual, Galvano Della Volpe. Both Della Volpe and Colletti were dedicated to the ruthless critique of idealism in the Marxist thought produced within and around the PCI, a mantle that Tronti himself would take up in his earliest publications.[19]

Our collection begins with a talk delivered by Tronti at a conference in April of 1959.[20] At the conference, which explored the relationship between Marxism and sociology, Tronti responded to a presentation by Lucio Colletti which proposed that Marx's categories provided tools for understanding social classes as agents in subjective struggle. Tronti discussed how *Capital* was "at the same time a work of theory and a work of practical action," and how the October Revolution was simultaneously "a great practical movement and a powerful theoretical discovery." He underlined how "this continual unity of diverse moments" could be found in not only the work but also in the biographies of Marx and Lenin.[21] Already then Tronti stressed the importance of reading Marx politically as well as incorporating the force of historical and political events into theory.[22] This could not be accomplished without extending the concept of unity to oneself: to be a Marxist meant to practice the "living unity" of researching, theorizing, and acting politically.[23]

An opportunity to practice a unity precisely of this kind emerged at the end of 1959, when Raniero Panzieri, former editor of *Mondo Operaio* [Workers' World], the theoretical journal of the Italian Socialist Party (PSI) [Partito Socialista Italiano], began putting together an editorial board for

Nesbitt (Durham: Duke University Press, 2017), 93–112.

19. Tronti, interview in Milana and Trotta, *L'operaismo degli anni sessanta*, 590. See also Tronti's "Autobiografia filosofica" [Philosophical autobiography] in *Dall'estremo possibile* [From the extreme possible], ed. Pasquale Serra (Rome: Ediesse, 2011), 234–42; also available online: https://www.centroriformastato.it/wp-content/uploads/autobiografia_filosofica.pdf. The reader can consult my introduction to the young Tronti for a longer exploration of the philosophical dimensions of this journey; see Andrew Anastasi, "A Living Unity in the Marxist: Introduction to Tronti's Early Writings," in "The Young Mario Tronti," ed. and trans. Andrew Anastasi, dossier, *Viewpoint Magazine* (October 3, 2016), https://www.viewpointmag.com/2016/10/03/a-living-unity-in-the-marxist-introduction-to-trontis-early-writings.

20. This was before the editorial body of *Quaderni Rossi* [Red Notebooks] had been constituted. Nevertheless, at this stage Tronti was already in communication with Raniero Panzieri, who himself had developed close contact with Della Volpe in Sicily.

21. Tronti, "On Marxism and Sociology," 50.

22. See Harry Cleaver, *Reading "Capital" Politically* (Austin: University of Texas Press, 1979).

23. Tronti, "On Marxism and Sociology," 50. In an essay from 1958 Tronti had drawn attention to a formulation written by Antonio Gramsci that was analogous, albeit expressed in more universal terms, that a person is "a historical bloc of purely individual and subjective elements and of mass and objective or material elements with which the individual is in an active relationship." See Antonio Gramsci, *Selections from the Prison Notebooks*, ed. and trans. Quintin Hoare and Geoffrey Nowell Smith (New York: International Publishers, 1971), 360. For Tronti's reference, see Mario Tronti, "Some Questions around Gramsci's Marxism (1958)," in "The Young Mario Tronti," ed. and trans. Andrew Anastasi, dossier, *Viewpoint Magazine* (October 3, 2016), https://www.viewpointmag.com/2016/10/03/some-questions-around-gramscis-marxism-1958.

a new Marxist journal. *Quaderni Rossi*'s research program would focus on the nascent stirrings of industrial workers, whose ranks had swelled in the big northern cities—Genoa, Milan, and soon most centrally, Turin—in tandem with the postwar economic boom. The new initiative was spurred by the tripling of the hours of work lost to strikes in 1959. From Panzieri's point of view, this phenomenon needed to be investigated, because the traditional tools of leftist analysis had foretold nothing of the kind. In 1955, the largest and most radical of the metal-mechanics' unions, the Metal-worker Employees' Federation (FIOM) [Federazione Impiegati Operai Metallurgici], which had previously dominated workplace organizations at FIAT Turin, lost half of its representative seats, shocking the left and indicating a crisis in its clout at the factory level, with the industrial proletariat apparently revealing its integration into the "Italian miracle" of postwar prosperity and development.[24] Although in 1959 there was an open struggle over the renewal of the metal-mechanics' contract in Milan, and the following year saw workers in the electronics sector also begin to struggle for a national contract, Turin, and particularly the workers at FIAT, remained to all appearances a sleeping giant. Panzieri and a group of sociologists carried out a series of inquiries, the results of which would be published in the first issue of *Quaderni Rossi*, released in October 1961. A highlight was Romano Alquati's innovative work to uncover what was going on at the shop-floor level—daily activity as well as passivity among workers, which constituted forms of embryonic refusal to collaborate in capital's plan.[25]

Although Tronti had not contributed any writing to the first issue of *Quaderni Rossi*, he was already involved in editorial duties and planning for subsequent issues. In a letter to Panzieri written in June of 1961, he began to develop a critique of the kind of Marxian thinking which hinged on a *deus ex machina* of economic collapse.[26] Tronti, rather than imagining revolution as a phoenix that would emerge from the ashes of a great crash, began in that letter to glimpse the "difficult marriage" which bonded working-class struggle and the expanding capitalist economy: the revolutionary process was "alive, actively and intimately, in the daily process of capitalism's development." He

24. Capitalist development in Italy produced extreme unevenness across the peninsula, provoking mass migrations from the South to the North and from the countryside to the cities. A powerful literary account of this process is found in Nanni Balestrini's *We Want Everything*, trans. Matt Holden (London: Verso, 2018).

25. See Romano Alquati, ed., "Documenti sulla lotta di classe alla FIAT" [Documents on the class struggle at FIAT], in *Quaderni rossi* 1 (Rome: Sapere, 1978 [October 1964]): 198-215, and "Relazione di Romano Alquati sulle 'forze nuove' (Convegno del PSI sulla FIAT, gennaio 1961)" [Report by Romano Alquati on the "new forces" (PSI Convention on FIAT, January 1961)], *Quaderni rossi* 1: 215-40. On Alquati, see Evan Calder Williams, "Invisible Organization: Reading Romano Alquati," *Viewpoint Magazine* 3 (September 2013), https://www.viewpointmag.com/2013/09/26/invisible-organization-reading-romano-alquati.

26. Colletti would carry out a not wholly dissimilar critique; see Colletti, "The Theory of the Crash," *Telos*, no. 13 (1972): 34-46. Asad Haider has dealt with this text and offers some important observations on crisis thinking in relation to workers' inquiry and Marxist theory; see his "Crise et enquête" [Crisis and inquiry], *Période*, March 7, 2014, http://revueperiode.net/crise-et-enquete.

insisted that *Quaderni Rossi*'s future issues should take up the problem of the "self-organization of the working class as a revolutionary class within the system of capitalism itself."[27]

The Working Class and Capitalist Development

Tronti's first essay in *Quaderni Rossi*, "Factory and Society," would feature as the lead article of the second issue, released in June 1962. While this essay does not contain within itself all the elements of Tronti's Copernican revolution, it nevertheless provides the reader with an important starting point for understanding the contribution to Marxist theory for which he is best known: the proposition that workers' struggles are the dynamic motor propelling capitalist development, and that, within capitalist society, the increasing political capacity and potency of the working class presents itself precisely as capitalist development.[28] In this essay, Tronti plants the seeds of this novel perspective through a re-reading of Marx, particularly the sections in *Capital*, volume 1, on the struggle by English workers to limit the length of their working day.[29]

In short, capital has a problem: individual capitalists, as a rule, are driven only by the prospect of increasing their own profit. One of the core means by which they increase profits is by increasing the exploitation of their workforce. The most basic way to increase exploitation is to extend the length of the working day, to increase what Marx called the extraction of surplus labor and the production of absolute surplus-value. If a worker produces in two hours the quantity of value that corresponds to her daily costs of reproduction (food, shelter, and other needs), and yet that same worker is compelled to work for eight hours per day, that means that three-quarters of her working day is for the capitalist's benefit, not for her own. Let's say the worker's boss decides that, if the worker wants to keep her job, she must now work for ten

27. Tronti, "Letter to Raniero Panzieri (June 1961)," this volume, 52–53.

28. Elements of this conception had been expressed by other thinkers, like Raya Dunayevskaya, who observed, from her own reading of *Capital*, that "[t]he struggles of the workers over the working day develop capitalist production." See *Marxism and Freedom: From 1776 until Today*, updated ed. (London: Pluto, 1975), 89. Although Tronti does not cite this passage, Italians in and around *Quaderni Rossi* and *Classe Operaia* did encounter Dunayevskaya's work by way of the French group Socialisme ou Barbarie, who had translated publications of the U.S.-based radical organization Correspondence, of which Dunayevskaya was a member alongside James Boggs, Martin Glaberman, CLR James, and Grace Lee. On this arc, see Asad Haider and Salar Mohandesi, "Workers' Inquiry: A Genealogy," *Viewpoint Magazine* 3 (September 2013), https://www.viewpointmag.com/2013/09/27/workers-inquiry-a-genealogy; Nicola Pizzolato, *Challenging Global Capitalism: Labor Migration, Radical Struggle, and Urban Change in Detroit and Turin* (New York: Palgrave Macmillan, 2013); and Christopher Taylor, "The Refusal of Work: From the Postemancipation Caribbean to Post-Fordist Empire," *small axe* 18, no. 2 (July 2014): 1–17.

29. Tronti would also work with the elements of Marx's analysis that had appeared *Capital*, volume 2, concerning capital's need to reproduce the conditions under which it can continue the production of surplus-value on an extended scale. Indeed, that volume was important for many of the operaisti, including Raniero Panzieri, who was the book's Italian translator.

hours per day at no additional pay. Now a greater proportion—four-fifths—of her working day is directly for the capitalist's benefit, and the degree of her exploitation has increased. The number of hours she must spend furnishing surplus-value for the capitalist has increased relative to the number of working hours for which she receives pay.

At the same time, the behavior of individual capitalists presents a problem for capital as a whole. The individual capitalist, if left unchecked, may lengthen the working day beyond the "natural" limits of what the human body can withstand. As Marx explains:

> By extending the working day, therefore, capitalist production, which is essentially the production of surplus-value, the absorption of surplus labour, not only produces a deterioration of human labour-power by robbing it of its normal moral and physical conditions of development and activity, but also produces the pre-mature exhaustion and death of this labour-power itself.[30]

The single capitalist, Marx explains, is often willing to take this risk. Blinded by individualism, he acts under the assumption that the long-term well-being of workers does not concern him. After all, the single capitalist reasons, if some of the people currently working for him die from exhaustion, there will be other workers ready and willing to take their places—immigrants from the countryside or from other nations. In short—and for Tronti, this is very important—no capitalist class consciousness can be assumed in advance. Marx continues:

> In every stock-jobbing swindle everyone knows that some time or other the crash must come, but everyone hopes that it may fall on the head of his neighbour, after he himself has caught the shower of gold and placed it in secure hands. *Après moi le déluge!* is the watchword of every capitalist and of every capitalist nation. Capital therefore takes no account of the health and the length of life of the worker, unless society forces it to do so. Its answer to the outcry about the physical and mental degradation, the premature death, the torture of over-work, is this: Should that pain trouble us, since it increases our pleasure (profit)? But looking at these things as a whole, it is evident that this does not depend on the will, either good or bad, of the individual capitalist. Under free competition, the immanent laws of capitalist production confront the individual capitalist as a coercive force external to him.[31]

Experiments and Explosions

30. Karl Marx, *Capital: A Critique of Political Economy,* vol. 1, trans. Ben Fowkes (London: Penguin, 1976), 376.
31. Marx, *Capital,* vol. 1, 381. The line in French, *"Après moi le deluge!"* [After me, the flood], is associated with King Louis XV's profligate reign.

Capital, Marx reminds us, "is not a thing, but a social relation," one which compels both workers and capitalists to act in certain ways.[32] In pursuit of profit, the capitalist devours the worker, the "living agent of fermentation" without whom the production process stagnates.[33] The preservation and expansion of what Marx and Tronti have called "social capital" therefore requires some additional mechanism, beyond the immediate profit motive of individual capitalists, to protect the capitalist system from the effects of their reckless self-centeredness.

In 1964 Tronti will suggest in the first editorial of *Classe Operaia* [Working Class] that, in order to discern the contours of the mechanism that holds capitalist society together and ensures its continued growth, "[w]e have to turn the problem on its head, change orientation, and start again from first principles, which means focusing on the struggle of the working class."[34] This rallying cry was intended not only to have a political effect. Tronti had become convinced, having confronted this problem of capitalists for capital, that to understand the capitalist system one must first understand workers in the plural, and not only the collective worker as a social mass, but the working class as a struggling subject, as an autonomous political power.[35]

Let's continue, as Tronti does in "Factory and Society," by considering Marx's reflections on the working-class struggle to shorten the working day, a process which takes place outside the bounds of the factory itself:

> It must be acknowledged that our worker emerges from the process of production looking different from when he entered it. In the market, as owner of the commodity "labour-power," he stood face to face with other owners of commodities, one owner against another owner. The contract by which he sold his labour-power to the capitalist proved in black and white, so to speak, that he was free to dispose of himself. But when the transaction was concluded, it was discovered that he was no "free agent," that the period of time for which he is free to sell his labour-power is the period of time for which he is forced to sell it, that in fact the vampire will not let go "while there remains a single muscle, sinew or drop of blood to be exploited." For "protection" against the serpent of their agonies, the workers have to put their heads together and, as a class, compel the passing of a law, an all-powerful social barrier by which they can be prevented from selling themselves and their families into slavery and death by voluntary contract with capital. In the place of the pompous catalogue of the "inalienable rights of man"

32. Marx, *Capital*, vol. 1, 932.
33. Marx, *Capital*, vol. 1, 292.
34. Tronti, "Lenin in England" [1964], in *Workers and Capital*, 65-72, 65.
35. Tronti, "The Copernican Revolution (May 1963)," this volume, 90.

there steps the modest Magna Carta of the legally limited working day, which at last makes clear "when the time which the worker sells is ended, and when his own begins." *Quantum mutatus ab illo!*[36]

Workers, refusing slavery and death, struggle "as a class" for a "social barrier" that limits the working day. And yet, Tronti would later point out, the "subjective demands" of the workers also fulfill the "objective needs of capitalist production."[37] This formulation might seem to confirm the cunning of capital, or suggest that workers' struggles for reform are simply petitions for a "golden chain."[38] Yet that would be seeing things from capital's perspective. From the working-class viewpoint, this same moment—the struggle by workers as a class to impose legislation on the capitalists—demonstrates that, not only do workers produce the surplus-value garnished by the individual capitalist, but the working-class struggle is the very lifeblood of "social capital." Workers' struggles produce the conditions that capitalist society requires for its own continued existence, and seeing the class as the beating heart of the system is necessary for participating in those struggles and deepening their reach.

Not only do workers' struggles prevent capitalists from undermining the foundations of capitalist society; they also provoke capitalist *development*. Capitalists increase the production of *absolute* surplus-value by extending the working day, a technique that runs up against physical limits, but they also seek to increase production of *relative* surplus-value. This requires intensive rather than extensive exploitation: speed-up on the assembly line, or investment in machinery, research, and science in the service of capitalist production.

These increases in productivity, which capital's ideologues call "innovations," are the core of capitalist development. The key point is that capitalists will not necessarily move to this terrain of their own accord; they must be compelled to develop the productive forces and increase relative exploitation. This compulsion often takes the form, especially in Marx's time, of legislation enacted by the state, prompted by and following on the heels of workers' struggles.[39] Progressive reforms, what Marx called "that first conscious and methodical reaction of society against the spontaneously developed form of its production process," must therefore be grasped not as regulations which intervene from outside the relation between capital and labor, but as an integral

36. Marx, *Capital*, vol. 1, 415–16. In a note on 416, Marx's translator Fowkes cites Virgil's *Aeneid*, book 2, line 274 for the Latin, rendering it as "What a great change from that time."

37. Tronti, "The Copernican Revolution," 89.

38. Marx, *Capital*, vol. 1, 769.

39. This claim distinguishes Tronti's project from those that understand capitalist development primarily through the prism of competition between individual capitalists.

mechanism of capitalist society itself, forcing weaker and older capitals to die off, concentrating capital in larger firms, prompting new investments in technologies, and injecting the capital relation into new environments.[40] Marx summarizes the process in the following way:

> If the general extension of factory legislation to all trades for the purpose of protecting the working class both in mind and body has become inevitable, on the other hand, as we have already pointed out, that extension hastens on the general conversion of numerous isolated small industries into a few combined industries carried on upon a large scale; it therefore accelerates the concentration of capital and the exclusive predominance of the factory system. It destroys both the ancient and the transitional forms behind which the dominion of capital is still partially hidden, and replaces them with a dominion which is direct and unconcealed. But by doing this it also generalizes the direct struggle against its rule. While in each individual workshop it enforces uniformity, regularity, order and economy, the result of the immense impetus given to technical improvement by the limitation and regulation of the working day is to increase the anarchy and the proneness to catastrophe of capitalist production as a whole, the intensity of labour, and the competition of machinery with the worker. By the destruction of small-scale and domestic industries it destroys the last resorts of the "redundant population," thereby removing what was previously a safety-valve for the whole social mechanism. By maturing the material conditions and the social combination of the process of production, it matures the contradictions and antagonisms of the capitalist form of that process, and thereby ripens both the elements for forming a new society and the forces tending towards the overthrow of the old one.[41]

Tronti's premises are all here: workers' struggles propel this development toward "specifically capitalist exploitation," from the extension of the working day to the increase in the intensity of exploitation, from the production of absolute surplus-value to that of relative surplus-value. Tronti, working through these passages by Marx, writes in "Factory in Society":

> Given capital's natural impulse toward the extension of the working day, it is true that the workers, putting their heads together and through living force, *as a class*, secured a law from the state, a social barrier which stopped them from accepting slavery "by means of a voluntary contract with capital." The working-class struggle constrained the capitalist to change the *form* of his dominion. Thus, the

40. Marx, *Capital*, vol. 1, 610.
41. Marx, *Capital*, vol. 1, 635.

pressure of labour-power is able to force capital to modify its own internal composition; it intervenes *within* capital as an essential component of capitalist development; it pushes capitalist production forward from within, to the point of driving it to penetrate all the external relations of social life.[42]

Struggles by the workers must be grasped as a force that "intervenes *within* capital" via a "political mediation."[43] If Marx had called the legislation around the working day a "social barrier," Tronti intuited that society as a whole was becoming "an *articulation* of production."[44] The "violent intervention of the state" served as a ramp to new levels of accumulation; it was a means by which the collective capitalist "seeks first to convince and then reaches the point of compelling the individual capitalist to conform to the general needs of capitalist social production."[45]

Herein lies the specificity of capitalist society. Capitalist society does not simply imply the existence of capitalists; rather, some agent of the collective capitalist must be established—here, that agent is the state—in order to ensure the reproduction of the conditions required to produce surplus-value: namely, the health of the workers. What's more, this reproduction must be, as Marx tells us, *on an extended scale*, that is, not merely a maintenance of the existing conditions of exploitation. Capital must constantly grow, which means it must constantly innovate. This cannot happen spontaneously, for a capitalist who has sunk millions into a plant that has become outdated will junk it only under duress. Growth requires compulsion, too:

> [T]he relation between capitalist production and society, between factory and society, between society and state, becomes increasingly organic. At the highest level of capitalist development, this social relation becomes a *moment* of the relation of production, the whole of society becomes an *articulation* of production, the whole society lives in function of the factory and the factory extends its exclusive dominion over the whole society. It is on this basis that the political state machine tends ever more to identify with the figure of the *collective capitalist*; it increasingly becomes the property of the capitalist mode of production and, therefore, a *function of the capitalist*.[46]

42. Tronti, "Factory and Society" [1962], in *Workers and Capital*, 12–35, 21.

43. Tronti, "Factory and Society," 23. If "politics," understood as subjective intervention, was always central to Tronti's framework, his attention to "political mediation" would grow over the course of the decade. Compare this passage, for example, to those in Tronti, "Report at Piombino (May 1964)" and "Within and Against (May 1967)," both in this volume.

44. Tronti, "Factory and Society," 26.

45. Tronti, "Factory and Society," 23.

46. Tronti, "Factory and Society," 26.

For Tronti, "capitalist society" only emerges once this circuit has been established, once the process of the regulation of "social capital" has been activated through workers' struggles that make demands on the state.

The Capitalist State and Democratic Planning

Tronti's second essay for *Quaderni Rossi*, titled "The Plan of Capital," develops the methodological discourse of "Factory and Society" and moves toward an explicitly political conclusion. This conclusion would in turn form the premise for the political work that he and his comrades would pursue through *Classe Operaia*. In this 1963 essay, Tronti argued that capitalist society can only be said to exist historically once all social production has become the production of capital, and once the collective capitalist has been produced as a "functionary of the total social capital." Against this figure of the collective capitalist there is "total social labour as a class of organized workers—social labour-power as a class." Capital's "plan," then, "emerges primarily from the need to make the working class function *as such* within social capital," in other words, to ensure that the working class's political action as a class serves capitalist development.[47] The plan of capital is the means by which social capital exerts total control over the working-class movements required by capitalist development. The "bourgeois brouhaha over state intervention" aside, centralized economic planning represents a step beyond the legislation that in Marx's day had regulated the length of the working day. Planning does not fetter the development of capital; on the contrary, it is a "very advanced form of the economic mechanism's self-regulation," which can also launch it to a "higher level." What *appears* to be "intervention" by the state "from the outside" actually serves as "a particular moment within the development of capital."[48]

This integration of the working class into the process of capitalist development includes the institutionalization of forms that workers have used to organize themselves, namely, trade unions, which acquire "decisive importance for the social interests of capital."[49] And, unlike the corporatist policies of the Italian fascist era, neocapitalist planning includes democratic participation, while also offering some measures of autonomy. The "true organic integration of the workers' unions within the programmed development of capitalist society" involves a careful balance to ensure the workers' collaboration in the process of development. Barring the explicit anticapitalist organization of

47. Tronti, "The Plan of Capital" [1963], in *Workers and Capital*, 36–64, 37.
48. Tronti, "The Plan of Capital," 45.
49. Tronti, "The Plan of Capital," 49–50.

workers according to an independent strategy, the unions function in service to capital.

> There is thus a tendential unity of authority and pluralism, of central direction and of local autonomy, with political dictatorship and an economic democracy, an *authoritarian state* and a *democratic society*. True, at this point there is no longer capitalist development without a plan of capital. But there cannot be a plan of capital without *social capital*. It is capitalist society which programmes its own development, by itself. And this is what *democratic planning* is.[50]

Tronti outlined the features of the capitalist state's particular form of despotism—democratic planning—in order to demonstrate that the presence of trade unions at the bargaining table with major employers and the state was not simply ideological propaganda, visualizing some pluralist fantasy, but a "material fact" that showed evidence of capital's need to incorporate the demands of the labor movement.[51] The unions' role in capitalist planning was to guarantee the continued subservience of the class struggle to capitalist development.

How does Tronti propose to counteract these processes of political subsumption? In this essay, he turns from analysis at a historical and theoretical level to an assessment of his contemporary political situation:

> Social capital's programming of its own development can and must be answered by a truly working-class planning of the revolutionary process. True, it is not enough to oppose the plan of capital at the ideal level; it is necessary to know how to use it materially. And this is impossible other than by counterposing to the *economic* programme of capitalist development a *political* plan of working-class answers.[52]

This working-class counterplan, which is a political strategy for building power and carrying out an organized revolution, involves a "long-term" strategy. This embryonic discussion of the "*political* plan" forecasts what Tronti will later call the "strategy of refusal": the refusal by workers to be integrated into capitalist planning, their refusal to bargain in an orderly fashion, and ultimately, their refusal to work.

> It is at this point that the working class must instead consciously organise itself as an *irrational* element within the specific rationality of capitalist production. The growing rationalisation of modern capital

50. Tronti, "The Plan of Capital," 50.
51. Tronti, "The Plan of Capital," 52.
52. Tronti, "The Plan of Capital," 60.

must find an insurmountable limit in the growing irrationality of the organised workers—that is, in the working-class refusal of *political* integration within the system's *economic* development. Thus, the working class becomes the only *anarchy* that capitalism is unable to *organise* socially. The task of the workers' movement is to scientifically organise and politically manage *this* working-class anarchy within capitalist production. On the model of the society organised by capital, the working-class party itself can only be the *organisation of anarchy*—no longer within capital, but outside of it, meaning outside of its development.[53]

By what means can the workers' movement organize such a refusal? How can this strategic perspective come to command forces strong enough to counteract capital? Tronti had already indicated in "Factory and Society" that a revolutionary process of this type could not be carried out "without the *political organisation* of the working class, without a *working-class party*."[54] But in "The Plan of Capital," he begins to broach the problem of strategy and the relationship it may have to the political project of revolution:

> The theoretical formulation of a total revolutionary strategy, at this level, is no longer only possible, it becomes absolutely necessary for the foundation of the revolutionary process itself. The objective anarchy of the working class within capitalism must now express itself at the highest level of consciousness. None of its elements can be left up to spontaneity any longer: everything must be tied to a scientific perspective for the revolution and to its consequent rigorous organisation.[55]

The working class's demand for power requires "*organising* the struggle for power."[56] "Workers," he reminds his readers, "do not move unless they feel organised," unless they are "*armed* in the struggle." Their action, the prerequisite of any serious Leninist politics, requires that there be "a plan for revolution which is also explicitly organised."[57] Organization is thus a matter of practical necessity not only for effective political activity but for constructing Marxist theory itself:

> The Marxist analysis of capitalism will not proceed unless it arrives at a working-class theory of revolution. And the latter will be useless if not incarnated in real material forces. And these forces will not exist for society unless they are politically organised in a class against this society.[58]

53. Tronti, "The Plan of Capital," 61. For a similar formulation, see "The Strike at FIAT (July 1962)," this volume, 73.
54. Tronti, "Factory and Society," 34.
55. Tronti, "The Plan of Capital," 62.
56. Tronti, "The Plan of Capital," 62-63.
57. Tronti, "The Plan of Capital," 63.
58. Tronti, "The Plan of Capital," 63.

The taste Tronti had acquired from Colletti and Della Volpe for the scientific method of experimentation, and his commitment to Marxism as the production of heterogeneous unities, would continue to shape his work for years.[59] The relationship between strategy and tactics, and between theory and practice, would not be one of mirror images but of links in a chain.

The Organization of an Imbalance

To proceed now from Tronti's methodological premises toward his novel contributions to political thought requires a half step back for historical context. Between the publication of the first and second issues of *Quaderni Rossi*, fractures in the editorial group had begun to emerge. The debate is often described as being about the relative merits of continuing to "analyze" capital and the factory, and attempting to "intervene" in the struggles that were beginning to rumble. Such differences in approach germinated among those investigating the workers' of FIAT in Turin, but the debate also circled around Tronti.

Vittorio Rieser, a *Quaderni Rossi* contributor and sociologist involved in the Turin inquiry, co-wrote an article in March of 1962 that warned of "Hegelian" elements in Tronti's framework, which Rieser and his co-author deemed too close to Colletti's method of determinate abstraction. They favored, instead, a Marxism committed to the patient analysis of capitalist processes by means of sociological inquiry.[60] On the other side, in April of 1962, at a seminar held by *Quaderni Rossi* on Marx's *Capital* and problems in the workers' movement, Tronti spoke for those more restless members of the group. There he argued that, indeed, it would be a "mistake" to simply return to the logical discourse of a Colletti or a Della Volpe.[61] However, the correct Marxist (and Leninist) approach would be to shift from philosophy not to sociology, but to revolutionary politics.

In May, asked about the growing schism in a letter from Alberto Asor Rosa, Panzieri acknowledged the feeling of "discomfort" beginning to plague the group. But he identified these as growing pains associated with a "leap in the objective situation." Moreover, he praised the theoretical advances made

59. In "Our *Operaismo*," Tronti has written that he "outgrew" Della Volpe and Colletti's framework "as far as content was concerned, while retaining its lessons with regard to method" (330). It would be interesting to consider Tronti's subsequent methodology in light of the critique by Louis Althusser of Colletti's model of "experimental practice." See "The Object of *Capital*," in Louis Althusser et al., *Reading "Capital": The Complete Edition* (London: Verso, 2015), 215-355, 285-86.

60. See Vittorio Rieser, "Sociologia e marxismo" [Sociology and Marxism], in *L'operaismo degli anni sessanta*, 160-62, an extract from a longer article written with Laura Balbo, "La sinistra e lo sviluppo della sociologia" [The left and the development of sociology], *Problemi del socialismo* 3 (March 1962): 169-93. See also "Interview with Vittorio Rieser" [October 3, 2001], trans. *generation-online*, October 2006, http://www.generation-online.org/t/vittorio.htm.

61. Tronti, "Closing Speech at the Santa Severa Seminar (April 1962)," this volume, 56.

by Tronti, "the only Marxist *thinker* we know of, these days."[62] The "Panzieri-Tronti Theses," distributed internally shortly thereafter in June, sought to settle the nascent tension between the more "sociological" investigators in Turin, who had produced the first issue, and those who began to call for more "political" intervention, grouped around Tronti.

The "Theses" held both "spontaneity" and "prefigurative groups" in contempt. Instead, Panzieri and Tronti emphasized the need for a party that is a "global" and "unitary" form of political organization. If the class composes itself "outside of capital," the party, as an "indispensable moment of revolutionary strategy," must remain "outside of the bourgeois state."[63] This emphasis on outsidedness echoes the stance that Tronti had been developing in his published essays on how to combat the integration of workers in capitalist society.

The authors also called for the need to establish "self-management within the revolutionary process."[64] One such moment of autonomy emerged in the extraordinary outbreak of militancy that shook Italy in 1962. Between 1960 and 1962, the number of working days lost to strikes in Italy quadrupled.[65] In 1962, the workers' offensive was concentrated in Turin, and over the summer 60,000 from FIAT awakened from their slumber and joined a city-wide struggle. Meanwhile FIAT's president Vittorio Valletta had endorsed the prospect of a center-left government led by the Christian Democrats (DC) [Democrazia Cristiana] with the PSI in tow. Valletta hoped that such a pact could lead to state planning of capitalist development in a rational manner that would smooth out regional and sectoral imbalances in productivity and modes of exploitation. He also hoped that planning could preempt the kinds of outbursts that had left his own assembly lines idle.

"The Strike at FIAT," one of Tronti's most lucid articles from this period, considered how this renewed labor militancy might yet be siphoned into a trade-union form suitable for capital, a "capitalist form of workers' control." This new institution could be as independent from the "workers' thrusts" as from the individual capitalists' preferences. The successful initiatives of certain sectors of workers between 1960–62 meant that wage gains and increases in productivity were distributed unevenly across the peninsula. The "plan" of capital for gradual economic development and wage growth required institutionalizing and rationalizing the workers' struggles, channeling them into regular bargaining schedules at the sectoral or even national level, and eliminating the need for strikes.[66] But for Tronti even a prospect

62. "Panzieri a Asor Rosa, 10 maggio 1962" [Raniero Panzieri to Alberto Asor Rosa, May 10, 1962], in *L'operaismo degli anni Sessanta*, 177–81, 178 (my translation).

63. "Panzieri-Tronti Theses (June 1962)," this volume, 67.

64. "Panzieri-Tronti Theses," 67.

65. Paul Ginsborg, *A History of Contemporary Italy: Society and Politics, 1943-1988* (London: Penguin, 1990), 270.

66. Tronti, "The Strike at FIAT," 71.

of this kind would not extinguish the struggles; capital's need for rationalization and reform afforded new material foundations, and consequently new political opportunities:

> The same organization of modern production that capital uses to decompose and destroy the class unity of the workers can be used by the workers' movement to recompose and excite that unity, in new forms, at a higher level. In this sense, there is no quality intrinsic to organized production that makes it always and only of service to capitalist power: everything always depends, in the end, on the relation of forces established in the struggle.[67]

The only way to escape and indeed destroy capital's plan was "*to organize the imbalance* of a working class that totally escapes the planned control of the capitalist class."[68] There could be nothing spontaneous about revolutionary activity, because the thrusts were precisely the lifeblood of capitalist development so long as they could be routed through orderly channels. The antagonism of workers would not be "explosive" to the system without finding permanent forms of organization that were networked in "capillary" form.[69]

This article had been written just before the watershed days of July 7–9, 1962. During those days, with the metal-workers of Turin still out on strike, the conservative-leaning Italian Labor Union (UIL) [Unione Italiana del Lavoro] would sign a side agreement with FIAT, undercutting the workers' struggles. A march and demonstration planned by the traditional workers' institutions—the Italian General Confederation of Labor (CGIL) [Confederazione Generale Italiana del Lavoro], the PCI, and the PSI—turned into a full-scale riot, centered around the UIL headquarters in Piazza Statuto and drawing unemployed workers and youth into the streets. The confidence of the class and its hostility toward accommodation with employers was growing, despite cries for moderation by the unions and parties.

By autumn, rising wages, inflated prices, and strong consumer demand for commodities combined to produce inflation. Small and medium industrialists cut back on their investments, and financial panic began to set in among those strata of Italian society whose savings were being eroded. The professionals and petit bourgeoisie who were most deeply affected were also the backbone of the DC, and the initiatives by the "progressive" wing of the Christian party to collaborate with the PSI on economic planning and social reform were shelved.[70]

67. Tronti, "The Strike at FIAT," 73.
68. Tronti, "The Strike at FIAT," 73.
69. Tronti, "The Strike at FIAT," 73.
70. Ginsborg, *History of Contemporary Italy*, 271.

In this context, Tronti's "The Plan of Capital," which began to circulate among the editors of *Quaderni Rossi* in late 1962, correctly portended a "plan" wrecked by uneven implementation.[71] The halting progress of the planning initiative indicated "dangerous *contradictions* for the capitalist class" and "miraculous *opportunities* for the workers' movement." The struggle to implement planning that was ideal for social capital meant that capitalist development itself, at this point, offered "the *possibility* of breaking the cyclical process through which capitalist social relations are produced and reproduced." The political opportunity arose not from a period of "catastrophic crisis in the system" but a political crisis concerning how best to respond to the growing pains of development.[72]

Tronti warned that "[w]e must not believe that capitalism and its functionaries have an absolute self-consciousness in all phases."[73] Nevertheless, the specter of planning did indicate a growing "self-consciousness" among the governing and business sets alike. "The total capital now needs the total labour to be standing visible before it, to make the necessary economic calculations for its own planned development."[74] If the struggle for higher wages was itself an indicator of the working class's combativeness in the face of the boss, that impulse could be weaponized by the enemy if the enemy were united and able to integrate the workers' demands in economic terms.[75] The question for Tronti was what action in this determinate moment would shift forces in favor of the workers. Organization and intervention were crucial for directing that antagonism toward the political realm, against the state, to rid the workers of it for good.

Tronti began to sketch out a work plan for how to attack this problem in a letter to Panzieri written in January 1963, in which he suggested they "launch a political newspaper directed at the workers of FIAT" and "experiment with a practical *model* of working-class organization."[76] A practical experiment was needed to unify the efforts of the editors and directly address the need for organization in the workers' fiercest struggles. It became not a matter of "testing" the discourse developed in *Quaderni Rossi* but of "directly *practicing*" organizational activity.[77]

71. Tronti's article arrived amid the growing rift in *Quaderni Rossi*, which had been exacerbated by diverging interpretations of the events of Piazza Statuto. Panzieri also leveled quite serious criticisms against the article itself; he and those Turinese editors who favored the original format of the journal decided to displace Tronti's "The Plan of Capital" from the lead editorial spot of the next issue and instead wrote their own article, which judged the time for intervention into the workers' struggle against the capitalist plan as not yet right.

72. Tronti, "The Plan of Capital," 43.

73. Tronti, "The Plan of Capital," 43.

74. Tronti, "The Plan of Capital," 54–55.

75. This would become important later for Tronti when he noted how severely wage increases were outstripping increases in productivity during the 1960s in Italy; see Tronti, "Within and Against (May 1967)," this volume. In subsequent years, of course, the relationship was inverted.

76. Tronti, "Letter to Raniero Panzieri (January 1963)," this volume, 79.

77. Tronti, "Letter to Raniero Panzieri (January 1963)," 81.

Over the winter of 1962–63, some of *Quaderni Rossi*'s "interventionists" would produce local newspapers for workers in various quarters of northern Italy. Tronti met with comrades on the side of intervention in Milan, where he delivered an important address that contains many of the assertions that would later appear in "Lenin in England," the inaugural editorial of the group's forthcoming initiative. In this discussion, Tronti argued "a bourgeois revolution as such has never existed," since the bourgeoisie did not constitute a class before ascending to political power in Europe.[78] Instead, it had gradually accumulated economic power.

Tronti then suggested that the working class, by contrast, cannot accumulate economic power. Instead it grows in political strength. For this reason, the moment of economic crisis was to be definitively subordinated to "the political revolution of the working class."[79] Rather than studying the laws of capitalist development, what now was required was to identify the "working class's own laws of development." Only in this way could one "forecast the future movements of the class" and provide oneself with "the opportunity to immediately organize them."[80] The class would not "spontaneously discove[r] communication and an organizational form allowing it to leap beyond the capitalist economic mechanism."[81] Instead, the organization would need to be methodically constructed.

But if spontaneous activity would not be enough, the existing left parties and unions function for capital as the "working-class articulation" of the total production process.[82] Rather than organs facilitating working-class liberation, they were in fact obstacles to it. They sought to leash the working class's antagonism and take it for periodic strolls along a pre-approved route of demands. The delivery of these demands was essential for capitalist development, and thus "refusal" becomes the key revolutionary watchword: when "the working class refuses to become the mediator of capitalist development," it expresses its own autonomous strategy. If the working class were able to force its institutions to quit articulating capital's needs, the "entire economic mechanism" could be blocked and a "serious revolutionary prospect" could emerge. By forecasting the moment in which "the workers themselves refuse to present demands to capital…refuse the entire trade-union level, refuse the contractual form of relation to capital," Tronti brought forward the components of not only spontaneous behavior but of revolutionary strategy in the class's movements.[83]

78. Tronti, "The Copernican Revolution," 85.
79. Tronti, "The Copernican Revolution," 90.
80. Tronti, "The Copernican Revolution," 86, 87.
81. Tronti, "The Copernican Revolution," 87.
82. Tronti, "The Copernican Revolution," 89.
83. Tronti, "The Copernican Revolution," 89.

Experiments and Explosions

Here arose, once again, the problem of unity. The development of capitalism provided "the material basis for this political unity of the class," but that unity had to be produced and reproduced through political organization. "The mass of total refusal—the 'no' opposed to the demands of the capitalists," Tronti insisted:

> can happen only when indeed this working class is not only a social mass, but a politically organized social mass, in other words, one that is politically functional to the point of actually expressing political organization in new forms, in forms that basically we do not yet know, that we still must discover. That is, how, at that stage, the political organization of the class, and the form it takes, will be expressed.[84]

Tronti's openness to the precise forms of unity that will be composed is important here. The forms of organization may not be known in advance, and the changing political composition of the working class would require continual investigation. Having criticized "preceding organizational forms of the class"—the union, the party, and spontaneous formations—what remained now was "the positive moment, of construction of the models of organization." This "experimental course" of constructing new models to see how they work in practice offers an opportunity for Marxian scientific practice, in which "the necessity of the experiment becomes functional to the construction of the the-oretical model."[85] The forms Tronti will later propose for such an experiment will include a network of "working-class editorial boards" and a cadre of factory workers to disseminate the political slogans proposed by the newspaper and test their capacity to rally the rank and file for organized struggle.[86]

Quaderni Rossi released its third issue in June of 1963. In July they would release the *Cronache Operaie* [Workers' Chronicles], a testament to the increasing pressure felt by Tronti, Antonio Negri, Romano Alquati, and others to address their literature to workers. This six-page leaflet included an unsigned article by Tronti on "The Two Reformisms." In this text, he argued that the unions acted as "active entrepreneurs of labor-power" and "offices for managing the working class on capital's behalf." Tronti further argued that the crisis of the center-left, that "first reformist political solution of capital," had been prompted by the "hot summer" of 1962, most notably by the workers at FIAT, who had given capital "its first strategic defeat of the postwar period." This strategic defeat took place as a result of the workers' expression of the strategy of refusal, however inchoate: "[t]he invitation to political collaboration with capital was picked up and thrown back by the workers in their attempt to subjectively reunify the

84. Tronti, "The Copernican Revolution," 92–93.
85. Tronti, "The Copernican Revolution," 93.
86. Tronti, "Letter to Antonio Negri (September 1963)," this volume, 102.

various levels of their own struggles."[87] Having rediscovered their own capacity for striking and street violence, and having rejected the unions' as well as the parties' attempts to mediate the struggle and channel it into the polite corridors of bargaining, the workers were on the march.

In this text, Tronti also reveled in the "anticapitalist sense" that the workers' struggle had assumed. If it were true that "each one of these struggles, at the outset and in the end, is always inscribed in an equally objective process of the development of capital," it was just as true that the process of this struggle "continually overturn[ed] the capitalist use of the struggle and repurpos[ed] it as a tool for working-class self-organization."[88] If the "signing of any contract is a working-class defeat," nevertheless "always, after the struggle, a particular power rests in the hands of the workers: an expanded political composition of the working-class mass, which seeks an anticapitalist organization."[89]

The need for the weapon of organization would only grow. What was required was a form capable of preventing reformist solutions from gaining traction in the factory, expanding the workers' refusal to collaborate, providing the geographical and temporal continuity necessary to sustain it, and articulating a revolutionary movement.[90] "There will be no workers' power until it is organized politically," he wrote.[91]

A Paper of a New Type

In a letter written to Antonio Negri in September of 1963, Tronti broached the question of the "organizational recomposition" of the group of militants who would split from *Quaderni Rossi* to launch *Classe Operaia*, a newspaper written for workers. Tronti hoped that its format would permit the group to shorten the time between issues, allowing "an increasingly direct intervention into individual situations, to both orient and transform them." Tronti believed that this quickened pace of publication would help to concentrate the "scattered forces" of the workers' struggle into a single point. If battles in the realm of theory could be conducted somewhat gradually, "at the political level, we must be right immediately, shifting material facts to our liking, with the simple violence of our own subjective forces."[92]

---

87. Tronti, "The Two Reformisms (July 1963)," this volume, 98.

88. Tronti, "The Two Reformisms," 99.

89. Tronti, "The Two Reformisms," 99.

90. For important reflections rooted in the context of the Bolsheviks' role in the Russian Revolution concerning the concept of "articulation"—in the sense of joining together diverse elements in order to facilitate movement—see Salar Mohandesi, "All Tomorrow's Parties: A Reply to Critics," *Viewpoint Magazine*, May 23, 2012, https://www.viewpointmag.com/2012/05/23/all-tomorrows-parties-a-reply-to-critics.

91. Tronti, "The Two Reformisms," 99.

92. Tronti, "Letter to Antonio Negri," 102.

That same fall, Tronti's notes on "A Replacement of Leadership" indicate that, from a very early stage, he planned for the work of *Classe Operaia* to proceed through successive phases. The initial problem, as he had indicated in his letter to Negri, was to organize the "new forms of working-class struggles," but at a certain point, the newspaper-cum-political organization's work would shift to a new level, "to organize the organization."[93] The goal then would be "to prepare the objective conditions for this leap to the new organization," helping to generalize "anticapitalist and antibureaucratic" forms of struggle that could cause a "political crisis and vertical collapse of the old organizations." The working class as a political force was already "full of political duplicity"; for Tronti the goal was to facilitate "class action to make the parties explode." Only then could the "correct recomposition" of the relationship between the class and party be accomplished. Here, "the problem of the party" and the "primacy of politics"—understood in a relationship of "unity-distinction" with theory—come into increasingly clear view.[94]

Over the winter of 1963–64, the PSI entered the governing coalition for the first time alongside the DC. With the specters of reform and planning continuing to loom, one-third of the PSI's members, including trade-union leaders and advocates of political autonomy from the government, quit to form a new party, the Socialist Party of Proletarian Unity (PSIUP) [Partito Socialista di Unità Proletaria]. At the same time, the weak economy was proving stubborn, and the Bank of Italy began to carry out deflationary measures. Prime Minister Aldo Moro argued that reforms could not be carried out under existing economic conditions.[95]

Meanwhile, *Classe Operaia*'s first issue was published in January with Tronti's "Lenin in England" as the lead editorial. The *operaista* manifesto affirmed the working class's "political capacity to impose reformism on capital, and then to make rough-and-ready use of that reformism for the purposes of the working-class revolution." This "strategic outlook" of the class, Tronti noted, was not yet embodied in its "tactical position," for it was still "a class without class organization." In the absence of the political organization of the class, the workers needed to harness their own capacity to "put brakes on capitalist development" rather than "give capital's reformist operations a free hand."[96]

Tronti's editorial suggested "strategic support for the general development of capital"—because capitalist development indicated the working class's political development—and "tactical opposition to the particular modes of that development." So, he underlined, "in the working class today, tactics and

93. Thanks to Matteo Mandarini for suggesting the importance of these notes in Tronti's trajectory during these years.

94. Tronti, "A Replacement of Leadership (Autumn 1963)," this volume, 107.

95. Ginsborg, *History of Contemporary Italy*, 274-75.

96. Tronti, "Lenin in England," 68.

strategy contradict one another." The "theoretical moment of *strategy*" and the "political moment of *tactics*" thus entered into a contradictory or even duplicitous unity, in which their non-identity was in fact a source of strength.[97] The strategic, theoretical moment of the class need not be weighed down by "immediate organizational tasks," but, at the same time, organization was not required to bend to a theory's law.[98]

In preparation for the release of the double issue 4–5, with its editorial "An Old Tactic for a New Strategy," *Classe Operaia* held a public event in the coastal town of Piombino. The gathering drew a large crowd of young militants. In Tronti's "Report" there, he offered reflections on the newspaper as the unique tool specifically capable of concretely unifying theoretical work and practical intervention in sites of class struggle, "made for unifying these two moments, which otherwise would seem to be completely isolated from one another."[99] The newspaper, with its capacity to present theoretical analysis alongside reportage on current events, congealed through the practical unifying labor of writing, editing, publishing, and distributing the paper among workers, made it an ideal venue for building a concretely united nucleus of radicals.

Organizational practice was seen as a key moment in conceptualizing anticapitalist struggle. This distinguished *Classe Operaia* from *Quaderni Rossi*, which Tronti indicted for its "pure and simple analysis also of the moment of intervention." Their new project was better suited to move to "practical forms of concrete actualization" and participation in the struggles themselves. The first proposed form was to be "an autonomous network of cadres," coordinated and committed to putting forward the newspaper's analysis to workers at the factory gates, or better yet, inside them. These cadres would not be like those of the old PCI, but "a new type of political militant" commited to "explod[ing] the traditional concept of the political organization in the party sense."[100] This dynamite would clear the ground for political organization to emerge in a new way.

The Party and the Problem of Organization

These discussions unfolded in a context of political instability at the national level. The center-left had failed to implement economic planning and instead continued deflationary measures, resulting in more than 300,000 workers being laid off from industrial jobs between 1964 and

97. Tronti, "Lenin in England," 69.
98. Tronti, "Lenin in England," 70.
99. Tronti, "Report at Piombino," 122.
100. Tronti, "Report at Piombino," 121, 122.

1966.[101] Private investment would continue to lag, and in June the first Moro government collapsed. It was quickly replaced by another government of the DC and PSI.

The center-left government continued to exclude the Communists, and talk of economic planning remained in the air. In August of 1964, Palmiro Togliatti, the long-time head of the PCI, died in Yalta. The vacuum of leadership in the Party now appeared to Tronti to offer new openings for political activity. That autumn, his articles "1905 in Italy" and "Class and Party" would cause some degree of disorientation among the group of editors by speaking explicitly about the PCI as a tool for revolutionary organization. In "An Old Tactic for a New Strategy," written in May, he had argued that "[t]he imbalance between wages and productivity is a political fact" that needed to be grasped and "used politically," thus granting workers' struggles in the factory credit for having prompted a crisis in the state.[102] Now, several months later in "1905 in Italy," Tronti asserted:

> It seems that all the contradictions and irrationalities typical of a capitalist society's development mechanism have been offloaded from the economic level onto the political level and concentrated there. Indeed, today the crisis always appears as a crisis of the state: what appears within the structures of production is, at most, a "difficult conjuncture." But, if this is how things appear, we should not be deceived. The dictatorship of capital rarely enjoys political stability. And, politically speaking, the capitalists are amateurs; it is always easy to beat them on this terrain with four well-combined moves. Their practical intelligence is all in economics. But the logic of profit does not mechanically coincide with the logic of power.[103]

Rebuilding the connection between the factory and the party—now understood clearly as the Communist Party—became the task of the day. In "Class and Party," Tronti affirmed that "[f]rom the workers' point of view, from within modern capitalism, the political struggle is the one that aims consciously to pitch into crisis the economic mechanisms of capitalist development."[104] Now the struggle for the wage—as the struggle for the working day had been in England for Marx—had assumed a political character, as the quicker growth of wages relative to productivity had put the government into crisis. This topic would increasingly preoccupy Tronti in the coming years. If he had already suggested a "new strategic approach" to invert "the relation between the

101. Milana and Trotta, *L'operaismo degli anni sessanta*, 361.
102. Tronti, "An Old Tactic for a New Strategy" [1964], in *Workers and Capital*, 73-80, 76.
103. Tronti, "1905 in Italy" [1964], in *Workers and Capital*, 81-88, 82.
104. Tronti, "Class and Party" [1964], in *Workers and Capital*, 89-100, 91.

working-class political movement and the economic crisis of capitalism," in the autumn of 1964, after the death of Togliatti, Tronti turned to the problem of tactics at the level of the party.[105]

> [W]hat interests us today is to foreground an element that we have thus far scarcely taken into account: namely, the subjective consciousness, which is internal and essential to the very concept of political struggle, and constitutive of all active intervention by the revolutionary will, insofar as it is the fruit of organisation. In fact, it is within this definition of the political content of the class struggle that we will discover, reaffirm and impose anew the irreplaceable function of the working-class party.[106]

The "correct relationship between class and party" meant determining the elements and roles of this concrete unity. The party was tasked with the "practical capacity to foresee and orient the class's movements in historically determinate situations," not only perceiving "laws of action" but "act[ing] concretely, on the basis of an intimate understanding of what might be called the theory and practice of the law of tactics." If "the working class spontaneously possesses the strategy of its own movements and its development"—in other words, the strategy of refusal—"the party has but to identify it, express it and organise it." The class could not act tactically in service of such a strategy; this required a party.[107]

To reconstitute this link, the PCI needed to enter into the factory. Its membership had eroded: between 1956 and 1966, amid rapid capitalist development, the Party had lost nearly a quarter of its membership,[108] and in 1965 only 3 percent of workers under the age of thirty in Turin, to take one city, carried cards.[109] The PCI was very clearly in crisis, but rather than abandon it for the political activity of small groups, Tronti was convinced that it could be renovated and wielded as a mass anticapitalist force if realigned under the banner of a new strategy. From the autumn of 1964 through the winter, Tronti would propose to regroup the formations on the left of the Party and go on the offensive, in both the factory and in mass political confrontation.

Amid an economic upswing in April of 1965, Tronti would remark, in a "Balance Sheet of the 'Intervention'" carried out by *Classe Operaia* up to that point, that the workers' struggle against the boss must be tied to the one "for the party." These were the "two faces of the workers' struggles in this moment,"

105. Tronti, "Class and Party," 91.
106. Tronti, "Class and Party," 91.
107. Tronti, "Class and Party," 93.
108. Ginsborg, *History of Contemporary Italy*, 290
109. Milana and Trotta, *L'operaismo degli anni sessanta*, 432.

but the operaista project had previously discounted the party, lulled by the rosy haze of the workers' immediate struggles.[110] On the same day that Tronti delivered this self-criticism before the group of editors, *Classe Operaia* held a public meeting in Turin on the subject of "the party in the factory."

Tronti's speech there sought to keep one eye on workers' struggles and the other on the development of capitalist planning, continuing to insist on the primacy of the former and searching for ways to take advantage of the latter. In his eyes, the enlightened sectors of capital, pressing for planning and a center-left government, had outpaced the politicians and administrators of the DC, which had found itself unable to carry out much more than the nationalization of the electricity industry. The capitalist class demonstrated a more savvy political reading of the situation than had the politicians in government.[111]

But now, in 1965, Tronti sensed a "convergence" between capitalists and politicians. The relationship between class and organization was unstable, as ever, but for the moment the renewed dialogue between big industry and the state indicated the possible "recovery of a deep unity." This increasingly harmonious relationship between the capitalist class and its state would soon, Tronti surmised, figure out a division of labor: capitalists would handle the production of profit, and the state would manage the distribution of income.[112]

The prospect of a strengthened alliance between capitalists and the state was worrisome especially because the workers' side was experiencing "*greater division between the Communist Party and the working class.*"[113] If the earlier season of militancy had the capacity to block "the process of unification between capitalist class and bourgeois political stratum," divide the capitalist class from its state, and "put the state and governmental structures of the Italian political apparatus into crisis," that time had passed and a temporary unity had been accomplished.[114] The problem was, then, to recompose the relationship between the PCI and the working class.

Given the "workers' openness to struggle" at the general social level, and the fact that there remained a blocked "channel of communication" between the workers in the factory, the intermediary cadres, and the leadership of the Party, *Classe Operaia*'s new initiative would be the tall order of rebuilding this relationship according to the strategy of refusal.[115] Tronti warned that it would not be easy; if aggression toward the bosses emerged from

110. Tronti, "A Balance Sheet of the 'Intervention' (April 1965)," this volume, 148.
111. Tronti, "The Party in the Factory," 129.
112. Tronti, "The Party in the Factory," 130.
113. Tronti, "The Party in the Factory," 131.
114. Tronti, "The Party in the Factory," 134.
115. Tronti, "The Party in the Factory," 136.

workers' immediate experience, the struggle "toward" the party possessed a different character. From his vantage point, the workers themselves had not deemed the PCI a useful tactical instrument—a judgment confirmed by their abandonment of the PCI in droves. But Tronti was sanguine; tactics could be carried out "only by an already existing political organization, and only by the party already reconnected to the class as such." Due to the lack of spontaneous adhesion of workers to the party, *Classe Operaia* needed "to organize a certain type of working-class thrust toward the party," the vehicle for working-class political revolution.[116]

Tronti saw the role of the militant theorist as articulating a material unity between these distinct dimensions of the struggle: party-tactics and class-strategy. Tronti proposed to restrict the party's ambit to tactically engaging the enemy, leaving aside the long-term plan of how to overthrow the domination of capital and its state. Rather than the domination of the party over the class of workers, he instead foresaw "workers' control over the party."[117] And not only was a dictatorship of the party undesirable; it was unlikely. The high intensity of the working-class struggle indicated an enduring "class hatred" unlikely to be quelled by reformist channels.[118] The PCI meanwhile was weak: its structures were in shambles, its means of communication were broken, and the leadership's assessment of the conjuncture was lacking.

For Tronti, the task was to direct the working-class pressure that already existed against the boss toward the party, in order to overcome its current leadership and begin practicing a new mode of political activity from inside the organization.[119] As he had already put Marxian economic concepts to work in a new political framework, pursuing "laws of development" for the working class, now he suggested that the party could "produce, accumulate, and reproduce" the workers' strength on an extended scale, providing an outlet for the political energy surging through the factory that otherwise powered capital's growth.[120] The workers' side needed to focus on "*preventing any planning whatsoever from functioning*," "putting the capitalist structures themselves into perpetual crisis," and calling forth a "*moment of permanent working-class struggle*," which, with an effective relationship between class and party, could give rise to a plan of a new type, the "*revolutionary plan*" of organization.[121]

116. Tronti, "The Party in the Factory," 137.
117. Tronti, "The Party in the Factory," 139.
118. Tronti, "An Old Tactic," 77.
119. Tronti, "The Party in the Factory," 138-39.
120. Tronti, "The Party in the Factory," 139.
121. Tronti, "The Party in the Factory," 141.

Tronti also reflected in this talk on the implications of his own Copernican revolution. The idea that working-class struggle drove capital's movements was both historically valid and a "political thesis" for short-term intervention into the transition, currently underway, from economic crisis to the plan which superintends national production.[122] Tronti's "*strategic overturning*" of the relationship between workers and capital, with the struggles of the former now provoking the development of the latter, had been necessary for grasping the working class's "separate and united" relationship to capital.[123]

He saw the need not for a new revolutionary party, nor for vanguard groups, but for the organization of "*the crisis of the workers' movement as such—what we in fact are calling the crisis of the Communist Party.*"[124] Shortly after the Turin meeting, during a gathering of editors in May, Tronti continued this line of argument by insisting that "before passing to organizations of a new type" the "obstacle of the reformist PCI" needed to be eliminated.[125] The "splitting of the PCI" could be a "formidable element" for the reconstruction of a "class party," he suggested.[126]

All this was unfolding against the backdrop of factional battles following Togliatti's death. By 1965, Giorgio Amendola had emerged as the spokesman for the right of the Party, offering a proposal for reunification with the Socialists in what he called the *partito unico della sinistra* [single party of the left]. Having watched the DC's own opening to the PSI fail, Amendola sought a new synthesis between social democracy and communism. Pietro Ingrao, on the other hand, represented the left flank of the Party, emphasizing the need to build a network of local, directly democratic sites of workers' control.[127] On June 3–4, the central committee of the PCI narrowly voted to approve the "single party" strategy, and although internal opposition would continue to rumble inside the Party under Togliatti's successor Luigi Longo, Amendola had the advantage.[128]

With this conflict in the air, *Classe Operaia* hosted a debate in Rome with representatives from the PSIUP and the PCI. There, Tronti suggested that the problem of the "general organizational reconstruction" of the Italian left should not be dismissed simply because the "political level of class" and the "level of political party" had failed to find each other.[129] In typical fashion, Tronti pointed to the bright side—the failures of the PCI had blocked capital's

122. Tronti, "The Party in the Factory," 143.
123. Tronti, "The Party in the Factory," 143.
124. Tronti, "The Party in the Factory," 145.
125. Tronti, "After the Reunion in Mestre." 150.
126. Tronti, "After the Reunion in Mestre," 151.
127. Ginsborg, *History of Contemporary Italy*, 293.
128. Milana and Trotta, *L'operaismo degli anni sessanta*, 477.
129. Tronti, "Single Party or Class Party? (June 1965)," this volume, 155.

plan for "full control," which was unrealizable without an adequate vessel to fulfill the mediating function.[130]

Tronti sought to put back into question not only the political line of the Party machine but also the structure of the Communist Party itself. Instead of asking how the leadership of existing parties might carry out their own unification, creating new acronyms in the process, Tronti encouraged focus on "a different concept of working-class political unity," namely, the "vertical relation between party and working class." Rather than the problem of how representatives of the working class might come to an agreement at the parliamentary level, the problem was how to reconstitute the mechanisms of the revolutionary party itself and its relationship to workers. This could only be done if the party were reconceived as the "class party" at the level of the factory, at the "mass social workers' level."[131]

Strategy and Tactics

By July of 1965, as Tronti began his "turn" toward the problem of the PCI and increasingly saw the limits of organizational work in small groups, he had also begun to consider closing the newspaper.[132] During these same months he wrote "Marx, Labour-Power, Working Class," an essay that would become the centerpiece of *Workers and Capital*, published the following year. In this formidable set of "theses" he renewed his reading of Marx and recast some of the theoretical hypotheses outlined in "Factory and Society" and "The Plan of Capital" following the experiment of *Classe Operaia*.[133] Although the essay charted new territory, it also returned to and elaborated on several themes already present in Tronti's work: the unity of the heterogeneous, the primacy of politics, and the non-identity of strategy and tactics.

In this essay, Tronti reiterated his thesis concerning the collective worker. "From the outset, the workers, like the capitalist's exchange-values, proceed in the plural: the worker in the singular does not exist."[134] With the workers' collective struggle as the motivating force of capitalist development, Tronti went on to articulate an explicitly antiteleological understanding of how capitalism develops in discrete national contexts. An assumption of shared linear development, he cautioned, would write out class struggle, which is essential for understanding how capital develops. It could not be said that "the class

130. Tronti, "Single Party or Class Party?" 156.
131. Tronti, "Single Party or Class Party?" 157, 158.
132. Milana and Trotta, *L'operaismo degli anni sessanta*, 505–06.
133. In the book *Workers and Capital*, those early "First Hypotheses" were followed by the "Political Experiment" of *Classe Operaia*, with the new essay of 1965 arriving as "First Theses."
134. Tronti, "Marx, Labour-Power, Working Class," 239.

situation of the more advanced countries explains and *prefigures* the class situation of the more backward ones," since from the workers' viewpoint "the important thing is precisely to impede this development in practice, to break it at some point—to impose a *non-normal* class situation," a refusal that is "*unnatural* with respect to theoretical-analytical models."[135]

As Marx had emphasized the historical nature of the capitalist mode of production, as one that was itself produced and reproduced through capitalist political intervention, so Tronti argued that a rupture in the reproduction of capitalist society required intervention by an organized working class. This was the only way to puncture the ever-expanding domination of capital. Marx himself erred, Tronti wrote, precisely when his analyses took the logic of capital as given, forgetting that capitalist development is also the historical development of the working-class struggle against the capitalist system:

> the production process—as a process that produces capital—is inseparable from the moments of class struggle…it is not independent of the movements of the working-class struggle. It is made, composed, organised by the successive series of all such moments. The development of the capitalist production process makes up a single whole, together with the history of workers' class movements.[136]

Marx's thinking was nevertheless rooted, Tronti argued, in the primacy of politics. For Marx, Tronti wrote, "the labour law of value is a political thesis, a revolutionary rallying cry," rather than a scientific law to be taken up by economics or sociology.[137] Instead, it was a matter of grasping that the "political conclusion" of Marx's project also constituted the presupposition for his economic analysis: "*Labour is the measure of value because the working class is the condition of capital.*"[138]

In the same text Tronti would also analyze the twofold character of labor, emphasizing that the dual condition of the working class as both *within* and *against* capital grounds the strategy of refusal. When these two points of view are "subjectively unified on the working-class side, the route is opened to dissolve the capitalist system and the practical process of the revolution begins."[139] In addition, Tronti proposed a novel distinction between *labor-power* as a component (albeit active, living labor) of capital and *the working class* as that which struggles against it—the working class as "a social power that decisively snatches the offensive weapon of power from the hands of the capitalists."[140]

135. Tronti, "Marx, Labour-Power, Working Class," 176; italics restored from the Italian original.
136. Tronti, "Marx, Labour-Power, Working Class," 202.
137. Tronti, "Marx, Labour-Power, Working Class," 228.
138. Tronti, "Marx, Labour-Power, Working Class," 228; italics restored from the Italian original.
139. Tronti, "Marx, Labour-Power, Working Class," 173.
140. Tronti, "Marx, Labour-Power, Working Class," 197.

In this reading, the crisis that offered a chance for revolutionary movement would be less economic than political:

> This is the new concept of the *crisis of capitalism* that we must start to circulate: there will no longer be an economic crisis, a catastrophic collapse, a *Zusammenbruch*, however momentary, that owes to the impossibility of the system's continued functioning. Rather, it will become a political crisis imposed by the subjective movements of the organised workers, through a chain of critical conjunctures provoked by the working-class strategy of refusing to resolve the contradictions of capitalism and by the tactic of organisation within the structures of capitalist production, but outside of and free from its political initiative.[141]

Political activity within a discrete conjuncture required a *combination* of class strategy and party tactics, not their immediate *identification*. Recalling Lenin's success in the October Revolution, with "the party here [taking] responsibility for the tactical moment, on the class's behalf," and lamenting the process by which "Lenin's tactic became Stalin's strategy," Tronti suggested that militants would need to "hold these two moments of revolutionary activity—*class strategy* and *party tactics*—together in theory, and rigorously separate them in practice."[142]

These two political moments were distinct components within the multifarious unity called Marxism, and the political work of balancing their unity and separation—even, indeed, their contradiction—was a "difficult art" conducted according to the needs of the situation. Pretensions to a "scientific politics" could only lead to defeat.[143] This also meant that revolutionary practice needed to retain a degree of autonomy from theory:

> [W]hat is right theoretically may be mistaken politically. Theory is understanding and foresight, and thus knowledge—even if one-sided—of the process's objective tendency. Politics is the will to invert this process, and thus is a global rejection of objectivity; it is subjective action so that this objectivity is blocked and unable to triumph. Theory is anticipation. Politics is intervention. And it must intervene not into what is expected, but into what precedes it; here lies the need for the twists and turns of tactics.[144]

141. Tronti, "Marx, Labour-Power, Working Class," 269. *Zusammenbruch* is a German word, once commonly used in Marxian theory to refer to an economic collapse.

142. Tronti, "Marx, Labour-Power, Working Class," 261-62, translation modified [to remove the word "never," which was incorrectly inserted before "rigorously separate them in practice" in the Verso edition].

143. Tronti, "Marx, Labour-Power, Working Class," 267.

144. Tronti, "Marx, Labour-Power, Working Class," 267.

If the historical PCI had banked on the "objective tendency" playing out to their advantage, for Tronti the unimpeded development of capitalist social relations would yield no ground to the working-class side. The "identity and non-contradiction" of theory and politics had long led to "opportunism, reformism, [and] passive obedience to the objective tendency," an inevitable trend discerned according to "science" alone.[145] Marxist theory should not prescribe activity based on economic models, but rather divide itself from practice and become "subordinated to it."[146] Only by recognizing the primacy of struggle over theory could the tactical repertoire of the movement evolve.

In "Marx, Labour-Power, Working Class," Tronti also deepened his reflections on unity. The erstwhile philosophical principle had been transformed by his practical experience as a militant in *Quaderni Rossi* and *Classe Operaia*. At this point, for Tronti, any purely philosophical or theoretical discourse was found to be not only wanting but a danger to the movement, "handing the weapons of knowledge proper to one's own camp over to the class enemy, without at the same time managing to provide weapons of another kind—of struggle, of organisation—to the class in whose ranks one fights."[147] Tronti updated the reflections on the "person of the Marxist" that he had outlined in "On Marxism and Sociology" six years earlier: "[T]he theorist on the working-class side and the revolutionary politician are one and the same: materially, they must coincide in a single person," he now wrote. Hence the necessity of partisanship: the "subversive reconstruction of the workers' direct movements can be achieved only from within their struggle, from the point of view of their organisational needs."[148]

Working-class theory thus possesses an "indeterminacy principle" because it seeks not to describe what exists but to "unfol[d] at the social level."[149] As an experiment, it would require tools of a party type:

> The class is only strategy, and strategy lives in a wholly objective form at this level. A strategic perspective, like the strategy of refusal, presents itself as materially embodied in the class movements of the working-class social mass. It can begin to live subjectively—in a conscious way or, in other words, in practical form—only when it arrives at that moment of political organisation which it still now seems best to define with the word "party."[150]

145. Tronti, "Marx, Labour-Power, Working Class," 267.
146. Tronti, "Marx, Labour-Power, Working Class," 268.
147. Tronti, "Marx, Labour-Power, Working Class," 268.
148. Tronti, "Marx, Labour-Power, Working Class," 268.
149. Tronti, "Marx, Labour-Power, Working Class," 268.
150. Tronti, "Marx, Labour-Power, Working Class," 269.

Tronti saw the instance of "organised strategic subjectivity"—the political organization, the party—conducting the revolutionary experiment through tactical forays, by carrying out subversive practice.[151] Revolutionary theory aims for a goal precisely opposite to that of bourgeois science, which was to explain the current state of affairs. Rather than "prefigure the future or recount the past," the working-class viewpoint "only contributes to the destruction of the present."[152]

Although Tronti did not categorically exclude non-party organizations from carrying out political work, in his estimation of Italy in 1965, a rejuvenated PCI was best situated to organize that destruction. Without its tactical support, the movement would find itself recuperated, propelling capitalist development forward once again.

A Working-Class Use of Social Democracy?

By January of 1966, Amendola had further strengthened support for his line within the PCI. At the same time, millions of chemical workers were out on strike, and the metal-mechanics, including major sections at FIAT, would soon join them, continuing their stoppages through the spring.[153] During these same months, the PSI and the Italian Democratic Socialist Party (PSDI) [Partito Socialista Democratico Italiano] had merged to form a new center-left party, the Unified Socialist Party (PSU) [Partito Socialista Unificato]. In the title of the lead editorial of the May 1966 issue of *Classe Operaia*, Tronti proposed a "united front against social democracy"—a fortification to prevent the PCI from being sucked into the social-democratic vortex. In part, this involved a campaign to bring militants from the PCI and PSIUP, which had formerly split from the Socialist Party, around a new left pole opposed to the newly minted PSU.

Shortly before that May 1966 issue was released, Tronti had spoken on social democracy at the newly opened Centro Giovanni Francovich in Florence.[154] His talk coincided with a formal proposal to his fellow editors that they end the production of *Classe Operaia*. His focus on reconstructing a "vertical" connection between workers and PCI, his push for a new strategic direction for the existing Party, and the new urgency of the situation with the PSU had put Tronti at odds with the impulses of the rest of the group.

In his talk at the Centro Francovich, Tronti discussed what he termed the "massification" of the trade-union struggles: strikes were achieving 90-percent

151. Tronti, "Marx, Labour-Power, Working Class," 269.
152. Tronti, "Marx, Labour-Power, Working Class," 271.
153. Milana and Trotta, *L'operaismo degli anni sessanta*, 523.
154. The center was named for a *Classe Operaia* comrade who had recently and unexpectedly died.

participation, workers in most of the big industries had joined in the struggle, and the "difference between vanguard and mass ha[d] practically disappeared." While the content of the demands had not changed markedly, "the level of working-class participation" was leaping forward. The question for Tronti was how these trade-union struggles could be extended and deepened to impinge on "the political stability of capitalist power."[155]

After acknowledging that a grassroots push for trade-union unity could helpfully divide the tasks of the union from those of the party, Tronti turned his attention to the concrete possibility of a "socialist management of capital" under a center-left government.[156] From capital's standpoint, this solution's appeal lay in the fact that capitalist Italy, "integrated into the international structures of capitalism," could no longer afford periodic political crises. But from where Tronti stood, capital remained politically fragile and the workers' struggles had reached a fever pitch. Social democracy could offer capitalists a "greater control over the movements of labor-power" by forging tighter bonds between the state, the unions, and the social-democratic Party itself.

Here as elsewhere, Tronti rejected "political determinism," insisting that the rise of social democracy in Italy was not inevitable, and that there was no way to predict the twists and turns such a process would take.[157] Rather than predictions based on a linear historical model, Tronti sought to furnish "positive directions" for immediate political work: the working-class side needed to marginalize social democracy, crush its capacity to ascend to the management of the state, and thereby provoke crisis in Italian—and, by extension, international—capitalist development. For the unified PSU to position itself as a responsible steward of social democracy, it would first need to demonstrate its capacity to gain the support of a majority of the workers' movement for its program of gradual wage increases amid planned and balanced growth across the country and across sectors.

The entire point of social democracy, as far as capital was concerned, was to limit the loss of work-hours and to avoid kindling the unpredictable anger sparked by workers on strike. The working class thus needed an autonomous "political movement that is itself already organized," and Tronti indicated that the PCI, ostracized from the scramble on the center-left for alliances, was an apt tool for nipping this social-democratic strategy in the bud and fostering the growth of a "political experience of a new type."[158] The priority was to

155. Tronti, "It's Not Time for Social Democracy, It's Time to Fight It for the First Time from the Left (April 1966)," this volume, 162.

156. Tronti, "It's Not Time for Social Democracy," 165.

157. Tronti, "It's Not Time for Social Democracy," 168.

158. Tronti, "It's Not Time for Social Democracy," 169.

avoid "political stabilization of the system over the very long term" and instead to maintain the "continual uncertainty" of Italy's political future.[159]

At the end of October 1966, Tronti's book *Workers and Capital* was published. Its introduction, "A Course of Action," was a momentous summing up of the previous five years. In this essay, he reiterated the need for a "new synthesis from the working-class side," "a stance simultaneously both *within* and *against* society," a "partial view" to "grasp the totality" and therefore to "destroy" it.[160] Working-class science was defined as a process that required practical, political activity:

> A discourse that takes itself as its own foundations runs the lethal risk of checking itself only by the yardstick of the formal logical continuity between its own successive stages. Rather, we need to choose the point at which we can consciously succeed in breaking this logic. It is not enough, then, to lower theoretical hypotheses down into lived experience in order to see if they function in practice. The hypotheses themselves need to be negated through an exhaustive political work that prepares the terrain for their real verification. Only when the ground is prepared politically can these hypotheses operate materially, factually, in practice.[161]

Organizational activity thus plows through theory, as if it were soil, and gives rise to new shoots of revolution. For Tronti, this intervention is fruitless if carried out by mere individuals; it must be embodied in the "organised strategic subjectivity" of a party.[162] If this collective aspect of the political subject remained crucial, "Lenin" remained an important referent, given the "elementary principle of subversive practice" to which the Old Bolshevik had always adhered: "never leave the party in the hands of those already in charge."[163]

Despite the confident and cutting tone of many of his polemics, Tronti also distinguished in "A Course of Action" between acuity and rigidity. The laws of tactics were not to be fixed but rather fashioned according to concrete situations. Tactics were "a harmony with real things and at the same time a freedom from any preconceived ideas," kindling "a kind of productive imagination that alone serves to make thought work amid the facts."[164] It was only right, then, to acknowledge that this process of organizational activity and political practice had transformed his thought:

159. Tronti, "It's Not Time for Social Democracy," 170.
160. Tronti, "A Course of Action," xix.
161. Tronti, "A Course of Action," xxi.
162. Tronti, "Marx, Labour-Power, Working Class," 269.
163. Tronti, "A Course of Action," xxviii.
164. Tronti, "A Course of Action," xxviii.

If you know how to look for them, in this book you will find a series of changes in the way in which we consider this problem. And it is only right that they remain there to see; this shows how these advances were made over time. There is no static equilibrium between political work and theoretical discoveries; there is a relationship-in-movement that makes the one serve the other according to the needs of the moment.[165]

As he had written in a letter to his publisher, Giulio Einaudi, "the whole thing should be presented as ongoing research, though caught at a decisive, transitional moment."[166] All writing in this vein was provisional because of what Tronti had called the "indeterminacy principle" of working-class science unfolding at the social level.[167] This supported his critique of stageist thinking: Italy could not be "fatally doomed" to a "normal path" of development, for such a conclusion would be an "error of pure strategy." The "political sensibility"[168] that would guide him in the coming years had become increasingly clear:

> We should, then, be talking about a party struggle to conquer organisation; a Leninist tactic within a strategic research project of a new type; and a revolutionary process at one point that can set the mechanism of the international revolution in motion again. Faced with the question of 'what is to be done', one possible answer has arisen—that all of us spend the next few years working guided by a single orientation: give us the party in Italy and we will overthrow all Europe![169]

The stakes of seizing the PCI had assumed international significance, because Italy—wracked by recurring political crises in government, with a substantial portion of the population living under capitalist social relations, with millions of workers struggling against their bosses, and with a vacuum of leadership and strategy in the largest Communist party in Europe—possessed what another Marxist theorist might have called, channeling Lenin, an auspicious accumulation of contradictions.[170]

* * *

165. Tronti, "A Course of Action," xxviii-xxix.

166. Mario Tronti, "Una lettera a Giulio Einaudi" [Mario Tronti to Giulio Einaudi, Rome, January 16, 1966], https://operavivamagazine.org/una-lettera-a-giulio-einaudi (my translation).

167. Tronti, "Marx, Labour-Power, Working Class," 268.

168. Tronti, "A Course of Action," xxix.

169. Tronti, "A Course of Action," xxxi.

170. See Louis Althusser, "Contradiction and Overdetermination," in *For Marx*, trans. Ben Brewster (London: Verso, 2005), 87-128, 99-100.

Tronti made the decision to close the newspaper shortly after the publication of his book in the autumn of 1966, despite protests from the other editors of *Classe Operaia*. In March of the following year, a final issue would be released, focused on the five-year economic plan offered by the Socialist Giovanni Pieraccini, Budget Minister in the new government.[171] In the last lines of the editorial of *Classe Operaia*'s final issue, Tronti would refer to the "monumental project of research and study" that would need to be explored in the coming years, and the "new level of action" that politics now required. Untying the "knot of the party" and developing "a new theory and a new practice of the party" remained his chief concerns.[172]

And yet this final editorial also outlined new courses of study: interests in the relationship between wages and productivity and the international dimensions of the conjuncture. In April–May 1967, after the closure of the newspaper, several former comrades of *Classe Operaia* met for a seminar on "political class composition" at the Francovich Center. There, Tronti delivered a talk that serves equally well as a postscript to the texts included in the present volume, as it helps to introduce the concerns that would occupy Tronti over the coming years, up through his 1972 talk on the "autonomy of the political."[173]

Tronti titled his presentation "The New Synthesis: Within and Against." He began by insisting again on the need to rethink his own Copernican revolution: rather than making the "strategic overturning between the working class and capital" operate "mechanically and immediately" in all cases, instead he now saw that a framework which emphasized the "historical-theoretical-political precedence of the movements of the working class" also required some "*concrete mediations*," pertaining to "historically specific" instances "of capital and its political initiatives."[174] In fact, Tronti now argued that *before* the great Italian workers' struggles over the wage in the 1960s, "there had been a *capitalist rediscovery of the wage* as a dynamic moment of the total structure of capitalist society and as a possible way to achieve overall control over this social structure."[175]

Here Tronti sought to understand the incredible wage gains that workers in Italy had experienced since the war. Citing the dramatic increase in the share of income going to workers relative to capital during the general

171. Donald Sassoon, *Contemporary Italy: Economy, Society and Politics since 1945*, 2nd ed. (London: Routledge, 2013), 47.

172. Tronti, "Classe partito classe" [Class party class], *classe operaia* 3, no. 3 (March 1967): 1 and 28, 28.

173. Tronti, "The Autonomy of the Political (1972)," trans. Andrew Anastasi, Sara R. Farris, and Peter D. Thomas, *Viewpoint Magazine*, February 26, 2020, https://www.viewpointmag.com/2020/02/26/the-autonomy-of-the-political. See the Appendix to this volume for writings that mark his transition away from operaismo.

174. Tronti, "Within and Against (May 1967)," this volume, 174.

175. Tronti, "Within and Against," 178.

economic growth of 1951–61, Tronti emphasized that wage gains had coincided with the "*capital's choice of democracy*." High wages served ideologically and materially to distinguish capitalist societies from both fascist and state-socialist ones.[176]

The Italian state's social policy and the "institutional mediation by the official workers' movement" meant that the "real terrain" of the class struggle had shifted away from the "traditional political terrain," away from "the explicit demand for power, or the violent, direct assault on the state machine," and toward the terrain "where instead the capitalist initiative was marching forward—the terrain of the income mechanism, of the wage, of profit."[177] The workers' constant struggle for "more money" thus entailed a refusal to be integrated into the system of capital, putting "the entire mechanism of the capitalist initiative back into crisis."[178]

Although the formal political terrain had been exhausted, the Communist Party's crucial task of generalizing the workers' antagonism remained unfulfilled. "[I]f the workers' political party had recognized the new terrain of the class struggle, and if it had assumed this as its area of organization," Tronti wrote, "a limitless revolutionary process would now be open in the capitalist West."[179] Rather than embrace "catastrophic conceptions of a new type," pertaining solely to capital's economic contradictions, Tronti reiterated his interest in capital "as a historical system of the reproduction of the working class."[180] He condemned the "damage" done to the working-class struggle by discourse within the PCI on the rotting "carcass" of international capital, forever on the verge of collapse. This not only impoverished Marxism theoretically; it "blocked the workers' struggle itself" from understanding capitalist development. In a trenchant rebuke of teleology and the abdication of strategy by Marxists in Italy, Tronti beseeched his comrades to "courageously learn to come to terms" with the "disconcerting vitality" of the capitalist system.[181]

His talk concluded with the possibility of a "*working-class use of social democracy*" as a means for introducing "workers' power at the apex of the state," with opportunities there for work to "smash the state machine." If the assumption of state power was a concrete possibility for the left, the pitfalls lay in what use the party would make of its position atop the citadel. From "the working class *within* and *against* capital" to "the party *within* and *against* the

176. Tronti, "Within and Against," 179.
177. Tronti, "Within and Against," 181.
178. Tronti, "Within and Against," 182.
179. Tronti, "Within and Against," 183.
180. Tronti, "Within and Against," 177.
181. Tronti, "Within and Against," 185.

state," Tronti aimed to set in motion a chain of events by which the working class would "utiliz[e] capital as the social interest."[182]

None of this could proceed without internal struggle over organizational direction. For Tronti, finally, one needed to be "*within* and *against* the party, such as it is.*" In order to "make it explode," militants could not remain aloof. They must "be there within" not only the Party, but the broader social-democratic movement, operating "tactically from the inside, but in a strategically alternative way."[183] This approach would characterize Tronti's political work over the coming years. It also offers an opening for us to reconsider his political revolution in Marxism today.

182. Tronti, "Within and Against," 187, 188. It could be fruitful to consider Tronti's reflections in this essay alongside Nicos Poulantzas's "Towards a Democratic Socialism," trans. Patrick Camiller, in *The Poulantzas Reader: Marxism, Law and the State*, ed. James Martin (London: Verso, 2008), 361-75.

183. Tronti, "Within and Against," 188.

Part One

From Investigation to Intervention

On Marxism and Sociology

(April 1959)

This talk was delivered as a short rejoinder to a longer presentation given by Lucio Colletti during a conference at the Istituto Gramsci in Rome. The conference, held April 13-19, 1959, explored the relationship between Marxism and sociology. Colletti was a Marxist philosopher who, in collaboration with Galvano Della Volpe, helped to break the stranglehold of Italian idealist philosophy over Marxist thought in the postwar PCI. Colletti condemned the split between dialectical materialism and historical materialism, instead emphasizing the unity of Marx's method and his critical study of capitalist society. Tronti's own contribution brought an additional component to the fore: the necessity of political practice.[1]

1. Translator's Note: For more on the Della Volpe-Colletti-Tronti relationship, see my essay, "A Living Unity in the Marxist." The dossier in which it was collected contained translations of three early works by Tronti: "Some Questions around Gramsci's Marxism," "Between Dialectical Materialism and Philosophy of Praxis: Gramsci and Labriola," and "On Marxism and Sociology," the translation of which has been revised for the present collection. Colletti's talk is available in English translation as "Marxism as a Sociology," in *From Rousseau to Lenin: Studies in Ideology and Society*, trans. John Merrington and Judith White (New York: Monthly Review Press, 1972), 3-44. All notes in this and subsequent texts are the translator's.

I will make a very short and very schematic intervention. I do this not so much to contribute to the discussion, but because I consider it appropriate to take a position on these questions, especially when they elicit different answers—in fact, I would say conflicting answers—within our movement.

In this sense, I believe that the worst thing would be to wish to settle these divergences in every way, not because I believe that the possibility of this agreement would be invalid if we were at the end of the discussion, but because I believe it is invalid to assume the possibility of this agreement in advance. The framework of this conference, at certain moments, has risked playing out in this way, as a traditional procedure: Seppilli presented the theses, Colletti laid out the antitheses, and Spinella wanted to produce the synthesis immediately.[2] In this way, Spinella has somewhat reproduced a general framework while also preserving a general law, which is that of the Hegelian dialectical trinity. At the same time, he has delivered an element of interruption into the proceedings of this conference.

I believe that the problem of this conference must be clarified in its own original terms, that is, the relationship between Marxism and sociology. In other words, to me this seems not to be a conference on sociology, but on the way in which Marxists understand sociology. This is the specific theme we must emphasize. Along these lines, I believe that, at the beginning of the discussion, we did not have two different interpretations of sociology so much as we had, I would say, two different interpretations of Marxism. And the two interpretations of sociology were a natural consequence, somewhat, of these two different interpretations of Marxism. I would say that if this conference were to clarify this theme, it would contribute to the conference's original problem, that is, the relationship between Marxism and sociology.

In Spinella's talk there was just a moment, a short passage, in which he said—as if it were perhaps an element of secondary importance, or even a presupposition—that he uses the term "historical materialism" because he understands Marxism to be more broad than historical materialism itself. Indeed, he understands Marxism to be dialectical materialism, of which historical materialism is an example or a particular application.[3] And so, according to this, certain general laws exist, and they exist prior to the practical application or research, which is to say that a general systematization already exists, one that is not implicit in historical materialism but which precedes

---

2. Tullio Seppilli was a Marxist anthropologist and Mario Spinella was a Marxist philosopher.

3. In an essay also published in 1959, Tronti further explores this artificial split between historical materialism and dialectical materialism: "It is the distinction between an *interpretation of history* and a *general conception of the world and of life*, as if they were two separate and overlapping things, the one a function of the other, the one subordinated to the other. That which will become, in the Marxist *orthodoxy* and *Vulgate*, the distinction between historical materialism and dialectical materialism." Tronti, "Between Dialectical Materialism and Philosophy of Praxis: Gramsci and Labriola."

historical materialism. This means that, in the moment in which one employs materialism, one presupposes the existence of this framework of general laws.

I would say that this point, which his talk only addressed in passing, is instead the fundamental point; in other words, his entire argument, his examination of problems related especially to sociology, flows from this premise. I believe that his particular conception of sociology is implicitly tied to this conception of Marxism.

I would say that this interpretation of Marxism—this division, this fracture produced within Marxism itself—could be the basis of two possible stances: either a stance of absolute powerlessness in the field of knowledge and thus practical research, precisely because at a certain point this general framework becomes an empty one that gives no practical grasp on reality; or the other stance that can follow from this formulation, of direct concessions to positions that are foreign to Marxism, for the reason that this general framework, precisely in its generality and abstractness, fails to sink its teeth, concretely, into a particular type of reality, and so it has an immediate need for something that can achieve this practical grasp on reality on its behalf. Thus, it needs to take an element from outside and not from within Marxism; and this is fatal, because whenever a general theoretical framework and thus general laws are assumed in advance, these cannot exist by themselves, independently from their practical application. When general laws are applied, they are immediately filled with a given content, which is clearly not controlled by these general laws but taken immediately from a determinate type of reality which is subsisting in that moment. To me it seems completely natural that, once the question has been formulated in this way—namely, the question of a general dialectical materialism that in itself contains the possibility of sociological research—it is inevitable that this sociological research would turn out not to be sociological research for Marxism, but something external to Marxism itself, in other words, a sociology that corresponds, at times, to bourgeois sociology.

Not only this, but I would say that, in doing this, we lose the scientific originality of Marxism. In other words, precisely due to this implicit need to appeal to something that is outside of Marxism, one retreats from that fundamental presupposition of Marx and of Gramsci, of the necessity, possibility, and reality of Marxism's autonomy, self-sufficiency, and originality, which therefore has no need in the course of research to appeal to elements external to Marxism itself. This is the question's fundamental point: that it is impossible to realize a precise, scientific grasp on reality when departing from this premise, and that when doing so one is likely to pick up a determinate element that has not been rationally tied to other elements, that has not been interpreted and seen within a general context, and thus one that has been isolated, transformed, and truly distorted, as if it had its own specific reality.

This gives some hint of what we can illustrate further: an element grasped in this immediate way very often exists in opposition to Marxism itself. In other words, insofar as the dominant ideas are always the ideas of the dominant class, we can see that, for a certain long period, we all had been historicists, and that, looking ahead, we are tending to become sociologists.[4] I mean this in the sense that—precisely because we fail to consider Marxism to be something autonomous and self-sufficient and think that it needs external support—previously we were forced to take this support at a moment in which a determinate tendency was dominant, namely, a moment in which idealist historicism was dominating the culture. This inevitably inserted itself right inside of Marxism. When a theory's dominance shifts, its dominance also shifts within Marxism; it is precisely this that manages to safeguard the autonomy and originality of Marxism itself.

Now, as historicism must not be rejected as a whole, given that it is not a matter of taking that type of historicism and filling it with Marxist content, the same can be said for sociology. In other words, it is not a matter of taking the dominant, bourgeois sociology and using it for Marxist ends, but of considering that just as Marxism presents itself as the only real historicism, in the same way, from this other point of view, Marxism presents itself as the only true sociology, that is, as the only science of society.

I agree with Pescarini when he said that the only sociology for us is Marxism, that is, the only scientific analysis of society that we have, the only science of society, is Marxism.[5] I would say something further: that this Marxist sociology is not something definitively fixed in established canons; rather, it is continual elaboration and development. Clearly, we must consider various problems that prevent this research from becoming overly specialized. For example, the problem is not to discover a national interpretive line for Marxism; in other words, it is not so much about finding a national Marxism. Rather, it is a matter of a concrete application, which Colletti explained very well: a model of a determinate situation that is concrete and therefore also national.

It is clear that no one rejects the necessity, or rather the indispensability, of the study and scientific analysis of the exact structure of Italian capitalism, but this analysis is impossible if we have not already understood the basic structure of a capitalist socioeconomic formation in general. On the other

---

4. "Historicism" was a trend in Italian political thought that tended to identify with Hegel and teleological visions of historical development. During the postwar period, historicist thinking dominated the PCI and authorized Togliatti's insistence that gradual progress in Italian society would pave the road for communism.
5. Likely Angelo Pescarini, a mathematician and member of the PCI.

hand, our understanding of this overall capitalist-economic formation is itself the result of a concrete research project that, indeed, is within capital. It is not, then, something that is alive before the research, but rather something born as a function of the research itself.

On page five of Colletti's report, which has been mentioned several times, he speaks of nothing but the concept of determinate abstraction, which is a characteristically Marxian concept, one that Marx not only repeats explicitly but applies concretely, typified in the concept of socioeconomic formation. This really is the specific example of a determinate abstraction, in other words, a concept in which the singularity of the particular object is not lost, but in which its specificity is actually preserved. In fact, it is the determinate abstraction that allows for the preservation of this specificity and this precision.[6]

I believe, returning to the initial problem, that the distinction between dialectical materialism and historical materialism is precisely what then causes and is at the origin of the distinction between economics and sociology—and not only this, but it is also at the origin of the distinction between theory and practice, as well as the distinction between culture and politics.

Comrade Barro yesterday took this thesis to its ultimate consequences, when he said that the economist studies society in general, and the sociologist studies things in particular, as if this tidy and physical dissociation could be made between two persons, one handling pure theory and the other only empirical research; as if this distinction were really legitimate within Marxism.[7] Well, this distinction—I find it again right at the origin of the fracture, the open breach in Marxism, which is, basically, the breach between dialectical materialism and historical materialism. Among other things, I believe that a historical study would show precisely this: that this is the breach through which all revisionist interpretations of Marxism have always passed.

To reject the legitimacy of that distinction means to accept the correctness of the opposite thesis, that is, of unity—which here is not an identity. Colletti should have been more precise and spoken at greater length on this: it seemed at a certain point that these two things were made to identify with one another immediately, and that therefore, the specificity and the determinacy of each moment was lost. But, on the contrary, it is precisely upon that unity of the heterogeneous that this question must be established. Indeed, just thinking of the figure of Marx makes it difficult to accept the conception of the distinction. How is it possible in the figure of Marx to distinguish the philosopher from the politician, the historian from the economist? It is absolutely

6. The "determinate abstraction" refers to the abstraction that is the result of a process of reasoning and analysis. For Della Volpe and Colletti, it was a scientific procedure developed by Marx and best understood by closely reading his "1857 Introduction," included now in Karl Marx, *Grundrisse*, trans. Martin Nicolaus (New York: Penguin, 1993), 81-111; see especially section three, "The Method of Political Economy," 100-08.

7. Likely Gianni Barro, a health reformer and member of the PCI.

impossible; one cannot say that first he was the philosopher and then he was the historian, then the economist, in parentheses he was the political person—no! He did each of these things; his first work, *Critique of the Philosophy of Right*, is the critique of the bourgeois state, the 1844 manuscripts are the economic-philosophic manuscripts—already we have the entire orientation for a whole work. How can one say that *Capital* is not at the same time a work of theory and a work of practical action? How can one maintain that "Critique of the Gotha Program" is not, at the same time, a political program and a formidable theoretical work about the state and rights?

So, there is this continual unity of diverse moments that one finds in Marx, and perhaps in a more obvious manner in Lenin; if *Capital* is at the same time a scientific work and a moment of political action that shifts the objective reality of things, one could argue inversely that the October Revolution or the Paris Commune is at the same time a great practical movement and a powerful theoretical discovery. I would say that the worst thing that one can do within Marxism is precisely to make this split and smuggle it into one's work, to not talk about it explicitly but to expect and take for granted this split between theorists and researchers.

Basically, here the question has been reintroduced: on the one hand the theorists, on the other the researchers. It is the first and last problem that must be eliminated, immediately. We absolutely cannot accept the existence of a researcher who offers material to the theorist, who then reworks it and produces theory. We cannot have a Seppilli who conducts social inquiries and then brings them to a Colletti, and a Colletti who organizes them into a general theory, just as we cannot have the purely theoretical type of intellectual whose only task is to offer materials to the politician, who applies them concretely. Instead there is a continual unity, precisely because this unity is already realized within Marxism, and thus it already is alive in the person of the Marxist.

And so, I would conclude with this figure of the Marxist scientist, who poses the necessity of unifying heterogeneous moments in theory, who is precisely the living unity of these heterogeneous moments. In other words, the person who achieves an equilibrium, which is precisely a scientific equilibrium—practical, not conquered once and for all, but daily, in research and in practical contact. An equilibrium of the concrete bond between theory, on one side, and practice—that is, with the class, with the party—on the other. A twofold path, which then is unified precisely in the labor of the intellectual, through which we rediscover both theoretical Marxism and the practical, political struggle of the overall workers' movement.

02

Letter to Raniero Panzieri

(June 1961)

This letter was written to the founder of *Quaderni Rossi* several months before that journal's first issue was released. Here, Tronti rejects two tendencies in Marxist thought—gradualist reformism and fatalist catastrophism—and begins to sketch the outlines of his own unique perspective: conceiving of capitalist development and proletarian revolution as intricately intertwined.

Dearest Raniero,

At this point, it is clear that the imminence of the "collapse" increasingly towers over us. It has come to dominate all our thoughts, it has upset the whole rhythm of our daily life, it has given a sense of industrious tragedy to the motionless idyll of these summer evenings. I have found the most complete image of the "collapse" in Gioacchino Belli: "The sun extinguished and the world shattered," along with what follows.[1] I confess to you that my "Roman Oblomovism" has been seriously shaken by these visions.[2] To the point that I have arrived at this radical conclusion: one needs *to develop the collapse*, or rather, transform the prospect of the collapse into a prospect of development.

In other words (now I will begin to talk seriously), the problem of capitalist development cannot be divided from the problem of *crises*. Due to this fact: the crisis is *a moment* of capitalist development. We must not understand development on the basis or in view of the crisis, but—quite the opposite—we must understand the crisis itself on the basis or in view of development. The analysis of the crisis can only be a dynamic analysis of the system and, in other words, the analysis of the system's dynamics. Hence the impossibility of envisioning the *final crisis*, as in the catastrophic collapse of the system.

The more one thinks about it, the more one is convinced that today the knot to be untied is entirely here, in this difficult marriage between *capitalist development* and *working-class revolution*. As a result of which the revolution must be alive, actively and intimately, in the daily process of the development of capitalism, and we must not limit ourselves to passively contemplating the "beautiful" appearances of its periodic crises. The new socialist experiment must be born precisely from this *material union* between development and revolution. And only this can stop the process of socialism's bastardization throughout the world.

The only alternative to *reformist gradualism* hitherto in existence has been the *catastrophic collapse*. The revolution is confused with the collapse, or better, the revolution is conceived only as collapse.

But it is exactly the opposite. The necessary and automatic collapse makes the revolution useless—the revolution as a *revolutionary process*, as the self-organization of the working class as a revolutionary class within the system of

<hr />

1. Belli wrote sonnets in the Roman vernacular, but in English one can see "Translations from G.G. Belli," trans. Harold Norse, *The Hudson Review* 9, no. 1 (Spring 1956): 71–85, 77.

2. Oblomov was the idle, aristocratic protagonist of Ivan Goncharov's mid-nineteenth-century novel by the same name. See Ivan Goncharov, *Oblomov*, trans. Marian Schwartz (New Haven: Yale University Press, 2010). In Russia after the October Revolution, Oblomov's lazy nobleman became a foil to Stakhanov, the ceaselessly industrious worker. See Kathi Weeks, *The Problem with Work: Feminism, Marxism, Antiwork Politics, and Postwork Imaginaries* (Durham: Duke University Press, 2011), 84.

capitalism itself. In this sense, there is only one "ideology" of the collapse, and it is an *opportunist maximalism*.[3] In other words, that typical form of centrism—revolutionary in words and reformist in deeds—which today dominates the class-oriented wing of the Western workers' movement.

If all this is true, then it is clear that the "ideological" aspect, the reexamination of some historical knots in the workers' movement's past, cannot be isolated from the positive analysis that one makes of the present. When speaking of development, one must speak of the ideology of development, and when speaking of the collapse, then one must speak of the ideology of the collapse. And I am inclined to make a single discourse from these two things—that is, I tend to understand the discourse on *collapse* as being completely enclosed *within* the discourse on development. For the collapse, in fact, I see the need for just one thing—a study that follows Sweezy's economic excursus in *The Theory…*, revealing all its *political* implications—the ideologies built on the theory of the collapse from Bernstein to Stalin.[4] But all this would be designed as a historical illustration regarding the current developmental tendencies of contemporary capitalism and therefore of the proletarian revolution. I could prepare this excursus myself. If you and the others agree, then let's move on *immediately* to planning the notebook (or two), not on the catastrophic collapse, but *on the revolutionary development* of capitalism.

Now, I realize that all this is not entirely clear, and that it is ambiguous. Indeed, I will ask Rita to describe for me your face when you were reading these lines.[5] After all, the fault is all hers: it is she who has "torn" from me this hurried letter, following your encouragement! Our *Rosa* is truly unique: patient enough to tolerate my "eccentricities" and determined enough to not take them into account. And, in addition, woman enough to understand *everything*. Now that she has come up, tell her to carry on.

Dear Raniero, see you soon.
Greetings to all, and greetings from everyone here.

Mario

02. Letter to Raniero Panzieri

---

3. The "maximalists" had been the left wing of the PSI. As "revolutionaries" rather than "reformists," they refused to collaborate with centrists in parliament. They also eschewed problems of political strategy and tactics, following their conviction that capitalism was guaranteed to collapse of its own accord. For more on this history, see Quintin Hoare and Geoffrey Nowell Smith's introduction to *Selections from the Prison Notebooks*, by Antonio Gramsci, ed. and trans. Quintin Hoare and Geoffrey Nowell Smith (New York: International Publishers, 1971), xvii–xcvi.

4. Paul Sweezy was a Marxian economist who co-founded the U.S.-based publishing initiative Monthly Review. His *Theory of Capitalist Development* argued that capitalist production was not heading for a specifically economic breakdown. See Paul Sweezy, *The Theory of Capitalist Development: Principles of Marxian Political Economy* (London: Dennis Dobson, 1962 [1942]).

5. Rita Di Leo was a member of the Roman section of *Quaderni Rossi*.

Closing Speech at the Santa Severa Seminar

(April 1962)

This talk ended a seminar on Marx's *Capital* held by the editors of *Quaderni Rossi* outside Rome from April 23 to 25, 1962. The purpose of the gathering was to engage in a study of Volume One from the point of view of the rapidly developing capitalist economy in Italy. The agenda included lectures on Marx's logic, presentations about the electronics manufacturer Olivetti, and analyses of capitalist development in the countryside. Tronti introduced the seminar, and he also presented the following closing remarks, which suggested the need to incorporate an understanding of the "collective worker" into revolutionary planning. The occasionally elliptical text is based on stenography by Liliana Lanzardo, with editorial interventions in brackets.[1]

1. Notes for an introductory presentation at Santa Severa are also available, but their authorship is unclear. They can be found ascribed to Panzieri, who had intended to introduce the seminar but ultimately did not attend, in the Fondo Panzieri in the archives of the Fondazione Feltrinelli; see the editorial notes in Milana and Trotta, *L'operaismo degli anni sessanta*, 169. The introductory notes were presented and attributed to Tronti in Mario Tronti, "Intervento al seminario di S. Severa, primavera 1962" [Opening speech at the Santa Severa seminar, Spring 1962], in "Quattro inediti di Mario Tronti" [Four unpublished works by Mario Tronti], dossier, *Metropolis* 1, no. 2 (June 1978): 14-17.

We cannot produce a discourse on method for our analysis until we manage to produce a discourse, or rather, find a method, that is able to judge the validity of this analysis. It is a mistake to go back to speaking of determinate abstraction: we must attempt an analysis that takes place at distinct levels, not because we see them as separate, but because we recognize them as such. The hypothesis remains that the most valid method is the one that Marx employed in *Capital,* and it is a matter of applying it in a new way to a precise investigation.

We can understand the totality as Marx did in the third volume: production, circulation… but then, he does not unite them, because their unity and the determining character of the first with respect to the others are already implied. It is not a distinction that is only logical; rather, it first considers the production of capital as such, and then it moves on to the generalization of this production and the formation of a capitalist society.

This overall process of capitalist society cannot be grasped by embracing the process's complexity, by starting from a general, global viewpoint. The process's complexity can be understood only in a unilateral way: the unmitigated, scientific one-sidedness of the workers' movement that grasps capital. One-sidedness is a sure, general method of investigation, and it permits the transition to the moment of intervention, in which there is also one-sidedness.

Here emerges the problem of a unitary recomposition of working-class thought alongside the recomposition of the working class.[2] These two processes have an objective substance, since they are dictated by a certain type and by a determinate level of capitalism. [*Description of the current level of capitalist development, decomposition of the class, etc.*][3] …I do not consider this to be inevitable: if capitalism manages to decompose the class, working-class thought no longer exists, and therefore the working class does not either. There are two objectives necessary for this development to acquire a determinate meaning, in other words, for there to be a revolutionary process: on the one hand, functional unity in the working-class struggle, and on the other, reunification between the class and the revolutionary strategy of the class, without which the former cannot be achieved.

We lack a specific discourse concerning the figure of the collective worker as it pertains to the figure of the collective capitalist [*even in the talks given at this seminar*]. At this point we have a clearer picture of the collective capitalist than we do of the collective worker. This is because we have the continuous

---

2. Because Tronti's understanding of "class" is resolutely political, the reader should understand that "working-class thought" need not only be practiced by a wage-earning worker in manual industry, nor should it be understood to encompass the sociologically defined working class in a broader sense, by also including all unwaged workers. For Tronti, "working-class thought" is that which contributes to the struggle against capital.

3. All bracketed text and ellipses were originally present in the Italian editions of the texts. For citations of the originals, see the Appendix to this volume.

action of the capitalist before our eyes, and because there is a collective capitalist realization that is not reflected in a realization by the working-class side of a certain type of capitalist development.

We have not managed to grasp this material figure of the collective worker. We have not managed to see it concretely, and this is one of the outcomes from this seminar: we must make an effort to see the collective worker. There is a possibility of doing so. But we must not see the collective worker in the terms in which the figure of the collective capitalist allows us to glimpse it; this is a hypothesis that cannot be subjected to concrete verification. This is not the path by which we can identify this historical figure (which does not always exist, not even within the history of capital). Our discourse should follow other paths; and very important in this regard is the problem of the generalization achieved by capitalist production in a determinate, national and international context, whereby there comes to be a collective homogenization of certain contradictions present over the whole arc of capitalist society.

The constitution of a capitalist society is tied directly to the fact that those two fundamental social classes, which had been hypothesized from the beginning of capitalist development, actually begin to constitute and establish themselves in pure form—those two classes which, at first, remained mixed up in a series of relations (the whole problem of historical survivals), which prevented capitalist society from unifying at the two poles and splitting definitively. This process is fundamental: at the moment in which capitalist society tries to achieve maximum unification, a process of division opens up at the level of capitalist society itself.

This process has an ambiguous character: there may be a stabilization of capitalism, but the concept that we have scrutinized, that of growing *proletarianization*, which we have subjected to a scientific and not only generically theoretical analysis, does not lead us there. We need to understand this process as it takes place within the capitalist process. This same term can become generic if we fail to grasp the specific features that it assumes today; we must be able to explain it with a proper analysis and no longer through a theoretical argument.

We must not wait for this process to finish in order to reveal it: it must be anticipated, albeit at an untested level. We need only think of the relation between agriculture and industry, and the discourse on the collective worker. This historical figure cannot appear in history so long as inside of the capitalist system there remains, as a survival from the past, this dichotomy that poses to the workers' movement false problems of alliances with other strata, and which also hides the specific function of the collective worker, which pursues a process of homogenization internal to the wage worker as well as the capitalist.

On this problem, let us take note of another fact: the discourse on agriculture is clearer than the discourse on industry, and it gets to the level of theoretical analysis—it manages to find the point of contact. The discourse on seeing the collective capitalist at a specific moment (Rieser) encountered the discourse on the collective capitalist produced in agriculture (Greppi), but there was not the same evidence and clarity concerning the relation between its two moments as there had been in the discourse on agriculture.[4] There is an objective reason: in agriculture, capitalist development is still in the classical vein, and our instruments are better prepared to grasp this. The social relation inside the modern capitalist factory takes on a specific complexity—not the generic complexity of a discourse, which is always established at a determinate level, but it derives from the fact that this reality of the factory immediately acquires a face, a dimension that is very much distorted. The pure development of the process of capitalist production, having burned through every other survival, makes it so that the overturned relation is detected in a clearer way than the relation of present capitalist production and the elaborate interplay which appears in the material process of capitalist production itself.

We cannot use one type of analysis at a practical level and a different type of analysis at a theoretical level, two different types of analysis—unity becomes necessary. If this does not occur, the discourses at the two levels do not encounter each other. The danger is that we fail to have the whole discussion, comprising both the production process and the political level, if we do not have the conversation continuously on two levels; we must find it again on two levels.

How do we understand the collective worker? We do not go looking for the collective worker in our analysis of the factory, but instead we are looking for things that may be useful only when understood through the figure of the collective worker. How capital decomposes the class, and how it may be recomposed—we must see how this mechanism unfolds in the factory. Otherwise, we cannot grasp it, and if we do not grasp it theoretically, we cannot then propose the need for an organization.

We have the analysis of the factory as an objective, but we do not have [*have not had in our work*] an object to analyze in the factory (collective worker...). If it can be grasped in this way, it can be made to function on the social level and on the plane of the class struggle.

4. Vittorio Rieser, a Turinese member of the left wing of the PSI, was a sociologist of workers' inquiry and one of the key members of *Quaderni Rossi*, who also remained at the journal with Panzieri after the split. Claudio Greppi, also from Turin and part of the left of the PSI, would by contrast leave *Quaderni Rossi* with the *Classe Operaia* comrades, after which he helped to establish the Centro Giovanni Francovich and later participated in the experience of Potere Operaio [Workers' Power].

The blockage is at the beginning of the analysis. This complexity is an objective, material fact, not an instance to be brought from the outside but one to be grasped specifically and analyzed theoretically. We have refused some traditional conceptions of the divided bourgeois society: the difference between society and the state, etc. Having recovered this unity of capitalist society, its possibly organic character—even capitalist society can be organic—just as we recover this unity between the economic level and political level within capital, we must also recover it at the workers' level. The unity of economics and politics at the level of capital is rediscovered easily, but the one between trade-union struggle and political struggle in the working class is difficult.

This, then, is the problem of the organization of the class, which is simplified with the advance of capitalism. We must not rule out any problem of economics or politics, and so discussions concerning the theory of the political party of the working class, the problem of the political organization of the working class—this weighs on our work. We cannot give up the need for a discussion about the party: the Leninist policy that fails to grasp the collective worker, all the processes that take place inside of the party, the bourgeois mechanism inside of the workers' party—these are things that revolve around the overall discussion.

It is necessary to judge the development of capitalism at a certain stage of its development: there was a moment in which the historical alternative presented itself as possible... But we speak of development, not of stabilization: the capitalist has passed [*through this bottleneck*] but has not yet destroyed the worker, hence the discourse on the plan, which is an open problem because it is a new one, because it seemed impossible to the workers' movement that one could speak of capitalist planning—which, as it happens, we can quite easily find in Marx's discourse. The possibility of capitalist planning means, at its limit, that the capitalist comes to a realization concerning the collective capitalist, not at a scientific level but rather at a political level. We can speak of a certain type of rationality in capitalist development. Capitalist rationality cannot but appear to us distorted in its anarchy; the empirical grasp on capitalist planning gives us a framework that does not correspond to the real development process, which proceeds today with precise awareness of developments.

Any alternative planning is destined to be functional to capitalism: it cannot be a disruptive element with respect to the system while inside of that system. The capitalist wants the balanced development of the Italian economy, and therefore to instrumentalize the workers' movement in service to a capitalist plan. Balanced development of the Italian economy leads only to the elimination of the contradictions of capitalism.

But should the workers' movement be opposed to capitalist planning? The workers' movement is not opposed to capitalist development as such but uses this type of planning for its own purposes. From the inside or from the outside? Here is the problem. The strategic plan of the workers' movement is posed precisely on the basis of the capitalist plan. The workers' movement must use planning in a knowing way to break the system.

Today, the theoretical composition of a strategy for the workers' movement only appears possible precisely because these facts exist, precisely because there is for us the possibility of seeing things over the long term. We must evaluate capitalist planning with an eye toward a response that escapes from capitalist planning. The strategic plan takes shape alongside the forecasting capitalist choices, not only with judgments of capitalist choices that capitalism has already made. The planning of development allows us to plan the revolutionary process of the workers' movement.

Now our discourse takes a leap. The leap is in this sense: the revolution is a revolutionary process. Before, the revolution could be understood as a bid for the conquest of power in certain countries. The conquest of political power remains, but it must be seen as a long process of continual, revolutionary response by the working-class to a type of capitalist development. The working-class response to capitalist choices must strive to put these choices into crisis, not to help the capitalist make better choices.

At this point, the question is rightly posed: what is workers' power? For now, we can say that it is not the workers' state. Once we have conquered political power, we will not already have workers' power. How does workers' power take shape? Political management by the working class within the system, not management of capitalist development. The working class lives in capital, but it cannot be exhausted inside of capital, and the capitalist must necessarily integrate it if he wants his own development: not through the integration of political parties, but by making the working class no longer exists as social class. In this case, it achieves stabilization. The working class must block this; this truly is the greatest instigator of crisis. But for this to happen the working class must place itself within capital, facing it as a class in the political sense. Workers' power is political power but in a specific sense: not the preservation of its parties, but bringing power to the place where the capitalist refuses to allow it. Political power must be demanded at the level of the production process, because there it divides capitalism from the working class and makes its integration impossible.

* * *

[Salvaco: Having arrived at this point, you demand for the class the "management of insubordination."[5] Tronti: Certainly, if this means "planning the revolutionary process," and if there is nothing random in it.] [A collective discussion follows concerning the significance of trade-union struggles on this point, their limits, political value, etc. In any case, bargaining brings any struggle that has taken a "political" course onto the trade-union terrain: how to continue to keep this political element alive? The class realizes "the plan": the insertion of insubordination, etc.]

A possible intervention: We build this type of workers' power where we believe it is possible. That is, the immediate problem of the demands for working-class self-organization at this stage. There is a serious gap here, between our capacity to discuss this problem and incorporate it into a correct and organic discourse, and our capacity to realize this objective. This may remain an instance that we are unable to grab hold of within these matters. This working hypothesis which has guided the analysis has remained at a theoretical level. This leads us to reconsider certain types of analyses and forecasts of the future development of the class struggle, but it never provides us with the transition to actualization: while we are moving the analysis forward, activity is not moving forward.

There is this discussion of the organizations: the relation between union and party does not hold, nor does the one between these organizations and the class. It is a matter of starting all over again. And we lack even a model for how to start over, because the models we have are wrong.

I agree with Panzieri on the argument "concerning the dynamism of everything except for the organizations of the workers' movement."[6] Indeed, if one could make such an assertion about the latter, there would be a flaw in our analysis, but none of our hypotheses are futuristic, because behind our analysis there is a moving reality. In addition to our forecast of the strategy of the workers' movement and that of capitalism as such, the level of capital effectively helps us. Here the relation between party and class takes a leap: between political organization of capitalism and capitalism itself. The collective capitalist today materializes in the figure of Moro.[7] This type of capitalism has manifested its own political stratum.

And on the figure of the workers' party: the same type of awareness materializes in the party of capitalism and not in the workers' party. Scientific

5. Maria Adelaide Salvaco was a Bolognese comrade who helped to craft *Quaderni Rossi*'s early workers' inquiries. Several letters that Panzieri wrote to her were included in the collection Raniero Panzieri, *La crisi del movimento operaio: Scritti interventi lettere, 1956-60* [The crisis of the workers' movement: Writings, interventions, letters, 1956-60], eds. Dario Lanzardo and Giovanni Pirelli (Milan: Lampugnani Nigri Editore, 1973).

6. A source for this quotation could not be located.

7. Aldo Moro, in 1962 the national secretary of the Christian Democrats, would soon become Prime Minister, a post he held from December 1963 until June 1968, and again from November 1974 until July 1976. In March 1978, he was kidnapped and, after more than fifty days of being held hostage, murdered by the paramilitary Red Brigades. For a classic account, see Leonardo Sciascia, *The Moro Affair*, trans. Sacha Rabinovitch (New York: New York Review of Books, 2004 [1978]).

awareness of the process, which the capitalist has mastered, has contributed to a strong capitalist party and to the workers' party such as it is. The relation between party and class has the relation between class and class as its preliminary relation.

This creates the possibility of crisis, which is already underway: for years we have all kept hope in the center-left, because the possibility of the crisis of the organizations lies there. There was confidence that the total reaction of the workers' movement would not happen: the greatest danger for capitalism is that the class struggle assumes the real level proper to it, because so long as it unfolds at the bourgeois political level it is functional for capital. Capital accepts this possibility of confrontation at the class level when it thinks that it can integrate the class: then it needs to present the class as class, because there is no solution to this problem for capitalism. The recuperation of the class struggle itself, which cannot [*but*] occur at the level of social relations of production, can only blow up or put into long, passive crisis the same organizations that had been formed by a different confrontation between classes at the level of institutions: the parties are destined to be integrated into the system. One of the workers' parties is already integrated. The other laments its inability to integrate into the system, despite its daily efforts, because effectively its relation with the class remains—a relation which objectively expresses the fact that the working class is not integrated into the system. This strange monster is immobile; it suffers the consequences of precisely that alternative: it prevents stabilization from going forward despite itself (since it represents the unintegrated masses), and it is unable to embark upon that other path. It is an equilibrium that we cannot posit as eternal. There is a danger that this equilibrium may also become functional to the stabilizing system of capitalism, but on this point we find that the other alternative remains open.

Forecasts: if action continues at this level of struggle, this would provoke perhaps a rather long process of crisis. None of us thinks of going back inside the organizations (in the traditional manner), back inside the parties. Our very participation in the struggle is an element of the crisis, which does not mean working inside of the organizations, in other words inside the parties, because, although the decisive point of class action is indeed there, this activity is one which hastens the crisis of the organizations themselves. We want nothing other than the political outcome of the crisis of the organizations: the self-organization of the class becomes an element of the total destruction not of the organizations, but of capitalist civilization.

Panzieri-Tronti Theses

(June 1962)

This outline of the key principles undergirding *Quaderni Rossi*'s approach was co-authored with Raniero Panzieri and circulated among comrades inside and outside of the journal's editorial board. It also represented something of an attempt at reconciliation between the various factions within the group. While it was intended to be presented in some form in the September 1962 *Cronache dei Quaderni Rossi* [Chronicles of the Red Notebooks], a publication aimed at workers, the text did not appear before a wider audience until 1975.[1]

1. See "Tesi Panzieri-Tronti" in "Raniero Panizeri e i 'Quaderni rossi,'" ed. Dario Lanzardo, special issue of *aut aut* 149-50 (September-December 1975): 6-10.

1. Gap between the logic of *Capital* and analysis of the factory.[2]

Enchantment of method and blockage of research. Terrain of study and of experimentation (hypothesis): no formula resolves the problem.

1.1 The verification is given by/in the struggle.

> struggle as anticipation
>
> hypothesis as provocation (consciousness)
>
> theory as thought of the revolution

2. Scientific concept of the factory.

Critique of the ideological concept (merely the premise for defining the correct concept).

The ideological concept presents itself as vulgar materialism and as empiricism in sociology (empirical sociologism).

Essential to recover the concept of the factory in political economy, that is, in the critique of political economy: unity of economics, sociology, and politics.

2.1 The two levels.

Error of separating the two levels as idealistic illusion of the passage of the first into the second. The unity of economics, sociology, and politics contained in the scientific concept prohibits stopping at one of the two levels.

2.2 Demystification of ideology and verification of the hypothesis in the collective worker = non-correspondence between critique of ideology and working-class science (insubordination). The first is only the premise to be conceived according to the second.

The abstraction of empirical sociologism (illusion of critique at the level of capital) appears, by way of example, as critique:

> of dynamism
>
> of capitalist planning
>
> of the political state
>
> of alienation

From these critiques are extracted:

> the institutionalization of workers' organisms (union and party) in the dynamic development of the system

---

2. "Capital" was capitalized but not italicized in the original.

democratic planning

the democratic road

the struggle for socialist humanism

That is, the critique of ideologies becomes the impotence of scientific analysis and the illusion of an objective social science. Reduction of Marxism to generic sociology.

As functional premises for scientific analysis (recovery and critique of political economy) the "critiques" should lead respectively to:

the collective worker

revolutionary strategy for self-management

dictatorship of the proletariat

laws of development of total capital

That is, for each aspect, the passage from the critique of ideologies to scientific analysis always implies the verification of the hypothesis of the collective worker, which is never implied in the sphere of the critique of ideology, while it is always implied in working-class science.

2.2.1 Bourgeois science and working-class science.

Impossibility of reducing bourgeois thought to ideology—that is, the level of working-class science reveals bourgeois science.

Moment of capitalist development in which bourgeois science takes shape as generalized rationality of the system. The anarchy intrinsic to the system is mediated by bourgeois science—which for this reason is, at the same time, functional to the stabilization of the system and revealing of the crisis (and culture itself in crisis).

3. Analysis of the factory = social relation of the factory.

Verification requires a revolutionary strategy of the class.

3.1 Revolutionary strategy as driving force of the analysis, as guiding hypothesis.

3.2 Verification not in the struggle as given but in the one that contains elements of revolutionary insubordination (verification and hypothesis).

3.2.1 Since revolutionary insubordination is such insofar as it is strategy, as a testing ground it must have a global and a determinate character—in other words, one that is generalizable and specific with respect to capitalist society.

3.2.1.1 The circumstances of capitalism's transformation in Italy, at the level of the laws of development of collective capitalism, mark it as place of significance for capital at the international level.

3.2.1.2 Revolutionary insubordination can be measured by its anticapitalist content, in its aspects of generality and determinateness (insubordination as determinate abstraction).

That is, verification excludes "co-research" and testing the refusal of capitalism through prefigurative groups, and it implies the global, unitary recomposition process of the class.[3]

3.3 To be considered as false problems are both the distinction between micro- and macro-economic (or micro- and macro-sociological) analysis, and the separation between short- and long-term action. The first of these false problems is typical of bourgeois thought, the second of reformist praxis, even in its anarchic version.

4 Political organization of the class as constitution of the class completely outside of capital.

4.1 Constitution of the class completely outside of capital is not the overcoming of the party, but rather the condition of its foundation. In reformist praxis that seeks to constitute the class within capital, the political party of the class does not exist.

4.2 To the current praxis of the mass, democratic-centralist party, there corresponds, as mere negative relief, the idea of the spontaneous organization of the class.

To the hypothesis of the complete overturning of the system, there corresponds maximum organization and violence.

4.2.1 Critique of the parties according to a new theory of the party (critique of ideology and positive analysis).

---

3. Co-research refers to a political process undertaken by some operaisti, most notably Romano Alquati, that sought to move from investigation by militant researchers of workers ("workers' inquiry") to the creation of a new, collective, political subject in which the traditional relationship between researcher and researched in the production of knowledge would be overturned. For a thought-provoking synopsis, see Gigi Roggero, "Notes on framing and re-inventing co-research," *ephemera: theory & politics in organization* 14, no. 3 (2014): 515-23. See also Romano Alquati, "Co-research and Worker's Inquiry" [1994], ed. Matteo Polleri, in "Against the Day: Militant Inquiry, History and Possibilities," dossier, *South Atlantic Quarterly* 118, no. 2 (April 2019): 470-78.

4.3 The class party as indispensable moment of revolutionary strategy. The need for a theory of the party is internal to the elaboration of the strategy and it conditions its practical process of development.

4.3.1 The political party of the class is not a prefiguration of workers' self-management within capitalist society, but establishment of self-management within the revolutionary process.

4.4 As the class is constituted outside of capital, so its political party is constituted outside of the bourgeois state.

4.4.1 As the constitution of the class outside of capital is the concrete way to blow up capital, so the constitution of the political party of the class is the material means for smashing and pulverizing the machine of the bourgeois state and substituting for it the dictatorship of the proletariat, in other words, the class that organizes itself into a state of a new type.

4.4.1.1 Characteristic trait of the political party of the working class is the conscious organization of its own extinction. Characteristic trait of the workers' state is its immediate process of withering away.

5 The organization of labor in *Quaderni Rossi* is the organization of political work.

5.1 Such political work rules out the contradistinction between the two levels, that of research and that of practical commitment in the struggles.

5.2 Activity is programmable within the development of the revolutionary strategy of the class.

The Strike at FIAT

(July 1962)

During the summer of 1962, tens of thousands of workers across Turin were out on strike, including, for the first time in years, the metal-workers of FIAT's gargantuan Mirafiori plant. Tronti wrote this dispatch, in response to a series of questions posed by the journal *Problemi del Socialismo* [Problems of Socialism], just before the revolt of Piazza Statuto, which exacerbated the growing split in *Quaderni Rossi*.[1]

1. See Michele Filippini, *Leaping Forward: Mario Tronti and the History of Political Workerism* (Maastricht: Jan van Eyck Academie, 2012), 18-19, for an assessment of how these events triggered and reframed debates within *Quaderni Rossi*.

The resumption of class struggle at FIAT is an ordinary event. It acquires exceptional significance within the particular context in which it has broken out: forecasted neither by the employers' bloc nor by the workers' organizations on such short notice. It is true that the strike network had long been well woven by the "sectarian" trade-unionists of Turin.[2] This does not mean that the first news of the 60,000 outside of FIAT struck everyone with all the welcome violence of a "wildcat" strike. The workers had encircled FIAT, which was silent; there were struggles everywhere else, and what's more, "political" struggles this time, seeking to articulate the power of the union against the power of the boss, from the firm to the sector, in a new system of global and permanent negotiation. Without a doubt, one of the underlying motives that drove the FIAT workers to struggle again consists in this *qualitative* leap taken by the workers' struggles. The FIAT workers have not moved for years partly because, for years, the model of struggle proposed to them covered their backs, but it did not open, as today, the prospect of greater power, which is the only perspective today that has importance at that level. However, we need not delude ourselves on this ground: the character of the current working-class struggles does no more than empirically register the actual, determinate level of capitalist development. The complete generalization of these struggles *illustrates*, before anything else, that a particular condition of exploitation, that is, a particular point in the development of capitalist production, is being generalized. Everyone today knows that FIAT is no longer an island of progress in a sea of backwardness: technological leaps and the well-being of workers now are becoming common features of the entire sector, which they tend to unify and homogenize at an equal level of development. Hence the potential reunification of the working class in that sector may have two different and even opposing results, depending on the relation of forces established in the near future.

For a long time, FIAT has had an interest in keeping around in its own backyard a lagging capitalism, one of caste privilege and bosses' fascism. The old corporative integration of the worker into their own company was the natural, internal *counterpart* to this historical, external situation.[3] Old-style industrial capitalism in Italy still needed the peasant South, and *therefore* it could not but *also* have need for the historical bloc with the landowners and the political right in government. Capitalist development itself now seeks to bury this past, and the democratic struggles of workers are an important internal component of this development. At a certain point within this development, there is a leap. Capitalist production is such that it does not tolerate

2. "Sectarianism" was a charge often lobbed by Palmiro Togliatti and others in the PCI against militants whose activities challenged the leadership's national-popular program.

3. "Corporative" is a reference to the fascist-era organization of workers into "labor corporations."

the category of the particularity; it tends by its nature toward the plenitude of the universal. Having reached a certain level, it needs to *generalize* this level before leaping to the next one. The working-class struggle often helps capital by grasping the *necessity* of this leap; it helps it by accelerating and organizing the successive moments of its own development. The working-class struggle gives capitalist development "tight deadlines." The stabilization of capitalism does not, as a matter of fact, imply the end of struggles: it implies their institutionalization.

Valletta has scolded his industrialist colleagues harshly for the encirclement of workers around FIAT; he wanted to make believe that FIAT had fallen due to external working-class pressure that other capitalists had been unable to control.[4] But as a modern representative of capital, his intellect must have secretly told him something more. It took the full-scale strike of his workers to make him openly say "yes" to the center-left. This means many things simultaneously. It means that the period of imprisonments,[5] retaliations, and discriminations at FIAT is definitively over; that the period of the corporative, company union is over; that the period of a "particular" monopoly policy toward the costs of capitalist society, in general, is over. Now Valletta can play the part of the collective capitalist directly: he faces not only *his own* workers but *all* the workers. At this point, the unions may be equally allowed, with equal rights, to join in the toasts at the bargaining sessions, sitting together in a triangle with La Malfa and the bosses, planning the balanced development of Italian capitalism together.[6] Because this, at bottom, is the ultimate dream of modernized capital: an "autonomous" union—autonomous, in an impartial manner, from the choices of the single capitalist and from the pressure of the organized workers; a "modern"

4. Vittorio Valletta, president of FIAT from 1946–66, who had collaborated with the fascists and Nazis during the war, announced himself as a supporter of the center-left in Italy in 1962. Throughout the postwar era, he kept close ties with U.S. anti-Communist efforts and would later visit President Kennedy to encourage financial support for the Socialists. See Paul Ginsborg, *A History of Contemporary Italy: Society and Politics, 1943-1988* (London: Penguin, 1990), 23, 192, 264.

5. The "imprisonments" [*il confino-FIAT*] refer to a practice, common during the 1950s at FIAT, of taking workers who were active in Communist politics and trade-union activity and isolating them in departments with horrendous working conditions. For a series of interviews with prisoners of one of these departments, see Aris Accornero, *Fiat confine: storia della OSR* (Milan: Edizioni Avanti, 1959). For a powerful visual reconstruction of this history in light of contemporary exploitation in the Italian logistics sector, see the documentary directed by Danilo Licciardello, *Democrazia sconfinata* [Democracy unconfined] (2010), available online: https://vimeo.com/18307344; see also the photo essay by Alessandro Leogrande, with photographs by Maila Iocovelli and Fabio Zayed, "I prigionieri delle fabbriche" [The prisoners of the factories], *Internazionale*, October 27, 2014, available online: https://www.internazionale.it/reportage/maila-iacovelli/2014/10/27/reparti-confino-in-italia-9.

6. Ugo La Malfa, member of the Italian Republican Party, was appointed Minister of the Budget under Italy's first center-left government in 1962. In May of that year he issued a "Nota aggiuntiva" [Additional note], appended to the ministry's report on the Italian economy in 1961, in which he argued that planning between the state, the unions, and industry would be required to sustain "balanced" economic growth. See "Nota aggiuntiva alla Relazione generale sulla situazione economica del Paese per il 1961" [Additional note to the general report on the economic situation of the country for 1961] [May 22, 1962] (Rome: Edizione Janus, 1973), available online with commentary: http://www.fulm.org/articoli/economia/nota-aggiuntiva-relazione-generale-situazione-economica-paese-1961. For context, see Ginsborg, *History of Contemporary Italy*, 268. Also see Palazzo, "Social Factory," 151.

union, a capitalist form of workers' control—control over the movements of labor-power, the rationalization of the irrationality that the workers' thrusts have from the bourgeois point of view.

The FIAT strike, then, expresses and illustrates *this* determinate level of capitalist development. It is born from a delay in the bosses' initiative in the face of changed working conditions for the worker; it imposes the necessity of a *leap* that manages to momentarily resolve the contradiction arising between the new needs of capitalist production and the old bosses' despotism, or rather, between the stabilization of the old process of valorization and the new forms of domination of capital over labor. Everything can be reduced in the end to an advance in capitalist exploitation, in its rational recomposition at the company level and its generalization at the sectoral level. The disordered outburst of the workers' struggles, their present character of being *outside* of capitalist planning, and the FIAT strike as a "wildcat strike," as far as capital is concerned, demonstrate one thing above all: that the old attempt to integrate the working class into the system has largely failed. The formation of a "labor aristocracy," which then would become the *political* leader of the workers' movement in its entirety, has failed; the traditional form of capture of the workers' organizations, the classical road of socialist reformism, no longer serves anyone, not even the capitalist. The modern production of capital *in itself* contains tools for smashing the class unity of the workers, for organizing their real division scientifically, and, moreover, for preventing any possible "formal" reunification among them. Then, once they have been divided and beaten, it is easier on this basis for the capitalists to unify. The FIAT strike very quickly split the bosses' bloc in two: signing a "modern" contract with *all* the metal-workers will enable its unitary recomposition at a higher level.

But the opposite could happen if the workers' movement were *organized*, if its current organizations were to correspond to its coming needs in terms of development—if, in a word, a *political* organization of the working class were to exist. The confrontation between classes at FIAT demonstrates once again that this enormous process of capitalist development in Italy *excludes* the Italian working class *in its entirety*. And this is the point of the contradiction we must leverage in order to put that development into crisis. The FIAT workers have given their reply to the nationalization of electric energy.[7] They are responding to the modernization process within the capitalist structures by directly bringing the working-class struggle into these structures. In doing

7. Italy began the process of nationalizing its electricity industry under the first center-left government in 1962-63. Nationalization of electricity was a key component of the center-left program of planning capitalist development—the shift to public ownership would allow the state to direct investments in the development of electricity infrastructure in accordance with the needs of social capital. The process was completed under a subsequent center-left government at the end of 1964. See Ginsborg, *A History of Contemporary Italy*, 268-70.

so, the *capitalist* nature of the system and the *working-class* leadership of the struggle that fights it develop simultaneously: in other words, a real socialist perspective is opened. Those who want "balanced" development of the Italian economy must know that this ultimately involves programming the workers' struggles within the plan of capital. To make this plan explode, on the contrary, what is needed is *to organize the imbalance* of a working class that totally escapes the planned control of the capitalist class.[8]

The same organization of modern production that capital uses to decompose and destroy the class unity of the workers can be used by the workers' movement to recompose and excite that unity, in new forms, at a higher level. In this sense, there is no quality intrinsic to organized production that makes it always and only of service to capitalist power: everything always depends, in the end, on the relation of forces established in the struggle. The FIAT workers found themselves all on strike, outside of the factory, based on the organization of production *inside* the factory. At that moment, they were strong enough to take what the boss had used against them for years and overturn it, directing it against the boss. But this movement cannot live off spontaneity alone. The future unitary recomposition of the workers at the sectoral level does not hold together in an autonomous way, or in any case, it does not become explosive within the system, if it does not ultimately find permanent capillary forms of organization at the level of the firm, of the plant, of the department, of the team. Articulated bargaining, the negotiation of all the aspects of the work relationship, the union in the factory—these are demands that must together obtain this single objective. This is the sole guarantee that they do not become reabsorbed, one by one, into the most rational development of modern capitalism.[9] Organizational forms of a new type, factory-based organization of the class, the immediate political content of this new power at the moment in which it is counterposed to the power of the boss—these are elementary rallying cries that the workers' parties today need not invent, because the workers have done it for them. There is a revolutionary *working-class use* of large-scale capitalist production that we still have to learn. The FIAT strike should reopen this problem, if nothing else.

8. This passage bears a striking resemblance to one in Tronti's "The Plan of Capital," published in June 1963 in the third issue of *Quaderni Rossi* but first circulated in the autumn of 1962. "It is at this point that the working class must instead consciously organise itself as an *irrational* element within the specific rationality of capitalist production," he wrote. "The growing rationalisation of modern capital must find an insurmountable limit in the growing irrationality of the organised workers—that is, in the working-class refusal of *political* integration within the system's *economic* development. Thus, the working class becomes the only *anarchy* that capitalism is unable to *organise* socially. The task of the workers' movement is to scientifically organise and politically manage *this* working-class anarchy within capitalist production. On the model of the society organised by capital, the working-class party itself can only be the *organisation of anarchy*—no longer within capital, but outside of it, meaning outside of its development." Tronti, "The Plan of Capital," 61. Thanks to Antonio Del Vecchio for highlighting this comparison.

9. "Articulated bargaining" was an evolution in "democratic planning" that combined national-level trade-union confederation negotiations with plant- and company-specific agreements.

Part Two

The Strategic Overturning

Letter to Raniero Panzieri

(January 1963)

After the militant uprising in Piazza Statuto, the editors of *Quaderni Rossi* were labeled provocateurs by the mainstream labor movement. While Panzieri responded by attempting to repair their relationship with leaders of the historical organizations of the working class, the "interventionists," Tronti among them, sought a different course—one in which they would play a more directly political role. In this letter to Panzieri, Tronti underlines his growing frustration with the priorities established by *Quaderni Rossi* and proposes they instead refocus their efforts by initiating a newspaper aimed specifically at the workers of FIAT in Turin.

Dearest Raniero,

The "new course" is in full swing around here: for everyone it provokes immediate agreement and great enthusiasm, and substantive objections to it cannot
be found. It is a matter of practically reconverting some of our tools in view
of a "war economy." Having reached this point in our discourse, we can no
longer limit ourselves to *saying* certain things: the very fact of saying them
forces us to try to do them. The subject matter we are dealing with is such that
it cannot be formalized in a purely theoretical guise; it must lead to immediate
practical results of organization and of action. There is an internal coherence
to the discourse that takes us then *outside* of the discourse as such, a logic
to the theory that delivers us then into the hands of a practical *experience*.
On the other hand, the form that this experience takes must be a function
of the particular theoretical analysis that has preceded it; it cannot take any
levels for granted other than those on which the theoretical construction has
been based. And *vice versa*. The terrain on which *Quaderni Rossi* exercises
its political influence *cannot* be the formal political terrain presented by the
traditional organizations, it must be a *new type of political terrain*, the same
one on which *Quaderni Rossi* is exercising its abstract theoretical discourse in
a new way. It is clear that, on this point, we are all in full agreement: it is only
a matter of seeing if the time is ripe for drawing the necessary, operational
consequences from it. I am convinced that a *first* fullness of time has already
come.

We must *begin to speak to the workers*. If all of what we are saying is not
just the chattering of disinterested intellectuals, but suggestions of political
struggle for the workers' movement, it is indispensable that we establish a
permanent and direct dialogue with the workers. If we want to escape the
fate that always threatens an experiment such as ours—an Italian "New Left"
instead of an English one, a pressure group that addresses itself to an enlightened elite—we must then give our political discourse a *working-class base*.
Everyone knows that only this path ever initiates a crisis in the organizations:
another path has not been found and *need not* be found. It is true that for a
task of this kind our forces are paltry, our ideas are confused, and the political
unity between us is itself incomplete. Yet we must attempt this experience
today, and we must do so at a *particular* point that may then be *generalized*
immediately. To make a cut at one of the system's nerve centers, *only one*, in
which the level reached by capital and the level of the working class are counterposed in a classical way, in a pure way, free from "external" interferences.
To strike this nerve center not only with the tools of theoretical analysis, but

with the resources of an initial political organization. This point can only be FIAT. The high degree of concentration and permanent *passive* mobilization of this nucleus of workers, the high degree of national and international socialization of this part of social capital (and there are other reasons), suggest that this is the most favorable terrain for a new political initiative, capable of *single-handedly* opening new prospects for the entire Italian workers' movement. Everything lies in attempting to connect with the collective worker at FIAT, on the direct basis of our political positions, with a discourse addressed to the workers and then made by the workers: a genuine dialogue, an exchange of theoretical and practical experiences, in which it is not true that theory must always come from us and practice must always come from the workers, but in which exactly the opposite could happen. Alongside the analytical and theoretical labor of *Quaderni Rossi* (which must become increasingly analytical and increasingly theoretical, in the sense of being more *abstract*), there is a need to launch a political newspaper directed at the workers of FIAT (not to all the workers, but *only* to *this* nucleus of workers). Alongside the theoretical model of capital's development (which then develops practically on its own), we must experiment with a practical *model* of working-class organization (which is only developed through our most violent exertion of willpower). This must become the *center* of all our work, not to the exclusion of everything else, but back to which everything else must continually refer. We need a point capable of judging all our various initiatives unequivocally: but this point cannot be a bureaucratic center that organizes *general* political forces around a precise perspective. This central point of political leadership of the movement can only be provided by a practical *experience* endowed with specific characteristics, such that it immediately rejects all that remains extraneous to it while accepting what goes in the same direction of travel.

If we accept this perspective, many of the things for which we had budgeted fall apart. The idea of the *Cronache* falls apart, that is, the idea of repeating the same *Quaderni Rossi* discourse at the level of the political battle. A false idea, because *Quaderni Rossi*'s political battle cannot take place on the traditional political terrain; it cannot accept this terrain without perverting its own nature, without, in other words, ideologizing its own theory.[1] Speaking to these intermediary party cadres, to the intellectuals in crisis, to the various little groups of Trotskyists, and perhaps even to a *general* public of workers—this is something we do not need to do, something which does not interest us, which is sterile from every point of view, and deadly boring. What also falls apart, in my

---

1. The *Cronache dei Quaderni Rossi* was published in September 1962 as an effort to more closely reach the "workers' level." This project was continued in a shorter format as *Cronache Operaie* for two issues, the first in July of 1963 and the second in October of the same year, after the *Quaderni Rossi* split. Helpful context is provided in Wright, *The Weight of the Printed Word*.

opinion, is the idea of making the Istituto Morandi the driving force and central engine of all our affairs.[2] It falls apart for the reason we mentioned previously. Leadership of this kind could very well be exercised even from Rome, which exposes how a leadership of this type is a *misconception*. In Milan, if I have understood correctly, we cannot do anything *decisive* today: it is a city that escapes us, which even our intellectual tools have failed to get a handle on, which threatens to drown us all in its reformist political sludge, with a *social* structure that produces and reproduces in modern form the *old* terrain of political struggle within the workers' movement and perhaps even against capital. Tell me if I am wrong, but in my opinion the piazza of Milan must, *for the moment*, be abandoned. All the available forces of *Quaderni Rossi* must undertake a long march toward Turin, concentrate themselves in the basement of the Centro Gobetti, show up in front of FIAT […].[3] It is difficult to say from here what the likelihood is of establishing political contact with the collective of FIAT workers. Certainly we can no longer, at this point, reduce our relations with the working class to personal conversations with the individual worker; nor can we wake up suddenly every time the struggle ignites in order to bring subordinate aid to the spontaneism of the masses. The same work of analytically reconstructing the theoretical foundations of the class struggle must present itself again at the grassroots level as the practical reconstruction of the initial political tools that organize the struggle itself. In each case, it takes strong and *continual* initiative on our part. I am deeply convinced that we will not manage to *hold* our current positions without continually *attacking* the positions of others, which are directly, in this case, the positions of capital.

The initiative of the FIAT newspaper could also fail. Nevertheless, it would leave us with an *experience* worth more than all the others we currently have combined. On the other hand, if it succeeds in the slightest, if we manage to establish, from our positions, some minimal political relationship with this nucleus of workers, thus establishing a model that could be generalized broadly, I believe that we could not foresee, not even then, what prospects for political struggle in Italy would immediately open. Certainly, for an action of this kind, we need courage first and foremost: the courage to quickly replace some of the tools of our own struggle as well, reconciling the gaps, exposing ourselves more with fewer defenses. But even in our work some *leaps* must be conceived and organized, leaps born from a certain ripening of the discourse and of forces, and even perhaps from objective necessities that are independent of us.

2. The Istituto Morandi, located in Milan, was named for Rodolfo Morandi, a leading postwar figure in the PSI and a mentor of Panzieri. It was the major source of funding for *Quaderni Rossi*.

3. The Centro Gobetti is a research center and archive in Turin, founded in 1961 and named for the liberal antifascist Piero Gobetti.

The worst thing would be to consider this initiative to be one of so many things that we may do today. It is necessary instead to make our comrades grasp, *today*, the exceptional and absolutely original character of an experience of this kind. To remind everyone of that intellectual audacity which cannot be limited to the discovery of new theoretical models, but which must then launch us toward the solution of complex practical problems. An experiment such as ours cannot go on as it does today, with all this sluggishness, this indifference, this scattered thinking among comrades—all things that derive, in my opinion, from lacking a center of experience that would practically guide everyone's action. Before this idea of "speaking to the workers," I confess, dear Raniero, all my infantile enthusiasm. Let me now explain with a degree of clarity that *instinctive* indecision which I had about coming to Milan and taking up *that type* of political commitment (those things that are first felt through intuition and then understood through reason).[4] The problem for me, today, is not that of living in a city of the North, to breathe in the industrial *atmosphere*: the problem is that of *specific* experiences, within industry and with the workers. Those words which close my last article were not written lightly.[5] It is not a matter of testing that discourse in practice, but of directly *practicing it*: putting it into practice is the most correct continuation of the discourse. Making this attempt is part of the theoretical work that I do and that *I will continue* to do. Moreover, it is part of *everyone*'s work and so it is affirmed as the highest form of organization proper to our work.

We should now discuss these things with all the comrades. In Rome, we have already done so, finding immediately a monolithic unity. I mentioned it to Paci who should have talked about it in Milan. Mauro told me that he wrote about it to Monica.[6] Before writing to you about this with such certainty, I asked around for substantive objections, in vain. Let us definitely set an editorial reunion for the 19th–20th in Turin or Milan (as you wish). From Rome, this time, everyone is determined to come (Alberto, Umberto, Gaspare, Rita, Mauro).[7] You really should mention the subject of the reunion to the comrades of the other cities (Florence, Genoa, Padua, etc.). I can stay longer to talk with you about everything. But let me know your

4. Panzieri had proposed to help Tronti find employment with the publishing house Einaudi Editore in Milan.

5. Tronti is referring to his "The Plan of Capital," the penultimate paragraph of which reads: "Thus we find the impasse in which discourse is caught when it wants to be both sectarian and totalising. It is caught between its will to set off calmly looking for the objective reasons that guide a long historical process and the need immediately to find the subjective forces which are organising to overthrow it. It is caught between the patience of research and the urgency of the response. The theoretical void that stands between the two is a void of political organisation. There is a right to experiment—indeed, this is the only right worth insisting upon. Until that is done, everything will be expressed through abrupt clashes between immediately contradictory concepts. So, we are *forced* to jump ahead. We do so without mediation, out of hatred for opportunism." Tronti, "The Plan of Capital," 64.

6. Massimo Paci and Monica Brunatto were members of the *Quaderni Rossi* circle in Milan.

7. Alberto Asor Rosa, Umberto Coldagelli, Gaspare de Caro, and Mauro Gobbini were members of the Roman contingent of *Quaderni Rossi*.

initial response: I am convinced, based on past experiences, that these last few days you have been thinking these *same things*. Now I will say goodbye; I am afraid I have written you the longest of letters, so long that I am careful not to reread it. Take it as it is.

Until soon, Mario.

The Copernican Revolution

(May 1963)

After tense meetings throughout the spring over the future of *Quaderni Rossi*, and the question of whether to prioritize the analysis of capitalist exploitation or the leap into workers' struggles, Tronti spoke with a group of interventionists in Milan on May 27th. The basic perspective he put forward, of understanding the working class as a growing political subject, would serve as the animating principle for *Classe Operaia*, the newspaper that he, Alquati, Negri, and others would soon found.[1] The present text first appeared in 2008, based on a transcribed tape recording of the meeting. Milana and Trotta, the Italian editors of the *L'operaismo degli anni sessanta* collection, gave it this title and offered summaries for certain portions of the discussion, now in brackets.

1. Panzieri would later refer to this talk as "a fascinating summary of a whole series of errors that can now be committed by a workers' left." He criticized Tronti's proposals for amounting to a "philosophy of the working class," in which capitalism "lives only by auto-suggestion," and indeed this registered the major claim of this talk: the history of capitalism must be rewritten with the working class as its protagonist. Raniero Panzieri, "Separare le strade" [Separating the roads] [August 31, 1963], in *L'operaismo degli anni sessanta*, 312-14 (my translation).

[*At the opening of the meeting, the comrades from Rome, and comrade Tronti in particular, were asked to clarify the way in which they understood the relationship between the work of analysis and political work, above all in reference to the criticisms that were leveled at the comrades from Milan for the framing of the first issue of* Potere Operaio.[2] *This, of course, was only the initial prompt for the discussion.*]

Tronti—We can and we must speak, from the beginning, of the socially organized worker, and so we can and we must be able to speak, from the beginning, of labor-power being born and putting itself forward as the working class, and therefore as a social class. And it is precisely this social proposition made by working-class labor, by wage-labor, of the social class, that clearly forces, on the opposite side, the class of capitalists to catch up, with a kind of class-based social organization that tries to directly replicate—without ever, in the entire arc of capitalist development, succeeding—certain social forms of the collective worker.

This means that, at this point, we directly overturn a certain type of argument, one that even we have made. This is the argument that, basically, at the level of capitalist society, history has always been proposed as the history of capital, as the history of the various determinations of capital, whereby capital explained everything else, and in fact, all of history. As in, capital explains ground rent.[3] Starting from capital, history in general is brought back to the drawing board, and thus a materialist conception of history is elaborated.

Today, we must instead find the theoretical courage to say that within capitalist society, ultimately, the highest point of development is by no means the level of capital; the highest point of development is the working class. Hence Marx's thesis, that capital explains everything behind it, is probably no longer true, because clearly there is something today that explains capital, and which alone can explain capital, and that is the working class itself. Along these lines, we can clarify a formulation that we previously gave in a more general sense, which is the fact that all research and all analysis must start out from the workers' viewpoint. At this point, in my opinion, we can concretely specify what the workers' viewpoint is.

2. *Potere Operaio* was a title shared by several newspapers launched in 1962–63 by members of *Quaderni Rossi* who were partisans of "intervention." Their targets were auto and petrochemical workers in Milan, Turin, and the Veneto. Tronti here refers to an issue of the Milanese *Potere Operaio*, released May 1, on which Alquati, Pierluigi Gasparotto, and Romolo Gobbi likely collaborated. See Milana and Trotta, *L'operaismo degli anni sessanta*, 285.

3. Tronti is referring to the perspective outlined in Marx's "1857 Introduction" and developed by his former mentors, Della Volpe and Colletti: "Ground rent cannot be understood without capital. But capital can certainly be understood without ground rent. Capital is the all-dominating economic power of bourgeois society. It must form the starting-point as well as the finishing-point, and must be dealt with before landed property." Marx, *Grundrisse*, 107. For another perspective, see Louis Althusser's critique of Colletti in "The Object of *Capital*," particularly the section "Marxism Is Not a Historicism," 268–95.

The workers' viewpoint is—once again, in a Marxian sense—the comprehension of reality starting out from the highest point of development, and the highest point of development within capital, within capitalist society, is clearly the working class. The greatest form ultimately produced by capital, which it is forced to produce and reproduce, is precisely the working class. And so, [...] a theme presents itself, according to which, as capital explained preceding categories—whereby ground-rent could [not] have existed without capital, but not *vice versa*—so now there is the necessity of seeing that the working class explains capital, precisely because we can speak of a working class without capital, while the opposite process is not given. That is, we absolutely cannot speak of a capital without a working class. At this point, separately from the discourse on the concept of class, a determination, something we must come to define with precision, is reintroduced into this framework. Namely, it is the concept of revolution itself, of the revolutionary break on the part of the working class, which then is related to how we analyze the type of social-class struggle that the working class itself is.

If the preceding premise and hypothesis are true, namely, that one can only speak of a social class at the level of social labor-power and therefore of the working class, we must ultimately go so far as to say that we can speak of a revolutionary process in a specific sense—of a revolution, of a revolutionary break—only at the level of the working class. If it is true, in other words, that a bourgeois class did not exist prior to the existence of the working class, then the very concept of the bourgeois revolution ends up falling apart. That is, we come to discover that, at bottom, a bourgeois revolution as such has never existed, and that the specific bourgeois form of capitalist development is a form of continual, gradual transition, one that proceeds within a specific economic process, and which is able to pose the political objective of seizing power only once this economic process has ripened on a broad scale—the bourgeois road, in other words, of seizing power.

Here, indeed, enormous research opportunities are opened for historical analysis: the whole problem of the transition from feudal society to capitalist society; reenvisioning the roads that exist in Marx's discourse in general terms, even if Marx also speaks of two roads, a revolutionary road and a reformist road, in the construction of capitalist society. These themes are proposed in a new way: the existence of capital is proposed as the existence of an economic category that lives and grows gradually within the economic mechanism of a preexisting society, and only in the end, in a secondary manner, is the problem posed of seizing political power and therefore of a political revolution. For this reason, the bourgeois political revolution is actually the transition; it is the sanctioning of a process that has already taken place. That is, at the very moment in which the bourgeoisie put forward the object of conquering power, its own specific type of revolution had basically been accomplished already, because it already had the fundamental economic power in its hands.

Nowadays, the workers are completely unable to repeat this type of development associated with the bourgeoisie, because we understand, as long as we do not accept a reformist conception of the transition to socialism, that the working class by no means experiences growth within bourgeois society as an economic category, does not at all grow through a seizure of economic power or through its capacity to economically manage a predetermined social structure. These are all characteristic of a reformist perspective that seeks to replicate, within the working class, a type of transition to constructing a new society that is specific to the bourgeoisie, to capital itself. The specifically revolutionary movement of the working class instead consists precisely in the fact that the seizure of power, the revolutionary break, and therefore the growth of the working class within the economic system of capital presents itself immediately as political growth.

In short, it is not labor-power that grows. For this reason, I suggest that we put the discourse on labor-power aside for the moment and go back to discussing the working class, because it is not labor-power that socializes itself and then becomes economically powerful within capitalist society; it is instead the working class that increasingly demands that its own position, its own power, its own place in society has political content. For this reason, at its limit, the working-class movement within the old society is even the exact opposite of the bourgeois movement within its old society. In this movement, as a matter of fact, what really grows is the political strength of the working class; in other words, what really grows is the transition as a political goal, and so this immediately suggests a directly political revolution. As a directly political revolution, this one arises as an actual revolution, precisely because the other transition was directly reliant on its gradual nature, on the possibility of not breaking, of never violently destroying the old relations, but of coexisting with them, until the entire process reached maturity and enabled the transition.

Clearly, we are dealing with formulations that remain hypotheses and thus with very abstract research. Yet, in my opinion, centering the discussion today on this topic is also quite useful in a political sense, because now we are really beginning to sort out the definite and specific forms of working-class struggle, the reasons why the working class struggles in these ways, going as far as discussing, establishing, and analytically elaborating some of the working class's own laws of development. Just as Marx began to work out the laws of capital's development, saying that capital moves in this way, that it is determined historically and continually in these ways, today we must manage to see how the

working class has come about historically, how it has been determined historically as such, by establishing objective and necessary laws of development.
Establishing these laws of development for the working class is the only way
to scientifically forecast the future movements of the class. Forecasting them
gives us the opportunity to immediately organize them. So here, once again,
we are proposing an organic relation between, on the one hand, the theoret-
ical-scientific-analytical moment, as the forecast of the movement, and, on
the other, the moment of political intervention, which precisely organizes the
forecast which has been made. And at this level, in this way, precisely within
the revolutionary movement of the class, we get back to a different relation
between these two moments.

[*Tronti says that this is what he has been thinking about these days, and that
these things could eventually be presented in complete form in the next issue
of* Quaderni Rossi. *He mentions that other comrades in Rome are doing work
around these theses, seeing implications of a historical character in them especially, and thus trying to see how and when a concept of class struggle presents itself, how it is established "on the working-class level, how it has been established
at the bourgeois level; if one can speak of the bourgeois class, in what sense must
one instead speak only of the working class, and therefore in what sense can we
differentiate between the struggle of the working class and the struggle of the
bourgeois class."*]

Gobbini—[*We can consider the problem of the continuity of the workers'
struggles, of communication about them within the working class, to have something to do with the conversation about the political growth of the working class.
It is also a problem where the two levels of our work, abstract and revolution-
ary-political-organizational, truly present themselves as tightly bound together.
How can we more precisely understand this continuity and this communication
of the struggle in light of the class's political growth?*]

Tronti—[*It is certainly a matter of further specifying what we mean by political growth, and of seeing how*] today we must go back to criticizing every
spontaneist excess within this political growth. However, the critique of spontaneism that we reintroduce today must happen at a higher level than the one
on which the entire Leninist framework was posed. If there is a point at which,
perhaps, Leninist discourse enters into the argument that we are making, it is
precisely this: the hypothesis that there will not, at any moment, be political
growth of the class such that it then spontaneously discovers communication
and an organizational form allowing it to leap beyond the capitalist economic
mechanism. What changes with respect to the Leninist proposal, are the practical forms of organization suggested for this leap from spontaneity to organization. Before reaching that leap, the significance of the class's political growth

must really be explored. On this point, we can also begin to put forward theses that are more precise than those produced thus far.

Certain forms of struggle and organization repeat themselves at different moments in the working class's development—for example, what today we are calling the refusal form, the form of the workers' "no," the refusal to collaborate in development and thus the workers' refusal to positively propose a program of demands. This is a form of struggle that has developed in its own unique way within the history of capital, within the history of the working class, because this form has, ultimately, existed since the beginning, from the moment the working class constituted itself as such. However, the more the working class grows, and the more it grows quantitatively and organizes itself around precise points, the more the refusal form grows in value. In other words, the process of labor-power's accumulation, unlike the accumulation of capital, has a directly political meaning, because it is not the accumulation of an economic category, but the accumulation of a political demand, an accumulation which boils down to just one: the demand for power in the hands of the workers.

So, this refusal form is one that grows together with the working class, which is why we emphasize that, when we consider its historical trajectory, the mass of working-class demands reduces in volume and becomes increasingly simplified. The demands undergo a process of unification up to what we may forecast as the maximum level: the disappearance of all demands except for one, the demand for general political power. For this reason, the different transitions that can be reconstructed between these moments are historical transitions between categories, between which we must begin to distinguish. For example, as today we generally distinguish between the bourgeoisie and the capitalist class—the capitalist class which is itself in contrast to capital, the bourgeoisie which is basically a sum of individual capitalists—I believe that we can indeed begin to speak of a difference between proletariat and working class. In other words, it is typical for proletarian demands to be split up into a menu of positive demands, which then all consist in a request for the improvement of economic conditions and the functioning of labor-power—a request that is practically a demand for the improvement of the conditions of exploitation, one that is bound to a whole, long, trade-unionist and reformist current of class organization, which indeed, in this specific way, replicated some of the forms taken by the attempted economic organization of the working class itself.

Now, the process is such that we can make a forecast: at a certain point the relation between the working class and capitalism will be directly overturned, in the sense that there will no longer be working-class demands directed at capital, but rather there will be an organization of the working class so politically functional that it will limit itself no longer to making requests but to refusing what is requested of it. In other words, we can forecast a higher form of development of the class struggle in which the requests, the demands, will be made only by the capitalists. We are seeing this at certain points of capitalist development: a capital which continually asks for the collaboration of the working class, which even expresses its objective needs through some subjective working-class demands.

This, for example, is characteristic of the current phase of Italian capitalism. In other words, the objective needs of capitalist production present themselves, ultimately, in the form of the workers' subjective demands. The union proposes a platform of demands, and this platform is nothing but the reflection of the objective needs of capitalist production. But capitalist production cannot submit these demands directly; it is obliged to pass through the working-class articulation, hence the importance for capitalist production of the organizational structuring of labor-power, of the working class through the union, the party, and so on. What happens when the organizational form of the working class is no longer the traditional form of the union or the party that passively accepts the reality of being an articulation of capitalist production? What happens when the working class refuses to introduce certain demands in its own name, demands that are really capital's own, in particular, the demand for planning a certain type of development that progresses through some leaps in the labor relation, some adjustments to the contracts between capital and the working class?

When the working class refuses to become the mediator of capitalist development, at that moment the entire economic mechanism comes to a standstill, and there is nothing to be done. This is the only premise for a serious revolutionary prospect at this advanced level of capital: when the workers themselves refuse to present demands to capital, in other words, when they refuse the entire trade-union level, refuse the contractual form of relation to capital. At that moment, clearly, capital itself, the capitalist class, is forced to directly make some demands, precisely because this need cannot be mediated through the mere existence of the working class within the productive process. At that moment, the capitalists will make a proposal to the workers directly, and this will be the highest point of the revolutionary struggle against capitalist society. At that point, the working class truly becomes the dominant political class within society, because it refuses, says "no," to the demands coming from the capitalist side. Because the working class's subaltern status within capital lies precisely in the fact that the working class is forced to submit its requests to capital, and capital has the ability and gets the opportunity to refuse them—this is the subaltern status of the working class. Probably the high point of revolutionary struggle in a classical capitalist country will emerge precisely in this way, with the relation of domination between the two classes overturned, with the demand coming from the capitalist side and the "no" coming directly from the workers' side.

But what does this mean? It means that, at that point, clearly, the working class has already developed so much political strength that in that moment it is the dominant class, not because it holds the power to economically manage society, but because it has organized for itself an autonomous, political, class power of its own, a power that dominates capital and thus practically forces it to break. It is clear that, at that moment, there will also be a problem in the economic mechanism of capitalist development; at that moment, we can truly speak of a crisis in the economic mechanism. But indeed, this crisis of the economic mechanism is ultimately subordinate to—in other words, comes after—the political revolution of the working class. Hence, in that moment, the necessity will arise for the working class to also reclaim, in addition to its particular political power, the economic management of the entire society. At that point, the failure of the capitalist economic mechanism, of the capitalist appropriation of production, emerges—and therefore a general crisis of the system emerges. Now, if this can be suggested as the general perspective, it indeed remains an extremely general perspective, and so all the other problems within it remain open still. In other words, with respect to this program, which is, after all, very far off, how can a movement that takes the ultimate necessity of this development into account be practically organized?

Asor Rosa—[He believes that the crucial argument in Tronti's discourse is the one regarding the working class as the only political class, considering its growth in a political sense within the capitalist system. This way of understanding the working class shifts from the traditional perspective of discourse made within the workers' movement, and which can still be found in some texts of Marxist theory.] You have refused the explanation of history as a materialist explanation of history, and you have cast aside objectivist determinism in whatever shape, no matter how refined. I would have liked you to specify in a more exact manner, or at least to have clarified the point regarding the character assumed by the working class when defined as a preeminently political force. In other words, with the evaluation of the working class as an economic category having likewise been discarded, and thus with all immediately and directly economic factors having been taken away from the explanation of the class's movements, an explanation clearly remains to be given of the political character of the class. From this derives the whole discussion that will need to be had about the specific organization of the class as a political class. In other words, you speak of the political growth of the class, and you foresee a political development of the class, at the end of which is the refusal of the capitalist plan in all its forms, that is, the refusal of capitalist demands, which puts the economic structure of capital into crisis and thus moves forward the revolutionary process, in the fullest sense of the term. I would have liked you to specify the character of and the reasons for this political growth. Exactly because it seems to me that, with the problem posed in this way, in the type of discourse that you are making, some elements return that could seem to be—that probably even are, in the objective reality of the class—voluntaristic.

Tronti—It can be said that here the problem reemerges of how the working class is born. When we start from the presupposition that labor-power within capitalist production is born already as a social fact, as a socially organized fact and therefore already as a collective fact—for which reason one must speak of "worker" always in the plural; the workers are born "in the plural" because a factory is not born with a worker, but with a capitalist and the mass of the workers—we then see that at the beginning of capitalist production there is precisely this relation: single capitalist—mass of workers. Within this mass of workers, what happens?

Not only are they born collectively, and not only are they organized collectively within the production process, around the production process, but they are directly organized in a very specific, very material way, such that from the beginning division does not, at bottom, exist between the workers. On the other hand, the relation between the individual capitalists is basically expressed through struggle, mutual competition and so on, to the point that it must be mediated by the market, to the point that analyzing capital means analyzing the relations between the moment of production, the moment of distribution, the moment of consumption, and so on. Conversely, when we confront the problem in terms of production, we see a social mass that lacks internal divisions, that indeed not only lacks internal divisions of mutual competition, but that directly organizes itself subjectively by means of a tool that, in the tradition of the workers' movement, is expressed by the word "solidarity." In other words, the primitive form of the workers' organization within a factory, or between factories, is precisely the moment of class solidarity. Hence, within a class, there is this massification of labor-power and thus of the workers as such. This, in my opinion, is the origin of a sociality within the working class that then is the basis of its political character; a sociality that expresses itself through the moment of production itself.

When we are analyzing the working class, we find ourselves before this fact: that it is necessary and sufficient for us to stay within the analysis of the production process. By contrast, when we are analyzing capital, we must continually keep in mind the other mediations, precisely because the capitalists need various mediations between themselves—they encounter each other on the market, they encounter each other at the moment when profit, rent, and so on are distributed, at the point when they reach an agreement concerning the overall management of political power—and so we are obliged to have this general analytical range. For the working class it is sufficient for us to analyze the production process, and it is no coincidence that when we carry out these analyses we always subordinate these other moments, emphasizing that our contempt for them is necessary. None of us begin to discuss distribution or circulation or consumption, precisely because we believe that if we want to conduct a serious analysis of the working class, we must remain within the production process.

Within the production process, we already have the whole working class. Within the production process, this working class is already a social fact, already a social mass. When we speak of its political character, basically we are speaking first about this sociality, about this fact which is global at the social level of the class, about this absolute lack of divisions within the class, such that the workers are all born with the same interests. There is no division between worker and worker, and so true is this that the first demands that the workers mutually organize are collective demands addressed to the boss. By means of this series of demands and refusals—if it is true that we want to interpret even the primitive demands of the workers as refusals, as refusal-demands—the ever-increasing politicization of this social mass is really organized as a process.

Here, indeed, the problems that we spoke about earlier are reintroduced. Is this political growth, this politicization of this social mass, a spontaneous fact, a fact driven by capital? No. What is driven by capital is only the growing sociality, the growing socialization. Capital absolutely cannot eliminate the fact that this social mass grows, that it increasingly becomes a coherently organic, internally consistent social mass. This stands in contrast to everything demonstrated by sociologists, according to whom the division within the working class grows. The real process is exactly the opposite: the unification of the working class grows, and this process is driven by capital itself as a necessity. So, the only spontaneous process is this one, the fact that the material basis for this political unity of the class grows, and then there is the moment when this growing sociality of the class becomes an autonomous political power. In the latter, diverse forms of class organization are proposed at different moments of this development, such that we should expect that the form which previously we called the mass of total refusal—the "no" opposed to the demands of the capitalists—can happen only when indeed this working class is not only a social mass, but a politically organized social mass, in other words, one that is politically functional to the point of actually expressing political organization in new forms, in forms that basically we do not yet know, that we still must discover. That is, how, at that stage, the political organization of the class, and the form it takes, will be expressed. Here, everything truly remains to be sought, especially since we have preceding organizational forms of the class to criticize—union, party, spontaneous forms of organization. So, we have now the critical moment in our possession. However, ultimately, we still do not have the positive moment of construction of the models of organization, and this is truly a course of research that is not only a course of research. Here, it really is an experimental course of constructing these models and seeing how they may function. It is a terrain on which truly the necessity of the experiment becomes functional to the construction of the theoretical model.

Vegezzi—[He asks if it might be possible, in this interpretation of the working class as political class and of the development of its refusal to collaborate with capital, to insert the discussion about certain organizational forms and tools of the class that have presented themselves at certain historical moments, whether and how these might present themselves again, today.][4]

Tronti—It is absolutely necessary to once again put forward, alongside the negative analysis of certain classical forms of organization, analysis of some positive forms of workers' struggle that have achieved precise historical results, that have made the working class itself take some political leaps, even in this way demystifying it, ridding it of certain ideological encrustations that were stuck to these historical experiences by the reformist part of the working class. We might go back, for example, to the point of transition represented by 1848, taking things back to a long time ago, starting over from a situation seen directly by Marx. And '48, June of '48 in Paris, saw basically the first working-class form come to the fore in open political struggle, an experience that was also disastrous, with a kind of defeat and a kind of working-class response that followed this defeat. Marx's analysis is extremely rich, not only with regard to the moment of rupture, but also concerning the moment that followed the workers' defeat, in which the working class in Paris threw itself into different situations of struggle. It then acquired its own, truly specific and characteristic forms—of working-class passivity, of refusing to continue a certain kind of revolution once that revolution had been seized as a moment of development for capital—realizing, then, what had been a basic error, of having itself taken an initiative that only served others.

4. Augusto Vegezzi took part in *Quaderni Rossi* and *Classe Operaia* and would later work on *Quaderni Piacentini* [Piacenzan Notebooks].

But in the general picture of all the other forms of workers' struggle, our discourse concerning the Commune needs a complete overhaul, still making use of remarks by Marx and Lenin, but going beyond them. I say this because on this point, in my opinion, they—Marx more than Lenin—clearly remained victims of a certain mythology of working-class revolution, and so ultimately a certain kind of enthusiasm impaired the critique of some of the forms in which that type of revolutionary confrontation developed. (I would say that, on the other hand, Lenin says on more than one occasion that the Commune should not be exaggerated, that it should not be considered the classical example of working-class revolution.) We should look there, too, to see how this was functional to the development of capital, but also how simultaneously, on the other hand, it represented a development, a rupture directed by the working class, once again at a particular level of development.

In general, it is a matter of following all these revolutionary ruptures, including 1905 in Russia: that type of democratic revolution which reworks the entire Leninist framework, and which must be subjected, if not to a decisive critique, then in any case to a particular reconsideration, one which takes into account various developments in the working class's leadership of a bourgeois democratic revolution, with everything that follows, with everything that has followed in the international workers' movement... Indeed, we must reconsider certain moments of working-class initiative in Petersburg and Moscow in 1905; at certain determinate moments, there are clear, working-class initiatives that go far beyond the indications of the social movements, even of the official party, initiatives that here too constitute particular forms of struggle. The same goes for the entire theoretical framework concerning these problems: certain discussions which took place at a high level of working-class thought, the whole discussion between Luxemburg and Lenin on the various forms of organization in these struggles, all the way to a critique of the Leninist conception of the party.

Other moments that are essential to this analysis include the Weimar Republic, including all of German social democracy's reformist misinterpretations, but also including a discussion that followed a real movement by capital. This discussion which disappeared in the international workers' movement after the turn, with the Stalinist victory, the creation of popular fronts, etc. The Turinese experience.

The Two Reformisms

(July 1963)

This compact text was published anonymously in *Quaderni Rossi*'s *Cronache Operaie*, an experiment deriving from the interventionist fervor to produce a more direct line of communication between theory and the factory. Alongside roundups from several different struggles, Tronti's lucid essay strove to explain how capitalist and trade-union reformisms each sought to integrate the working-class struggle—a struggle, he argued, that was nevertheless still able to pitch both into crisis, on the condition that it be organized on an autonomous and anticapitalist basis.

The present stage of the class struggle in Italy has a particular characteristic: the will to struggle belongs simultaneously to both sides; the need for movement and confrontation finds its origin in the respective class situation of the workers and of the capitalists. There are moments in which the struggle is imposed by the boss upon the workers, and other moments in which the workers impose it on the boss.

The situation today sees the capitalist boss and the exploited workers having the same urgent need for struggle. In the two camps, the same process of development is underway: growing social cohesion of the two antagonistic classes, each one within itself. Planning of production and reform of the state on the capitalist side, class reorganization on the workers' side: these are the two objectives, respectively. Struggle is the only means of winning them.

Capital has taken a strong, historic initiative in Italy: an initial, broadly mature economic system wants the stability of political power to be absolutely assured over the long term. Once achieved, this political stability must then serve to put forward again the huge job of modernizing the capitalist structures themselves, using the irregular and particular course of the class struggle and recovering it at the level of balanced social conflict. Capital's reformism starts with the general needs of the capitalist social system and passes them through the democratic mediation of the state's despotism, so that they may then command the particular movements of the production of surplus-value, and organize the capillary levels of productive labor. This sets off from society, passes through the state, and arrives in the factory with all the strength of the power bloc that has been accumulated along this journey.[1] If capital were successful today in ruling over labor-power in the factory, its reformist operation would have succeeded. The working-class production of capital would directly organize, in planned and rationalized forms, the total social movement of capitalist development.

1. "Power bloc" [*blocco di potere*] is a tricky term to unpack, especially because although it has a Gramscian ring, Gramsci himself did not use the term in his prison writings. He did, of course, develop the concept of the "historical bloc," which Peter Thomas concisely defines as "a dialectical unity of structure and superstructure." See Peter D. Thomas, *The Gramscian Moment: Philosophy, Hegemony and Marxism* (Leiden: Brill, 2009), 174. In a 1958 essay on Gramsci, Tronti himself noted the richness of the "historical bloc" concept, which entailed an "organic unity" between "material forces" and "ideologies." See Tronti, "Some Questions around Gramsci's Marxism."

The term "power bloc" was, however, commonly used within the PCI. From at least June 1962, PCI Secretary Palmiro Togliatti wrote of Gramsci's analyses of "class positions" that had combined together into a new "fascist power bloc." See Palmiro Togliatti, "La voce di Gramsci in Parlamento" [The voice of Gramsci in Parliament], now collected in *La politica nel pensiero e nell'azione: Scritti e discorsi, 1917-1964* [Politics in thought and action: writings and speeches, 1917-1964], eds. Michele Ciliberto and Giuseppe Vacca (Milan: Bompiani, 2014), 2771-72, iBooks digital edition. The term would appear no less than eighteen times in the published proceedings of the PCI's Tenth Congress, held in December 1962, where the "traditional power blocs of Christian Democracy," a "power bloc of dominant classes," and one of a "landowner-industrial" type were discussed. See Partito Comunista Italiano, *X Congresso del partito comunista italiano, Atti e risoluzioni* [Tenth Congress of the Italian Communist Party: acts and resolutions] (Rome: Editori Riuniti, 1963), 215, 287, and 288, respectively (my translation). The "power bloc" would later be conceptualized more fully by Nicos Poulantzas, who followed debates within the PCI, and who used the term from at least 1965 to refer to a "*contradictory unity*" of classes or class fractions "*under the dominance' of the hegemonic class or fraction.*" See Nicos Poulantzas, "Preliminaries to the Study of the State," trans. Gregory Elliott, in *The Poulantzas Reader: Marxism, Law and the State*, ed. James Martin (London: Verso, 2008), 74-120, 103-04.

Capital's reformism has its own particular needs. In order to articulate itself within the production process, for example, it needs to use the autonomous channels of an organized workers' movement; without these it fails to reach the real levels of productive labor and thus it cannot control the actual movements of labor-power.

The existence of a new type of reformist workers' movement then becomes necessary, one that meets capitalist reformism halfway, through an exactly inverse path of development, starting from the factory, passing through the state, and coming only in the end to sanction the general social interests. The capitalist function of the workers' organizations is no longer their being passive representatives of the workers on the formal terrain of political institutions, but their being active entrepreneurs of labor-power at the real level of the production process: offices for managing the working class on capital's behalf. The Italian capitalists' predicament is in no longer being able to count on these types of working-class organizations. The collective boss rightly feels as though his functionaries at the workers' level have misunderstood him; they fail to function within the factory and, precisely at this point, they actually block the entire process. Planning does not take because the unions bring the minister too few guarantees of orderly development of the workers' struggles: they manage to control a sectoral struggle, a monopoly struggle, but inside and outside of these, nothing is in their hands, and everything remains in the hands of the workers. The reform of the state, the recomposition of a real political power on the bourgeois side at this high level of development for capital—this does not proceed, because the workers' parties, which collaborate at the top to maintain the class dictatorship, have at their base, with the working class, the same political relationship as they have with the nomadic peoples of outer Mongolia.

The result is that capital today, in Italy, manages only in part to exercise trade-union control over labor-power, while by no means and in no place does it exercise political control over the working class. In the capitalist operation only just sketched out, this is immediately clear: the reformism of capital and the reformism of the workers' movement have not encountered each other. This is the root of their dual crisis. Keeping them divided is the immediate task of any serious political struggle. Keeping them divided is the only way of defeating them both. But who today has in their own hands this preliminary power of division? Clearly, the same ones who have up to now exercised it practically. Who is it that has put into crisis the center-left, as the first reformist political solution of capital? Who is it that has split the capitalist power bloc in two, precisely on this terrain?

Too many have already comfortably forgotten "the hot summer" of '62.[2] But when the hundred-thousand FIAT workers took back the leadership of the class movement, everyone could recognize the amazing weakness that was eroding the bases of capital's most solid structures. The relation of forces in that moment was being directly overturned: the initiative was in the hands of the workers, and capital was registering, precisely at its new political level, its first strategic defeat of the postwar period. Everything was being called into question. To the "clear and far-sighted vision" of the most reformist capitalism there responded a sudden realization, confused but near-sighted, of the most revolutionary proletariat.[3] The invitation to political collaboration with capital was picked up and thrown back by the workers in their attempt to subjectively reunify the various levels of their own struggles. Thus, a specific type of working-class response proved able, by taking the reins of the movement, to take a situation of permanent struggle that had existed for some time at the level of the structures of production, and bring it together again into one piece. Outside of capitalist control, all the terrain of working-class struggle was recovered and used, from the mass strike to street violence.

Progressing exactly this way and giving each their own: to the capitalist, the total shut-down of the production of capital; to the trade-unionist, the civil contempt of a few rocks in the offices of Piazza Statuto. The subjective recomposition of the struggles at a common level did not then find organized political expression; practically each situation of struggle flowed back into its own particular form. By this route, capital recovered the initiative quickly and decisively. The entire process was reunified at a higher point of capitalist development; and this will allow for an updated relaunching of the entire reformist political operation. But within this and outside of it, the workers' presence promises to be increasingly direct, solid, total, and united.

A working hypothesis guides this political discourse. It is the fact—visible to the naked eye, given the material evidence of it—of a subsisting and persistent political unity within the Italian working class. Even before beginning to identify the articulations of this unity—the various levels of working-class

2. The summer of 1962 saw widespread strikes coursing across the northern industrial zones. From July 7-9 in Turin's Piazza Statuto, hundreds of people, including FIAT workers and youths from the neighborhood, attacked the offices of UIL, the Socialist-aligned trade-union confederation that had recently signed an agreement with FIAT, undercutting the metal-mechanic workers' ongoing strike. The event deepened the rift between *Quaderni Rossi* and the "official" left. As the rebellion raged, *Quaderni Rossi* circulated a flyer advocating that the metal-workers' confederation, FIOM, denounce UIL. Subsequently, members of *Quaderni Rossi* were attacked from various quarters of the left as "provocateurs." The interpretation of the riot also led to fractures among the editors of the journal. Tronti, Negri, and Alquati saw the riot as a moment of working-class self-organization and thus an indication that continued political-organizational intervention was needed, while Panzieri believed that further and deeper inquiry of capital was required.

3. Tronti is referencing a line in Aldo Moro's 1962 speech in Naples to the Eighth Congress of the Christian Democrats, where Moro urged his party to adopt a long-term strategy open to the center-left. See Francesco Malgeri, *La stagione del centrismo: Politica e società nell'Italia del secondo dopoguerra (1945-1960)* (Rubbettino: Saveria Mannelli, 2002), 399.

political development, to each of which various and different forms of class struggle and class organization can correspond—what must be recovered well in advance of all this is the existence of this unity, and the particular ways in which it is forced to express itself politically. We must not stop at the traditional expressions: the class unity of the workers is not disproven by divisions in the official workers' movement, and it is not affirmed by the phony results of parliamentary elections. What is decisive is the anticapitalist sense objectively assumed by the working-class struggle, whatever the point at which it explodes and whatever the demand from which it begins. It is true: each one of these struggles, at the outset and in the end, is always inscribed in an equally objective process of the development of capital. Yet the course of the struggle, its duration, its intensity, the forms in which it is expressed, in some cases the organization that it assumes—these go extraordinarily far beyond any possible utilization of them by the boss. They continually overturn the capitalist use of the struggle and repurpose it as a tool for working-class self-organization; in fact, they impose an autonomous direction on their own movements, at the only point in which the workers feel that they have the strength to impose it: in the single factory, against the boss directly. It is at this point that the power bloc of trade unions and bosses always rushes to formally recompose the balance of development. Under these conditions, the signing of any contract is a working-class defeat. General power is completely handed back to capital. Yet always, after the struggle, a particular power rests in the hands of the workers: an expanded political composition of the working-class mass, which seeks an anticapitalist organization. It is all a process that happens at the elementary level of the single productive unit, and it is sufficient to prevent the boss's rule over labor-power in the factory. It is not sufficient to recompose the political pressure of the working class against capital at a general social level. It preserves a fundamentally unitary revolutionary potential; it does not organize it into new forms for the unique aims of conquering power. No one can think that this second process would take place through the spontaneous generalization of individual significant situations. There will be no workers' power until it is organized politically. And this presupposes a political reconstruction of all the movements of the working class, with the goal of putting all the tools of the workers' movement back into its hands. Preventing reformist solutions from passing into the factory, refusing any type of working-class collaboration at any level, seeking revolutionary organization—these are the premises of this journey.

Letter to Antonio Negri

(September 1963)

During the period of transition from *Quaderni Rossi* to *Classe Operaia*, after Panzieri had announced the need for a separation but before the interventionists had decided on how best to organize their new project, Tronti, Negri, and others thought deeply about the forms of theoretical and political work, and how their organization could best relate to working-class struggles. In this letter, the "newspaper" under discussion was the second and final issue of *Cronache Operaie*, an experiment born from within *Quaderni Rossi*. This letter illustrates how important the processes of organizing a tightly knit group of militant theorists was for Tronti's thinking.

Rome, September 19, 1963

Dear Toni,

I agree once again on the post-local and pre-national newspaper, unique and varied at the same time. It seems to me the right way to fill a period of transition. I would implicitly stress its temporary character, giving more space to particularly significant class situations, around which it becomes possible to *immediately* and preliminarily organize working-class editorial boards.

One of the intermediate objectives that we must propose today is the organizational recomposition, at the subjective level, of the group, which must first increase the quantity of its forces and transform them qualitatively if it is to start making progress again on decisive endeavors. The overall political discourse must be able to count on this solid material basis if it is going to impose itself, or even just express itself, as a real organizational moment of the class. Without this basis, the same discourse—and the political initiative that it presupposes—tends in a fatal way to wear itself out, burn itself out, until it becomes inadmissible for a long period of time. At the theoretical level, we can wait decades to be right; at the political level, we must be right immediately, shifting material facts to our liking, with the simple violence of our own subjective forces.

The week of passion and death (let us hope without resurrection) of *QR* (the arc from Milan to Florence) encourages serious reflection.[1] We must avoid finding a solution that is too easy for our problems. If it is true that we are carrying out the transition from one period of our activity to another, this transition will not be accomplished without a *leap*. *QR* paved the way for a theoretical alternative to the official workers' movement. We now must pave the way for a *political* alternative. And so far this is nothing new, partly because this second alternative is, in a more or less confused way, in each of our heads. The novelty must consist in this: in the need to adjust the means to the end. We can no longer tolerate that the political initiative we propose— the only strategic perspective open to the working class at the international level—be expressed today as it has been expressed up to now, in these absurd, artisanal, personal, corporative forms, on the level of pre-industrial, nineteenth-century capitalism, with the socialist romanticism of scarce resources for useful ends. We also must definitively close the organizational chapter of the group of "exiles," in clandestine activity on the outside and publicly in struggle on the inside.[2]

1. *Quaderni Rossi* held two final meetings: the first, on August 31 in Milan, during which Panzieri proposed to end the project; and the second, on September 7–8 in Florence, during which the interventionists debated how best to move forward with the idea of a workers' newspaper such as *Cronache Operaie*.
2. The "exiles" [*fuoriusciti*] were militants who had been forced out of or left the PCI.

The Weapon of Organization

The political transition to *open struggle* against the power of capitalists is a problem not only for the workers, but also for us. It is clearly the same problem, but this open struggle cannot bear being closed up in forms that are inadequate, that do not extend it, that do not organize it. The same goes for the forms, the modes, the tools of our political initiative.

I am thinking now of a political newspaper that no longer has any problem circulating at the workers' level or otherwise. This is itself an underdeveloped problem. A discourse and serious political work have already in fact overcome this problem. All the other capillary levels of organizational recomposition, which follow and anticipate the continuity of the workers' struggles step by step, can and must grow around this central level of intervention, which recomposes, with regularity and discipline, the successive moments of tactics and strategy of the entire class movement. The monthly cycle should be gradually shortened so as to increasingly unify the various experiences in time, to allow an increasingly direct intervention into individual situations, to both orient and transform them. This is the only way of watching and monitoring the growth of a material political influence with the same degree of precision with which one watches and monitors the growth of a production index. The baseline work is still that of offering a point of reference to all the innumerable, scattered forces that are tacitly available today for a class action, selecting and judging these forces, and above all *concentrating them* in one single direction. In this work, we must know how to use all the tools of communication that political democracy offers—for example, the newspaper, through all the normal democratic channels of commercial circulation. It is absolutely necessary to refuse to organize a clandestine struggle against the current "open" structure of bourgeois power. Doing this is also a sign that the discourse and the forces that carry it forward have reached some maturity.

We must speak as if we were the majority of the workers' movement, interpreters of the general interests of the working class confronting the general interest of capital. The political tool—even at the ordinary level of the newspaper—must *quickly* be adjusted to this task. Otherwise it will not even be born. It is worth giving oneself a little time to think and rethink these things, again and again, making the most of all these recent experiences. Nevertheless, from now on, we can say that a program of this kind seems by no means impossible. Two conditions seem absolutely necessary to me:

1) A subjective reorganization of the forces, and to be more precise, the constitution of a homogeneous political group along with a political network of organizers, above all at the nerve centers of capitalist production, and without so many formal theorizations and institutions, but with the simplicity with which, it seems to me, our group operates in Padua or Venice,

which should serve in this area as a model or, if you prefer, as a pole of development (here, then, the publication of the newspapers in Padua, Milan, and Turin is helpful).

2) (The search for financial resources.) Of fundamental importance for the life of any initiative. (All roads can be good ones.)

The Florence report seems rather unworkable as an introduction.[3] Besides, why an introduction? The discourse, it must be said, is a continuation. Concerning the class struggle at the international level, here too I would limit everything to the analysis of the experience of struggle. On these individual problems and on others, we can and will make our own contribution. But my thought—and that of the comrades of Rome—is that this newspaper, in this phase, is *our exclusive task*.

(Greetings follow, etc.)

---

3. This refers to the final meeting of *Quaderni Rossi*; see the note above.

A Replacement of Leadership

(Autumn 1963)

These notes were written in preparation for a talk likely delivered in September or October 1963 to comrades involved in the development of the newspaper *Classe Operaia*. They demonstrate that before the first issue would be published, Tronti already conceived of two phases for project, moving from struggle toward organization.

End of *Quaderni Rossi*

Political judgment concerning *Quaderni Rossi* and Panzieri

       (general areas of *Classe Operaia*)[1]

Our attitude / two phases—two years

       the last year

                    results: *Quaderni Rossi* 3

                    C[*ronache*] O[*peraie*] 1

the political space for a working-class left was left open

a new phase of work centered on political intervention is opening

specific areas of *Classe Operaia*

nuclei of workers to be organized

        to organize the struggle or

        to organize the organization?

the current phase is still that of the organization of the struggle/new forms of working-class struggles

to move in stages toward the second objective

the newspaper *today* must represent this transitional moment

        it cannot include decisive rallying cries aiming toward the new organization

        it must pose the political premises for this

        a political leap must be taken at a certain point in order to move to a subsequent phase.

       to prepare the objective conditions for this leap to the new organization.

the conditions are:

        1) generalization of specific forms of working-class struggle

        anticapitalist and antibureaucratic

           at the same time

        2) political crisis and vertical collapse of the old organizations, at the national political level

---

1. In these notes, Tronti does not enclose the words *classe operaia* inside quotation marks as he does *Quaderni Rossi*, but from context we might infer that the "generic" and "specific areas" mentioned here pertain to that new project, rather than to the working class "itself."

working class and workers' movement
particular attention to this relation
to specify the current attitude of the class toward the
movement
ambiguous attitude, full of political duplicity, and cautious
and slow attrition.

class action to make the parties explode
then, correct recomposition of the relation.
      at the political level this is all the problem of the party is.
      it is only at the theoretical level that it subsists as a problem.
unity-distinction between theory and politics
      primacy of politics.

replacement of leadership
a draft of working-class organizers
Bolshevik "center"

Report at Piombino

(May 1964)

By November 1963, *Classe Operaia* had established its editorial board, and in January they released their first issue, announcing the search for "a new Marxist practice of the working-class party."[1] Their "political monthly of workers in struggle" focused on insurgencies racing across Italy and Europe, while also keeping an eye on center-left reformism and the prospect of capitalist planning amid the growing economic recession. *Classe Operaia* also began to distribute agitational leaflets at sites of working-class struggle,[2] and in the opening editorial for issue 4-5, Tronti emphasized the need to continue addressing factory workers.[3] To mark the release of that issue, the editors hosted a public seminar that drew over one hundred participants, many of them young militants.[4] Tronti's contribution was the following text, which derives from a transcribed recording, in which he proposed a new organizational form: an autonomous network of political cadres rooted in key factories, which would aim to avoid both the error of becoming a groupuscule as well as that of acceding to the existing PCI bureaucracy. In addition to Tronti's talk, the conference also featured reports on possible points of intervention across Italy.[5]

1. Tronti, "Lenin in England," 72.

2. For one example of a flyer distributed by the group in Milan, see *"classe operaia*: un volantino a Milano" [*classe operaia*: a flyer in Milan] [January 1964], in *L'operaismo degli anni sessanta*, 351–52. In March, in a letter to Gobbini, Tronti stressed the immediate need for a flyer to address Milanese workers and goad them, in the midst of the economic recession and layoffs, toward an "attack on the social boss": "The field for an intervention of this kind is completely open...neither the union nor the party intend, for the moment, to lift a finger.... Let us attempt a little show of strength." "Tronti a Gobbini, Roma 24 marzo 1964" [Mario Tronti to Mauro Gobbini, Rome, March 24, 1964], in *L'operaismo degli anni sessanta*, 367 (my translation). Also noteworthy is a letter written to Tronti by Bologna during these same days, in which he reflects on distributing flyers and the need to "impose a strategic discourse" at sites where the working class was organizing, and that this ought to guide Tronti's reflections at the upcoming Piombino conference. See "Bologna a Tronti, 30 marzo" [Sergio Bologna to Mario Tronti, March 30, 1964], in *L'operaismo degli anni sessanta*, 368-70 (my translation). Lastly, see also Gobbini's reply to Tronti, which confirmed that 4,800 flyers were being distributed at Alfa Romeo and Pirelli, and moreover, that 600 copies of the newspaper's first two issues had been circulated in Milanese factories: "[S]ome workers who we know in these factories were surprised to find the newspaper read and discussed in almost all the departments." "Gobbini a Tronti, Bologna, 2 aprile 1964" [Mauro Gobbini to Mario Tronti, April 2, 1964], in *L'operaismo degli anni sessanta*, 371-73 (my translation).

3. The editorial of issue 4-5 was "An Old Tactic for a New Strategy," now in *Workers and Capital*.

4. For Tronti, Piombino marked a moment of great "unity" and "enthusiasm" achieved among the group of *Classe Operaia*; see interview in *L'operaismo degli anni sessanta*, 602. Gobbini also remembers it in glowing terms, recalling the happy impression that "the group was growing and assuming a national scale"; see "Mauro Gobbini" [Interview, Rome, May 12 1998], in *L'operaismo degli anni sessanta*, 679–95, 690.

5. Milana and Trotta, *L'operaismo degli anni sessanta*, 386.

In a discussion of political intervention, at least two premises must be established: the first is that we cannot isolate, not even with the best intentions, the problem of intervention in struggles from other moments of political work. This is because, upon initial examination, intervention turns out to be one of these moments, and indeed, we need to understand the role it plays within political work conceived in a more general way. The second premise of the discussion is the observation that this theme is hardly new among our usual topics of discussion. Actually, I would say that, if we go back to the beginning of the history of these attempts of a new approach to general political work, at the start we find this theme of political intervention in the workers' struggles. Probably—indeed almost certainly—these groups, which have evolved internally in recent years, were really born as groups for intervening in the workers' struggles, and a short history of these various attempts and the various approaches that have succeeded them helps to clarify the theme of political intervention itself. It is also necessary at this point, in my opinion, to acquire the capacity, which is characteristically Marxist, to see ourselves and to know that we ourselves have been conditioned by the concrete social situations in which we work, and particularly by the specific level reached by the class struggle. It is unlikely that the various attempts to intervene politically in workers' struggles were not widely and substantially conditioned by the levels reached by the class struggle during the period in which the intervention was being attempted.

This theme is mentioned in the first article of this issue of the newspaper.[6] We attempt a very initial approach, one which will be further specified and deepened, through our discussion of a specific characteristic assumed by the workers' struggles in recent years in Italy: a certain use made by these workers' struggles—and through them, the working class itself—not so much of the union, as of the trade-union struggle. From this particular angle—the workers' struggles in Italy—there arise two considerations regarding the organization of the workers' movement: the concept of the mass party, and conversely, in reaction to this, the attempt to organize groups for political intervention in the struggles.

In my opinion, a common root can be found for these two moments, in the sense that, not so much the theory of the mass party, but the practice that has come out of it in recent years is clearly a broad revision of the traditional concept of the party, the traditional Leninist, Bolshevik conception. Even if it did not disavow this tradition, the structure and internal substance of the workers' party has been modified in practice, giving it this mass-party character. In the face of this, it is possible that the traditional concept of the minority

6. See Tronti, "An Old Tactic for a New Strategy," 77.

group active at the workers' level and within the workers' movement has also itself changed. That is, in the face of this new practice of the mass party, a new concept of the revolutionary minority has emerged in practice, and has been partly generalized, in a series of groups. This new concept of the revolutionary minority has sometimes acquired characteristics similar to those of the so-called intervention groups in recent years, abandoning certain organizational traditions of the workers' movement, refusing to present themselves as organized groups, presenting themselves instead, directly, as intervention groups and nothing more, and starting again from that point to reintroduce a concept of the necessary political organization of the class within the workers' struggles themselves. So, if we were to search for the origin of these attempts at political intervention, we would need to find a new point on which to pivot, and rediscover the real origin of this within certain types of workers' struggles that took place in Italy in the postwar period, struggles which grew in a certain manner and in a certain way until assuming a more general character around the 1960s. It is no coincidence that these new attempts of political intervention were born precisely around these same years.

In this development of the workers' struggles up to the 1960s and beyond, we can basically pinpoint two characteristics. The first is the initial discovery by these intervention groups of what for a certain period was called the "trade-union channel of contact" with the working class. For a long time, there was a discussion about what the most direct channel for reaching the workers' level was, and for a time, the trade-union channel was chosen, somewhat consciously, as the one that offered the most opportunities for intervention at the grassroots, working-class level. The other characteristic, which was especially typical of the Italian workers' movement, is that the generalization of this intervention in struggles ends up again in what we could call a *Turinese* mold.[7] There, at a certain moment, it formed part of an attempt to more generally define a theme that was also resurfacing elsewhere, even though other places were not then able to generalize it.

What kind of intervention was being proposed then, around the 1960s? Precisely the kind found in *Quaderni Rossi*. The first issue of *Quaderni Rossi* spoke of "workgroups engaged in the struggles of the workers' movement," of workgroups that intervened in the workers' struggles.[8] If this was the definition, among other things inaccurate, of the content of the intervention that was taking place from 1960 onward, then, in my opinion, we must study a different fundamental characteristic that it had. In my opinion, it was an

7. Turin was the site of high-pitched struggles by FIAT workers and workers of other major industries, and so it often took on a particular significance—see Tronti's 1963 letter to Panzieri, above.

8. This precise quotation could not be located, but one can see *Quaderni rossi*, no. 1 (Rome: Sapere, 1978 [September 1961]).

attempt at political intervention in the absence, at that moment, of a political alternative. It was, in other words, an attempt at political intervention without an alternative political line, one that was distinct from the official, traditional organizations of the workers' movement. An intervention that, in a certain sense, preceded the composition and definition of a political line that was an alternative to the traditional one.

This explains some of the features particular to these interventions, and, most importantly, the fact that, due to this flaw within it, the intervention that took place still exhibited a subordinate character with respect to the traditional organizations of the workers' movement. In other words, whether it passed through the trade-union channel or whether it abandoned that and sought other channels of contact with the grassroots workers' level—that is, independent of the instruments continually chosen for moving toward the realization of this type of intervention—the defining characteristic was still this subordination, precisely because it did not yet express, at a general level, a type of politics that was new and which was either already partly elaborated or on the way to being elaborated. So, the political imperative that this intervention carried along inside it was, clearly, very generic. Moreover, the theoretical perspective that lay beneath it, that guided this type of intervention, was very confused. At both the political and theoretical levels, there was not then a clear alternative, a political line different from the traditional one. If we recall some of the most defining moments of this experience, such as the intervention at FIAT during the great strike, with the *Quaderni Rossi* leaflet and its rallying cry—"Workers, it is you who must decide"—what they needed to decide was left unsaid, and this amounted to a rather generic kind of political intervention. It is no coincidence that, from that period onward, a political slogan came alive and began to spread, a seemingly comprehensive one that was an alternative to everything then existing in the workers' movement—that of "working-class self-organization," in a certain sense as a counterweight to the official organization of the movement. But this slogan turned out to be a substitute for positive political directions: it was, in other words, typical of a moment in which the necessity of intervention had been identified, but in which this intervention had not yet come alive with the clear direction of a new politics.

An intervention of this type cannot yet be defined as *political*. It was lacking the positive indication of a certain number of goals to be achieved in that moment, with a certain form of struggle, and thus also with a certain organizational form. And, precisely at that moment, feeling the effects of this type of experience, we posed the problem of re-organizing other components that then turned out to be insufficient and flawed—primarily, there was the need to re-organize the theoretical component of our political work. That moment really underscored, perhaps beyond even certain concrete needs, the necessity of retrieving and establishing some categories at this general theoretical level, categories that would have been able to serve as a serious and deep basis for this new type of political intervention, which then needed to be relaunched at a certain point.

The course that this theoretical work has taken is clear to everyone: starting from the analytical moment of the working class, and discovering at that point the necessity—not just the possibility—of the "inverse path"; starting from the direct analysis of the working class to then come to a certain type of analysis of capital. It is within this largely theoretical journey that the issue of a precise political intervention was posed in direct form, an intervention at a determinate point that would not have been scattered across a range of easily identifiable places in the national structure of production, but a determinate point that would have been particularly indicative of and decisive for all the rest. This is the moment the possibility was identified of concentrating the intervention at the highest level of the working class—at FIAT—with the aim of starting from there to begin the process of politically generalizing the intervention. This was clearly a decisive point of transition, because it clarified a series of problems that turned out to have previously been very confused.

Today, we can also with a degree of clarity see the limits of that proposal, of concentrating the moment of intervention at one point that is decisive. And the limits were, once again, those in existence at the start of all these interventions: they resided still in the inadequacy of the political discourse, which itself also needed to be concentrated at the base of this intervention. The limits of a proposal of that kind, and the reason why it was not practically realized, consisted precisely in the fact that the concentration of this political discourse was made impossible by the asynchrony between the level reached by our theoretical work, on the one hand, and the degree to which the political discourse and political line were being elaborated, on the other. In other words, the attempt was made in that moment to pass from very general theoretical hypotheses to empirical and determinate realities without any mediating political discourse or line. This limit, in my opinion, can be found in certain concrete implementations of the attempt to locate this central point of intervention, this limit that can also be found in experiences such as *Gatto Selvaggio*, which is basically where this proposal of intervention was carried out in practice, albeit with this disjointed transition between the theoretical hypotheses, which were rather clear at that point, and the moment of practical political work.[9]

9. *Gatto Selvaggio* [Wildcat] was a newspaper exploring sabotage and wildcat strikes, produced in 1963 and

There is one aspect of this experience that, in my opinion, is very important: in its discourse, it abandoned the theme of organization in the mistaken
and premature sense in which it had been posed initially, with the rallying cry
of "organize yourselves, you decide, you do it," the pronounced spontaneism
of previous interventions that was still very much alive. It abandoned this
theme and, in part correctly, deferred it. The theme of struggle comes to the
fore, the theme in which the forms of working-class struggle serve as a possible opening to a different, permanent working-class organization. This is an
important transition. What was lacking, I repeat, was the moment that was
to have preceded the identification of forms of struggle, the elaboration of an
alternative political line of a general character, not in theoretical terms, but in
terms precisely of a political alternative, a political line. In my opinion, we can
then pinpoint three moments [...][10]

These three moments must be seen together as steps, as phases of transition in the revolutionary process, which proceeds on terrain marked out by
the watchword that the initiative takes as its presupposition. By specifying,
in other words, this series of successive transitions in our political work, we
can correctly retranslate the watchword at the base of our entire political discourse, the one ensuring that our proposals are not mistaken for the generic proposals of an old, maximalist type: the formula, the watchword, of the
revolutionary use of capitalist reformism. That is, the capacity to seize and to
utilize, in the organization of the struggle, those transitional moments of capitalist development that make a concrete political intervention possible, and
which occasionally make growth possible, a growth that is not continuous but
instead achieved through leaps in the objective organization of the working
class. Otherwise, we would be restricting that watchword to the formal political level once again, and we would be conceiving it in the exact manner of a
governmental formula, as the bourgeois political stratum has its institutional
formulae. It must instead be used concretely at the real level. It is clear that
this can only be done by keeping a firm hand on the entire strategic network
of the revolutionary process's political movement. By laying claim to this strategic continuity of the movement, we can pinpoint each moment of transition, each step and each phase, with each one requiring a concrete handle on
the class level as well as new concrete proposals at the general strategic level,
in terms of the objective.

distributed to workers at FIAT and Lancia by, among others, Romano Alquati and Romolo Gobbi. See Steve
Wright, *Storming Heaven*, 55.

10. Milana and Trotta note that this and the second ellipsis, in brackets below, were in the original tran-
scription of the recording of the talk. (The third ellipsis, presumably, does not indicate missing text but a
sentence left unfinished by the speaker.) They also clarify that the "three moments" in question are those of:
(1) Marxian theoretical analysis; (2) general political discourse of the kind worked out in the newspaper *Classe
Operaia*; and (3) direct intervention in the factory by a network of cadres guided by that discourse. See Milana
and Trotta, *L'operaismo degli anni sessanta*, 385.

The Weapon of Organization

I believe that precisely in this way we manage to bridge that gap, that vacuum about which I spoke earlier, that exists between the theoretical level and the political level. In my opinion, this gap is being bridged precisely in the discourse of the newspaper, which for the first time poses the necessity of these two moments being seen together: taking the moment of political discourse as being decisive, and bringing it closer, in practice, to the level of the theoretical discourse. The newspaper's discourse truly fills in the gap, deals with the asynchrony between the two moments, which in my opinion is the material, objective reason why a range of interventions are still limited, still incapable of directly grasping the real level reached by the class, and thus incapable of having a bearing on it.

It is only in this way—through the newspaper's discourse, which across each issue has grown, which will continue to grow in issues to come—that the relation between political and theoretical discourse is posed correctly for the first time. Our political discourse no longer takes the formulae and indications found on the theoretical plane and repeats them at another level, a level of mass vulgarization, but instead it translates them concretely, into real situations, through the work of concretely identifying actual moments of development. In other words, the political discourse begins to directly practice the point to which the theoretical analysis has arrived. Why is this necessary, this process of rapprochement, to fill the vacuum which had been created? Because we are seeing that the theoretical discourse has taken root, has by now acquired its autonomy, an intrinsic strength that is unlikely to be stopped in the coming years, nor by anyone today.

Our theoretical discourse has so much power to convince, such a prestigious political character, that it makes visible to all the possibility of creating for themselves an organic body of research and discoveries that would be an alternative to what has existed up until now. It will be no coincidence if, in the coming years, the program established here overturns an entire theoretical tradition, one which has more than 100 years of history in some cases, but which we are—today, due to certain achievements, certain levels reached—in a position to take, negate, and replace with other formulations, other types of analysis that absolutely no one can dispute. It is no coincidence that this kind of theoretical discourse has not been undermined in any way, that no one has attempted to attack it, because it turns out to be absolutely unassailable at all levels.

In my opinion, at this point, we must give this same fate to the political discourse produced by the newspaper. We must, in other words, resume the effort we made in the first issues of the newspaper to start from the beginning. The political discourse needed to be presented in this way, and we must continue this, because it is the only way to prevent the discourse's immediate liquidation. When we bring out a new political discourse, the first thing we must do is prevent it from being immediately criticized, because a new argument immediately runs the risk of being totally defeated. Liquidation is an objective fact in the workers' movement. Anyone familiar with the history of the workers' movement knows that the term "liquidation" points to a serious fact; there have always been immediate attempts to liquidate things that arose at determinate moments. This is a very grave danger, because liquidation breaks the legs of any new attempt and prevents others from arising on the same terrain. So, it is absolutely necessary that the political discourse be posed at that level. In this way, we present a political discourse that cannot be liquidated, and simultaneously one that is not absolutist. These are the two fundamental characteristics that we must confer upon our political discourse. It must have the same fate as our theoretical work. Why has this theoretical work not entered the conversations held in the traditional clubs of the Italian left intelligentsia? Because it absolutely cannot be absorbed at that level, and therefore it turns out that it cannot be liquidated.

The political discourse of the newspaper must run exactly this kind of course. That is, it need not even be discussed at the traditional political level, at the formal political level, because at that level it must prove to be absolutely unacceptable, unable to be absorbed. And if it proves unable to be absorbed, it is clear that it will not be discussed, because the things that cannot be absorbed by the official workers' movement are not even discussed. They are attacked and destroyed the moment they present themselves in weak and disorganized form. At that point, they are not discussed, they are refused, that is, defeated and rejected, and therefore destroyed.

Precisely this kind of concern must be adopted in the growing discourse produced in the newspaper, as it will afford greater openness, greater freedom of movement, and greater articulation—even, if you like, a greater weakness inside the discourse itself. It is clear, for example, that if one closely reads the most recent article in *Classe Operaia*, "An Old Tactic for a New Strategy," it is so easy to find weak points open to an attack by official, traditional discourse. Why could we do this at this point, presenting some elements, some spaces, that leave open the possibility for a direct attack? Because, it is evident: this discourse comes after a methodological approach that was serious, heavy, organic, and partly closed. So clearly, today, an attack on a political intervention of this type turns out to be very difficult, because it must also assail the other level, that of theoretical and methodological systemization. Today, a discourse of this type, more directly political and more attackable, has the possibility of functioning and the capacity to convince precisely because it has come from a strong foundation, one which was already planted by the preceding issues of the newspaper. At a certain moment, we will produce a much more articulate political discourse, one that has much more of a mass character, much more elementary, much simpler, with rallying cries that make it more exposed, and which make an even more direct attack possible. But clearly, at that point, even that type of opening, that way of articulating the discourse, will not open the possibility of attack and liquidation, because it will have been preceded by and based on this political systemization. At this point, after the political discourse given in the first three issues of the newspaper has been systematized, what instead becomes important is the ability to seize determinate political moments. Such an ability must simultaneously verify and go beyond the methodological approach to which the political discourse had been subjected, for the reasons discussed earlier.

This is a procedure of transition and development within the political discourse that has considerable importance, and it absolutely must not be underestimated. I believe that, on this point, in the transition from the still methodological discourse of the first three issues of the newspaper, to the need to seize a determinate moment of capitalist development and implant ourselves there, within a certain type of working-class attack or response—and without the formulae of needing to identify the moment when capitalism passes from one stage to another in the short term, a snapshot so to speak, and identifying the potential to introduce a political intervention there inside it. In this transition, in my opinion, it turns out that there has been a considerable delay on the part of the newspaper, in the response by individual comrades when faced with the need to carry this out. Perhaps due to a shortcoming in the newspaper's inaugural address, aimed entirely at identifying the strategic line of movement, there has been in recent months and weeks an inability to seize a precise moment of transition in which this long-distance, long-term vision could be concretely applied.[11]

I am speaking of the capacity to seize the conjunctural moment, to see what its causes are, and what kinds of possibilities it offers to the class struggle. In my opinion, the delay we have shown, in our ability to seize these transitions when they take place, opens a series of problems—or, better, one specific problem that we must try to clarify and resolve. At this point, a certain inheritance reveals itself, one that we might say is from *Quaderni Rossi*, because that experience was characterized precisely by this: namely, by pure and simple analysis also of the moment of intervention, which as such instead needs to go beyond analysis and move on to practical forms of concrete actualization. Likewise, the arguments made thusfar in the newspaper rarely manage to be

11. The "inaugural address" of *Classe Operaia* was the editorial of the first issue, Tronti's own "Lenin in England," now collected in *Workers and Capital*.

overturned and wielded as political tools for intervention into individual situations and opportunities of struggle, creating new opportunities and so on. The initial approach of the newspaper, for the reasons discussed above, provoked for most of the comrades a kind of flight toward political analysis, but a political analysis still carried out at a historical-theoretical level—hence the series of topics that continue to have a massive presence even in issue 4–5, the historical reconstruction of the movement. Indeed this is precisely the more methodological type of approach that the newspaper had offered initially, provoking the revival of all these rather traditional problems. Through the newspaper, a new type of political analysis has been discovered, but this analysis still remains at the theoretical or historical level; it has not yet acquired foundations of a practical character. This course must now be amended. That is, through the newspaper, we must demonstrate not only the capacity to organize or reorganize an alternative political line—which, in my opinion, has already been done in previous issues of the newspaper, even if incompletely. I do think we will need to return to some topics and problems, but, in addition to this, we must now move on to a different kind of work.

Today we can consider a certain new type of intellectual framework to be accepted, available for a certain type of analysis, for historical reconstruction of the problems of the workers' movement or for the theoretical discovery of new things. This is a terrain on which, truly, we are all now confident, and on which we need no further directions. What at this point must concern us, and what must become the newspaper's immediate task, is to work out the constitution and formation, in addition to this intellectual framework, of a genuine *political cadre* that works neither around the newspaper, nor within the newspaper, nor with the discourse of the newspaper, and no longer only on elaborating or forming or specifying the political line. Rather, a political cadre that works at the level of practical implementation, translating this line at the workers' level, at the grassroots level. In other words, if it is true that at this point our political discourse is being adjusted, albeit slowly, to the level that our theoretical discourse has reached—our theoretical discourse which today turns out to be generally unassailable, resistant to any attack—the moment of intervention, that is, the moment of practical politics, is still very far from these levels. [...]

In my opinion, we begin to do this in the latest issue of the newspaper, and in the next two issues we need to continue on this path, focusing only on the immediate workers' level, perhaps limiting the circulation of the newspaper for the most part to that level, precisely in order to rather forcefully correct that flaw which existed in the discourse's initial organization in the newspaper. And, analogously, we can say that, as our theoretical discourse has been translated into political discourse in a non-automatic way, so our political discourse, once elaborated at the level of the newspaper, will not then find automatic expression in a certain subjective capacity for political intervention. This, too, is an illusion that we must avoid. In other words, we must avoid believing that once we have properly organized the overall political discourse, once we have produced the newspaper for a year, and once we have offered this new political perspective, perhaps in an articulate and specific manner at every point, in every sector, and so on—we must avoid believing that at that point we will automatically acquire the ability to intervene in every situation and to immediately organize the workers, etc. This type of automatism must also be rejected absolutely. It may very well happen that we produce a year's worth of the most wonderful political discourse, that we perfectly construct an alternative political line, and that we then find ourselves in an impossible situation, with a practical, subjective inability to make it function, because during this time, perhaps, we had not attended to the need to organize, around and within this political discourse, a subjective network of individuals, of cadres who are able to practice this discourse.

If it is true that, during this period, we may begin to clarify this alternative political line, putting it into a form that we can call its "short-term form," something we had deeply underestimated before now—because we stretched ourselves to discover the long arc of the movement, we have been less able to indicate concrete moments of transition for political work—if this is true, we must now find the ways in which this short-term political discourse may also be able to function practically. In other words, how it might actually stand up and walk. Now, which routes can we single out that will help us achieve this political practice of the newspaper discourse? There may be more than one; indeed, several can be identified. We can think, for example, that the Italian situation should be broadly emphasized in the development of our political discourse, that we must do a better job of specifying, of going further into the real structure of capitalist power at one precise point, one that must be directly before our eyes, because only in this way can we see its articulations concretely, and embed ourselves within them in order to change them, to smash them, depending on the levels reached by the struggle in Italy.

At this moment, then, the international discussion—which the newspaper has also begun to treat at a methodological level, providing an illustration of discourse at a general level—even if this must remain an important strand of our work, I see it being less useful to the problem of political practice, of political intervention. This is because, if it is true that the international discussion should provide us with the tendency of development, to which Italian development is clearly also sentenced and within which it is confined, it can never be taken for a practical moment of concrete articulation of the political line. Actually, in some cases, it can become directly the opposite, functioning as a sort of political alibi. It is no coincidence that ambiguous forces on the Italian left preserve this international discussion, these weak forms of international cooperation, weak forms they would also like to see in the workers' struggles. But what is its usefulness? Clearly, this is a new way of escaping the real problems of political struggle and the class struggle at a determinate point. We must avoid this danger and instead emphasize a direction that at this moment offers unique, open possibilities, as the Italian situation clearly does. And certainly, within the Italian situation—this is another path that the discourse must take—the skeleton of capitalist production must be rediscovered, and within it we must firmly implant a permanent active presence. In other words, subjectively, we must have the skeletal framework of this structure clearly before our eyes, so that we may know the points at which we must strike, in certain instances and on certain occasions, to achieve general correspondence. Then, at those points, we must plant some presence of this political discourse independent of our rooting. In my opinion, a basic and essential condition must be found, such that the moment of intervention adapts to the moment of the political discourse. That is, we must pose for ourselves the goal of adjusting a certain quality that exists in our group concerning the newspaper discourse, an adjustment that increasingly emphasizes the political capacities of individuals—and even, in addition to their political capacities, their organizational capacities. I would go so far as to say that, alongside this need to increasingly articulate the general political line, we need to pose the problem of achieving something essential: the formation of an entirely new network, an autonomous network of political leaders.

The newspaper must apply itself to this task in an explicit way: no longer in a tacit way, but in a truly public and more explicit way. Political cadres can be drawn from various types of situations; clearly, the prerogative must be given to the constitution of an autonomous network of cadres in the factory, cadres of direct working-class extraction. This is the crucial point, though we should not overlook other possibilities. We could very well also draw cadres of a new type out from the traditional organizations. We must be able to fully exploit the political hegemony that the newspaper's discourse makes possible. It is a hegemony that in fact can be used at any level; you will not find people—or if you do, it will be rare—who explicitly oppose this line. In most cases, you will find people more or less aware that this line is a winner; you will find, in other words, a range of cadres feeling the objective effects of this discourse's hegemony, even if, for reasons we know well, they are not yet moved to make the political leap out from the organizations. In any case, this is a marginal problem with respect to ours, the constitution of an autonomous network of cadres, which must really emerge from the direct contact that we establish at the level of production, at the factory level, between the newspaper's discourse and the working class's concrete circumstances. I believe that we may begin to organize this in a sufficiently systematic way, precisely because in these cases, the capacity of knowing how to correctly interpret individual situations, within the framework of a general strategy, is very valuable.

We can think very easily of organizing the next conference to discuss the newspaper as a conference for political cadres from the factory—at a minimum, in two months from now, after the discussion of this issue and after the circulation of two issues directly devoted to identifying this new political cadre. I am emphasizing this topic, which it seems to me we have always underestimated and circumvented for who knows what reasons—perhaps because the very concept of political cadre arouses suspicion among us, immediately giving us the impression of a bureaucrat, etc. There is absolutely no chance of carrying forward grassroots political work, the practical application of political work, without constructing and being endowed with a network of cadres—and I speak of a network because this, precisely, is the concept. I would connect the development of our political work and the newspaper's discourse to *this* condition, because otherwise we will not be able, in practice, to present this new political line in an alternative way. It is clear that, if this has weight at the political level, it also has weight at all the other levels. Either we manage to achieve this form, in which we subjectively practice the political discourse, and then get back to everything else—in other words, it is worthwhile to continue to articulate the political line, to fix general theoretical categories, to reconstruct the history of the working class going backward, etc.—or…

Within these three categories of political work, we can foresee diverse tasks. I would rule out the absolute division of labor between the three levels, but objectively we will not succeed in avoiding it, because there are clearly comrades more adept at this or to that type of work. Bearing in mind the possibility that this division of labor will be codified, the discovery and building up of cadres is, in any case, to be privileged, in light of the problem we have at this point: we have a need not for people who study, but for people who work politically, who make politics in a new way around this discourse. Taking someone who approaches this type of work perhaps for the first time, they must overcome a serious prejudice against politics understood as only happening in a party, or as what one can only begin to do inside a party. If someone skips over this prejudice, then you have found an exceptional individual. Any time that one takes up this degree of political intervention outside the traditional organizations—not even within another organization, because we do not have to present ourselves as an organization as such, etc.—when this happens, an entire tradition of political work is turned upside down. Taking those who accept something like this, you find yourself in front of a pre-revolutionary cadre, absolutely. To help advance the kind of active politics that we are proposing here means to apply oneself to the building up of a new type of political militant, one who explodes the traditional concept of the political organization in the party sense, the bureaucratic organization—one who reintroduces the question, in the most correct form possible, of a political organization that is indeed of a new type, completely different from those traditions.

These are minimum programs, and we must fix the discourse and discussion around them. It is pointless to restate here the general argument regarding the need to reconstruct the relation between class and class organization. At this point, we must begin to see which are the most correct and most serious paths for coming to confront this problem in the most practical way possible. Once again, we must select a center capable of unifying the various levels of our political work.

Now, it is clear that the relationship between general historical-theoretical work and the moment of practical intervention into individual struggles cannot find a genuine point of mediation except for in the newspaper, in the structure of the newspaper, in the discourse of the newspaper, in the work of composing the newspaper, in the work of circulating it, etc. This tool was deliberately made for unifying these two moments, which otherwise would seem to be completely isolated from one another.

At this point, we must propose a new structure, in the manner of an organization even, within the newspaper, one that must absolutely serve this practical and immediate purpose. The newspaper—if it is true that it exists between these two levels—must also move between them in a positive way, increasingly distancing itself from the moment of the general proposition of political problems, and increasingly approaching the one in which political discourse is translated concretely into the positive, practical moment. Thus, it must stretch to become an increasingly direct moment, a practical moment of intervention, coming to identify itself with this moment. There must be a point at which the newspaper, having overcome this hurdle, this necessity of political mediation, identifies itself with the moment of the intervention. Then, step-by-step, it locates concrete situations, interprets them, and seeks to organize them in accordance with the general political discourse. The newspaper will need to move around in this way: we have issues of the newspaper that pose these problems and systematize them (for example the one coming out now, still one of systematization), then there can be issues of real, practical intervention, and then subsequently there can be a return to other equally massive issues focused on general problems (the problem of the party, for example), which we still need and which we have anything but exhausted. This year, the newspaper cannot but move around in this sense, providing issues that are more focused on political systematization and formulation, alongside more agile and direct issues focused on political intervention. In this way, we can simultaneously set our political work within a sufficiently rigid structure, one that allows us to identify modes of intervention in a definitive way, and in a way that is unified at the national level. If it is true that the question of intervention has only just now arisen in an organic form, under conditions in which theoretical and political systematization have already in part been achieved, we must first systematize the moments of intervention into a form that assumes features which are, if not definitive, then sufficiently valid for a certain period of time. So then, in my opinion, it is worth elaborating a series of theses on intervention that really must emerge from this type of reflection.[12]

12. The "theses" on intervention would be elaborated in the lead editorial of the subsequent issue, unsigned but likely written by Tronti. After assessing the continued political growth of the working class, and reiterating the call to build a network of cadres, the author clarifies that what must be exploited is "the happy condition of not being a party," and the freedom from certain formal and institutional burdens that would go along with that. At the same time, one must also avoid constituting a "minoritarian group." Ultimately, the goal is to transition "from the class to its political organization, through the moment of *the organization of the struggle*, which alone is able to impose a new structure for the workers' movement and guarantee its non-reformist character." See "Intervento politico nelle lotte" ["Political intervention into the struggles"], *classe operaia* 1, no. 6 (June 1964): 1 and 20, 20 (my translation).

Part Three

The Problem of Organization

The Party in the Factory

(April 1965)

During the summer and fall of 1964, Tronti's articles in *Classe Operaia* increasingly addressed the problem of organization, and more specifically, how the Italian Communist Party factored into the working-class struggle.[1] This talk was delivered at a large public meeting in Turin, held by *Classe Operaia* to coincide with the release of their third issue of year two, bringing together leftists from groups and tendencies inside and outside the PCI.[2] Here Tronti discusses reconstituting a proper division of labor between the working class and the PCI in light of the increasing unity between capitalists and their state.

1. See Tronti's "1905 in Italy" and "Class and Party" for the key instances.
2. According to the *Gazzetta del popolo del lunedi* of April 12, 1965, more than 200 people attended the public gathering; *L'espresso* of April 18, 1965 noted that Tronti's speech was given to an audience of 400. See Milana and Trotta, *L'operaismo degli anni sessanta*, 476-77. The editorial in question was "O partito unico o partito in fabbrica" [Either single party or party-in the factory], lead editorial of *classe operaia* 2, no. 3 (May 1965): 1-2.

Our judgment of the current phase of class struggle in Italy has so far been, and will continue to be, the guiding thread of all the discourse produced by the newspaper. Bringing this judgment to bear upon the present situation, we find a precise moment of transition in the capitalist structure that we may summarize in the following way: *after the conjuncture, before the plan.*[3] In other words, a phase in which, from the capitalist viewpoint, there is an attempt to reconnect these two moments: the conjuncture understood as a crisis of development in the short term for Italian capitalism, and the prospect of development over the long term, which is tied to the various, historical forms of planning and programming. Now, we know that in a capitalist system the conjunctural crisis is primarily and obviously an economic fact, in other words, a fact relating to determinate transitions in the structures of production, and to transitions in all other structures which depend directly on production. However, what we are saying (and we have already made this argument about the conjuncture) is that this economic transition in the system has had, may have, and concretely in Italy has had, certain political causes. In the same way, it may also have certain political effects—and we believe that the economic transition has had and is having such effects, especially in recent days.

We have outlined the political cause as a network of working-class struggles that preceded and provoked this conjunctural transition, to the point of forcing the economic structure of Italian capitalism to undertake general readjustment measures, because of its need to recuperate, within itself, a network of working-class struggles that were hitherto not controlled directly by the capitalist. This lack of capitalist control over the workers' struggles seemed and still seems to us to be the political cause of the conjuncture, insofar as it is a crisis in the country's structures of production.

3. In this essay, Tronti uses "conjuncture" to refer to a discrete encounter that comprises both economic and political developments: the recent economic recession, concomitant with capitalist restructuring and working-class struggle. The concept of "conjuncture" was current among Marxists in Italy: it features in Togliatti's postwar writings and appears in Gramsci's fragmentary *Prison Notebooks*, in which he had offered some provisional definitions of the term. The conjuncture could be defined as "the set of circumstances which determine the market in a given phase, provided that these are conceived of as being in movement, i.e., as constituting a process of ever-changing combinations, a process which is the economic cycle" (Gramsci, *Selections from the Prison Notebooks*, 177n79). Gramsci counterposed "conjunctural" crises and movements to "organic" ones, which were understood as being more long-lasting and permanent (178). This recalls Tronti's notion of capitalist crisis as a *moment* of development, rather than as a crashing *telos.*

But the "conjuncture" also had an important political dimension for Gramsci. For him, studying the conjuncture had an important bearing on "immediate politics," on "tactics" and "agitation" (177n79). In addition, in one of Gramsci's many notes on Machiavelli (a piece of context missing from the *Selections from the Prison Notebooks* and not yet available in the English translations of the complete editions), Gramsci also refers to a "strategic conjuncture" in a military sense, defining it as "the level of strategic preparation of the theatre of struggle," which importantly includes "the qualitative condition of the leading personnel, and of what may be called the 'front-line' (and assault) forces" (217). Tronti's analysis follows in this vein by demonstrating the origins and outcomes of the economic conjuncture in terms of working-class political activity.

Although the parallels may seem clear to today's reader, Tronti's use of the term would not appear to have been influenced by Althusser, who in this same period had already begun his own project to develop the concept, drawing from Lenin and Machiavelli. For an overview of how the "conjuncture" has been handled by Gramsci and Althusser, as well as by Nicos Poulantzas, Stuart Hall, and others, see Juha Koivisto and Mikko Lahtinen, "Conjuncture, Politico-Historical," trans. Peter Thomas, *Historical Materialism* 20, no. 1 (January 2012): 267–77.

Here, then, we find ourselves before a phenomenon that is characteristic of the relation between the political effects of the working-class struggle and its operation within the real structures of capitalist development as such. It was and is necessary, in our opinion, to provide a political interpretation of the conjunctural transition, because this political interpretation is and has been decisive for the comportment that follows within the same conjunctural transition—in other words, within the working-class struggles that explode in the crisis.[4] They could be pushed along and used as directly political struggles only if they had been understood as struggles that had provoked that conjuncture.

Later, this political interpretation of the conjuncture was provided by the capitalist side, particularly by the entrepreneurial stratum, which sought to use the conjuncture politically, organizing a political response to its direct cause: the workers. In this sense, we can say that, on this score, the entrepreneurial and industrial strata—in other words, the capitalist class in Italy—has outpaced, in terms of its awareness, the managerial political stratum, the political class itself (as those people say, inaccurately), imposing on it this political interpretation of the conjuncture. Because we have seen that in an earlier phase, the managerial political stratum tended to underestimate the political moment of the conjunctural transition; it tended, in other words, to respond to it entirely at the economic level. The hesitations in the various countercyclical measures taken at the level of government have derived precisely from the fact that the managerial political stratum (albeit taken in its entirety, since clearly for certain strata this consciousness was there) lacked an awareness that, by contrast, was present among the majority of the entrepreneurial stratum and capitalist class.

Within the conjunctural transition there was a development of the following type: the capitalist class as such knew how to apply pressure on the managerial political stratum and the government directly, so as to impose on the entire capitalist formation, across the board, a political response to the conjuncture itself. Indeed, in the second phase of the conjuncture we have seen a division of labor between the entrepreneurial stratum and the political stratum. The bosses said, "We will attack the workers directly" (and this was a form of political pressure on the government, in addition to political pressure on the working class) "because we think that there lies the weak point of the Italian capitalist structure, there lies the point that we must resolve in order to exit the conjuncture and implant the plan. It is the government's responsibility to set up a safety net of countercyclical measures that ought to operate

4. Here I follow Arianna Bove's decision to translate *comportamento* with "comportment," rather than the more generally used "behavior," because it literally signifies "how one carries oneself with others," and thus, the movement of collective subjectivity. See "Translator's Note," xxv, in Antonio Negri, *Factory of Strategy: Thirty-Three Lessons on Lenin*, trans. Arianna Bove (New York: Columbia University Press, 2014).

at the general level of society, toward redistribution and general equilibrium between the social forces, as they present themselves within the political state as well as within civil society."

There was, in other words, a precise division of labor between these two roles, which initiated a rather remarkable process, the most important process that we must understand: a convergence between these two sections of the capitalist formation, between the capitalist class and the political government. There was a moment of friction during a previous phase, a lack of confidence in their state, and this was an actual fact, in other words, a difference in how the industrial stratum and the political stratum, each taken as a whole, evaluated the class situation. In the latter part of the conjuncture, we witnessed a convergence between these two sections of the capitalist front, a renewal of rather intense dialogue, which leads, and will lead, undoubtedly, to the recovery of a deep unity between the industrial stratum and the political stratum, one that bears decisively upon our judgement of the coming situation and upon opportunities for political action within it.

At this point, we are witnessing a new division of labor at a higher and more functional level of the system's economic structures. You all have read the argument made by the industrialists, by Cicogna for example, the argument that essentially says this: let industry return to its particular function within the national social structure, because public interest as such must be taken up *en bloc* by the political stratum, at the governmental level, pure and simple.[5] This is a decisive transition, because it shows that the capitalist class now has control over the entire society, and that this permits it to reclaim a particular role directly related to the production of profit. On the other hand, this is the first real basis for a chance to plan the whole of development over the long term, because, clearly, at the very moment in which capitalists have this control, or in which they are thought to have this control over the general network of social relations—at that moment, the job of planning control over this development is entrusted to the state as such, that is, the public interest is handed back to the state. Today the industrialists' argument is precisely this: *"We will take responsibility for the production of profit; the state, the government, and the political stratum can take responsibility for and control over the distribution of income."*

It is essentially a division of this type that we find as the material starting point of a serious planning initiative. Here we see something very interesting. It has been said from many quarters that the relation between the conjuncture and the plan was clear neither at the governmental level nor at the capitalist

---

5. Furio Cicogna was the president of the employers' association Confindustria from 1961–66, during which time he strongly opposed the center-left.

level, and that therefore the conjuncture would delay planning in Italy. Today we notice that it is exactly the opposite; we notice, in other words, that the conjuncture at once established certain economic, political, and structural bases, as well as the bases for control over the movements of the working class which for the first time make a long-term planning initiative possible in Italy. In other words, it shifted the discourse about the plan from draft form to a phase of concrete realization. The planning that is being formulated today is precisely the result of this conjuncture. There is a very close link between the two—it is the link between two moments of the cycle of capitalist development, two moments that have been joined together by the capitalist class's control of the situation at the subjective level. The conjuncture has elicited this development within the capitalist formation.

It is interesting to consider the effects elicited by this same conjuncture within the workers' movement: here, it tended to seriously divide the working class from the organized workers' movement. This is the second political effect of the Italian conjunctural transition: *greater unity within the capitalist formation, greater division within the workers' formation.* Greater unity and greater division must be understood in this sense: greater unity of the capitalists is not greater unity between Christian Democracy and its allies within the center-left, because this is the old bureaucratic conception of upper-echelon unity. The real unity in the capitalist front is the relation that has been built, for example, between the Christian-Democrat leadership, united today around particular capitalist positions, and the capitalist class. This is the real unity we refer to when we say the bosses are more united today. And so, within the workers' movement, the division must not be understood as it often is, as greater division between the Communist Party and other parties of the workers' movement, such as the Socialist Party or other parties. It does not fit into this framework, and, in any case, the effects of this are rather weak and do not interest us.

When we speak of a greater division within the workers' formation, let us instead rediscover it as a *greater division between the Communist Party and the working class*; this is what we are saying when we speak of a further distancing, following the conjuncture, between class and class movement. Clearly, while the capitalist side has basically managed, at least during a certain phase of the conjuncture, to offer a political interpretation of the conjunctural transition, in other words, to take possession in political terms of the moment of capitalist development, the same has by no means happened within the workers' movement. Instead, what emerged from this was all the economism and syndicalism in which the workers' movement as a whole and the Communist Party in particular are objectively locked. The very fact that the Party has, during this period, completely delegated the workers' response to the capitalist attack to the trade-union level—this already shows the objective limit that the Party expressed in its awareness, in the control that it had over the development of the class situation.[6]

This is because, most importantly, when the capitalist attack was unleashed at the general level, bringing along those goals that we mentioned earlier, the working-class response through the trade-union channels did not manage to respond on an equal footing. At that moment, it needed political control over the conjunctural situation, a direct involvement by the Party in the workers' struggles, one that could take the reins of these struggles and respond to the political attack of capital with a political counterattack by the working class. As you all know, none of this happened. And not only was the working-class response delegated to the trade union at a moment when it, while certainly a place from which the struggle began, absolutely could not remain its endpoint—not only did this happen, but in addition, in the forms of the trade-union struggle, it did not go beyond the type of response that could only assume a political character if modified in form.

For our part, within this conjunctural transition, more than demanding the direct intervention of the Party in the struggles—which to us seemed correct to demand but almost impossible to achieve—we focused on the forms of the struggle, because it seemed to us that, with these having changed, even the trade-union struggle itself could take on a political content. In other words, our call for the struggle's generalization, our polemic against the articulated struggle, our pressing for the general strike in situations in which it could be achieved—to us, all this seemed to open up the possibility of a working-class political response to that capitalist political project which could be distinguished through a definite, correct analysis at that moment.[7]

This general response, this change in the form of the trade-union struggle to a general trade-union struggle—as you all know, this was in the end achieved only in certain cases, which did not then manage to break through onto the national terrain. Now, although the workers' openness toward this form of struggle was certain—because the capitalist attack was so strong that it could not but have an openness to general struggle as its counterpart on the workers' side—there was not, on the other hand, a concrete opportunity to generalize the struggle beyond trade-union levels. And this was not due to any subjective, anarcho-syndicalist limits that we had, but to the objective limits of the situation. This much is clear about that moment: never have we been more aware of the real difficulties present in grassroots political work absent a class organization, and of the possible use of a class party at those levels.

6. Here and below I have capitalized the word "Party" when Tronti's reference to the PCI appears most unambiguous.
7. For the "polemic against the articulated struggle," see the opening editorial, "Contra la lotta articolata" [Against the articulated struggle] in *classe operaia* 2, no. 2 (March–April 1965): 1 and 4.

We can conclude this part of our talk, then, with exactly this point: at the end of the conjuncture—and precisely because the workers' general openness to struggle was not gathered politically in the organized workers' movement, and particularly in the Communist Party—we must take note of a new division between class and party. I believe that if we wanted to confirm this, it would suffice to follow, with a modicum of attention, the development of the factory conferences of the Party, which had the fortune of being inserted into a sharp moment of class struggle, and which precisely in this way offered an opportunity to grasp the state of relations between workers and organization.[8] Right there, where the Party was taking the initiative and having a direct dialogue at the workers' level, this dialogue was broken off. It was broken off the moment the factory conferences were not connected—as they were not connected at any point—to the real moments of the working-class struggle, to the real needs of the working-class political response. The only way to prevent this new division between class and party would have been to actually throw the factory conferences into the workers' struggles, making them an element of those struggles or, vice versa, bringing the masses of workers into the factory conferences.

Reconnecting these two elements would have meant blocking the division between class and organization, which was clearly one of the capitalist side's political objectives precisely during the conjunctural transition. It is within this framework that we must discuss the need to push forward, at the general level, a rallying cry on which the newspaper has been harping for a long time, practically since last summer—one raised by our grassroots political work everywhere it has been successful and everywhere it has reached. The rallying cry is that of mass confrontation, of mass social confrontation, at this point in Italian capitalist development.

Mass social confrontation meant exactly this: to have already made a judgement concerning the conjunctural transition of capitalist development in Italy, to have glimpsed the greater unity that was being set up between the capitalist class and bourgeois political stratum, to possess the awareness that this foreshadowed the concrete possibility of their planning capitalist development in Italy over the long term, and that the only way of defeating the bosses' political project was to take advantage of a certain requirement that the capitalists have—that of reckoning with workers—and thus, to prepare a political response that indeed would have led to this general reckoning at the political level of class, offering a good chance to stop that process just as within this confrontation the existing relation between working class and its

8. The March-April 1965 issue of *Classe Operaia* included a special supplement, "Per la terza conferenza dei comunisti nelle fabbriche" [For the third conference of the Communists in the factories], which would be held on May 29-30. The PCI had held such events for the past several years.

organizations would have been put into play. The political objective that we wanted to draw from this rallying cry was not the general crisis of capitalism in Italy, the seizure of power by the workers, but rather the recovery of a new unity, the likes of which the capitalists were achieving on their own account in their camp: *a new and correct relation between class and organization*, between class and party. The objective was, in other words, to put the traditional relation between class and party back into play, something that can only be recovered in correct terms from within this mass confrontation. This is because there is no possibility of recovering it at a moment when, instead, the confrontation is subdivided, in which the struggle is articulated, and in which, therefore, there is no direct, general relation of the class as such with the party. When there is no general movement of the class, clearly its influence over the party is infinitely smaller. The opportunity for the general struggle was completely lost.

Some objections have been made to this: you are proposing a social confrontation of this type, but do you not expect this confrontation to end with a general defeat for the workers, one that derives precisely from its general character? And is a general defeat of this type not all the more possible when there is no party capable of concentrating the entire working-class thrust and throwing it back at the boss? It is an objection to which we must be sensitive, because it is among the few intelligent ones we hear. As a matter of fact, there is a risk of this type.

This rallying cry also originated from an analysis that we believe to be as precise as that of the relations within the capitalist formation, an internal analysis of the working-class situation, from which emerged an openness to struggle that was so strong, global, and total that a defeat of the working class in a general confrontation would have been unlikely. *In other words, our analysis of the class situation in Italy leads us to conclude that direct relation between the two classes right at this moment—and we do not know for how long—is more likely to end in the workers' favor.* With the existing relations of force, it would have been unlikely for a direct confrontation between the two classes to lead to a workers' defeat; it would much more likely have led to a block in the process of unification between capitalist class and bourgeois political stratum. It would instead have exacerbated the contradiction, which existed during the first phase of the conjuncture, between these two sections of the capitalist formation; it would have in large part divided them. It would have put the state and governmental structures of the Italian political apparatus into crisis, calling into question a set of relations even at the formal political level, as well as in the capitalist institutions in Italy, and we could have gambled on this to intervene and deliver the first points of rupture. We should add that, within this social confrontation, while the capitalist institutional struc-tures could have been put into crisis, by contrast, the institutional structures of at least a part of the workers' movement could have been recovered.

I have said all this because, very often, when some rallying cries are brought forward, above all at the workers' level, in the factory, they have the tendency to be seen as improvisations of personalities that sprout out from who knows where, with the idea of doing one thing instead of another, lacking awareness of the general limits of the political situation and the general class situation. With what I have said, I have indeed attempted to provide evidence that attests to the fact that our rallying cries, which we are advancing at the factory level at a certain point, are born of a careful and analytical interpreta-tion of the class situation in general, of the real movements of the two classes in struggle, as much as an interpretation of their respective political institu-tions, and that only in the end do we choose certain rallying cries rather than others to bring to the workers' level. *This point does not exhaust our work, because we are also trying to use our intervention as a moment of verification for the general discourse itself, and then picking this discourse up again after the experience to see if it functions or not.*

You all know that it does not depend on the immediate political result, because at the workers' level another element inserts itself, one that is decisive for attaining a certain result over another, and that is the possibility of moving forces materially, of *finding an organizational channel for these rallying cries that do not spontaneously function as such*, but which must be *carried along by a material organization*, that material organization we are going to seek, but only for the future—we do not possess it for the present. Our judgment of how correct rallying cries may be must not be tied to their immediate results, but once again, to an analysis of the general situation, and to the outcome it determines in the relations between class and state, between class and party, and so on.

We are seeking in practice to discover and use models of political action that we believe will emerge again at other moments of capitalist development, in Italy and elsewhere, which will emerge each time with far more material, organizational strength, and thus with a far greater chance of success. For us, it seems possible that political comportment within the conjunctural transition could serve as an example of political work that will be able to emerge again in the presence, simultaneously, of a correct relation between party and class and a short-term transition in capitalist development. And within that short term, there again will emerge the need for a working-class political response, one that cannot but refer to these previous experiences of political work, one that cannot but retrieve this interpretation of the facts, which is also tied to the long-term analysis of capitalist development. It is no coincidence that, from the political outcome of this conjunctural transition—if we want to consider it finished, and I think that perhaps we can consider it finished—from this we have drawn the necessity and urgency of proposing again, *en bloc*, the theme of the party in the factory.

* * *

The theme of the party in the factory is connected not only to the occasion of the Communists' conference in the factories, but also to the initial conclusions that we have drawn from this conjunctural transition, which poses for us, once again, the whole problem of the organization's existence at determinate, transitional moments of capitalist development, and *the political organization's existence not in general, but in connection with the real levels of the working class, that is, connected directly to the site of production.* The theme of the party in the factory is nothing but this.

Indeed, the lesson left at the end of this conjunctural transition, as far as this problem is concerned, is exactly this: the relation between party and class, and more precisely, between PCI and working class, endures in a rather negative sense, in the sense that, within the conjunctural transition, the channel of communication between class and party was not successfully located. In other words, *the workers' openness to struggle, which, at least at certain moments, had a general, global, and social character, did not manage to climb up inside the structures of the Party.* We believe that this is because of an actually existing, material fact, namely, because the channel of communication between class and party, from the site of production to the intermediary cadre to the upper echelons of the Party, *is a practically blocked channel.* Moreover, the possibility of generalizing the struggle and directly politicizing it was, at that moment, closely tied to the possibility of internal communication between the two of them. There was not, at that moment, any other force capable of politically generalizing that openness of the workers to struggle. The fact that there was not another force available and capable of carrying out this politicization, that the channel of communication between the class and the only organization able to do this was practically cut off—this is the objective limit that prevented, in practical terms, the unfolding of this general confrontation, which could have had those results we have already described, even beyond the relation in the factory between class and party.

So, taking up the theme of the party in the factory again, at this point, has validity in its own rather specific and immediate way. There emerges here a lesson that is quite important for us: not only had these channels of communication between party and class been broken due to the lack of a factory organization of the Party, but we also experienced something else, on which we must reflect at length even if we ourselves have perhaps reflected on it too little. Namely, the workers' openness to struggle against the boss does not correspond and does not replicate itself as the workers' openness to struggle—I would not say against the party, because we would not bring forward this kind of rallying cry at any point, but—as the *workers' openness to struggle toward, within the party*. The point to be emphasized is this: we are seeing that there is a certain type of passivity among workers regarding the problems of political organization; there is passivity among workers that is rather general, rather organized at the social level. There is a certain social indifference among workers to immediately resolve the problem of organization, or for that matter, to be associated with the argument we have put forward—which has made some very serious and important theoretical connections. At the level of the working class, the tactical moment is completely lacking. The tactical moment at the workers' level can be brought only by an already existing political organization, and only by the party already reconnected to the class as such.

If the moment of the party is missing, then the moment of tactics at the workers' level is missing. Within the working class, there does not exist the possibility of tactically using situations in which capital is weak, nor is there an immediate need for organization. With regard to this problem, therefore, it is necessary to organize a certain type of working-class thrust toward the party, something which absolutely does not spontaneously develop by itself. We can easily verify a concrete form of spontaneity in the workers' struggle against the boss, and this spontaneity must in turn be organized politically by the party; however, it is indeed the organization of *a spontaneity that exists*, whereas we cannot speak of a spontaneity among workers to resolve the problems of immediate political organization. These problems must be brought to the class level subjectively—brought directly from without, if we want to use this Leninist terminology.[9] It is a theme that is perhaps not yet completely clear, even for us, and I pose it here as a problem for further reflection.

However, what we can already conclude from this given reality is the necessity, at this moment in our political work in the factory, of *managing, on our part, to directly and subjectively reconnect the workers' struggle against the boss and the workers' struggle toward the party.* One pursuit to which we will commit ourselves in the coming months of grassroots political work, distinguishing this work in a new way, is to grasp the dual nature of the working-class struggle as such, to understand our political work as a subjective unification of these two

9. The phrase is from Lenin's *What Is to Be Done?* See Lars T. Lih's translation in *Lenin Rediscovered: "What Is to Be Done?" in Context* (Haymarket Books: Chicago, 2008), 745. Lih argues that Lenin's harsh critique of the limits of "spontaneous" working-class politics was a "tacked-on polemical sally," inessential to his argument. While distinct from Tronti's reading, Lih's exegesis is invaluable for considering the uses and abuses that have been made of Lenin's thought.

moments. Because unification of this kind does not exist spontaneously at the workers' level; it must be imposed subjectively, combatting even some forms of passivity among the workers. We cannot, in other words, count on a spontaneous working-class thrust upon the party, even upon the traditional Party, even upon the old organization. For this thrust to exist, it must be concretely organized within determinate struggles against the boss. Even here, we cannot think to organize a working-class thrust toward the party independently of a working-class struggle against the boss and against the capitalist directly. It is there that we think one may pose, that one must pose in concrete terms, the problem of political organization: the problem, that is, of working-class pressure on the party. If these two moments are divided, these two faces of the working-class struggle, then, in my opinion, the real development of the class struggle as such has not been grasped in its entirety, and there is a risk of carrying out political work that has no chance of producing immediate results.

This is why we are working on a hypothesis—and it is not a scandalous hypothesis, insofar as it has already been said of the experience that we have had—of today reopening, or trying to reopen, and leading a battle to reopen, these blocked channels between class and party, and, let us say, between working class and Communist Party. To reopen these channels at this point with the rallying cry of the party in the factory, understood precisely as Communist Party in the factory—this has the tactical value of renewing contact between these two levels, the class and the organization. Because the moment one puts the general relation back into play, one can conceive a moment of general crisis within it, and one can push that working-class pressure on the party through some already organized channels—the strength, presence, and so on of which, as we were saying, must be organized.

This is why we are also bringing forward the theme of the party in the factory in concrete terms, saying: alright then, we accept the rallying cry of the Communist Party in the factory. Here, too, there can be dozens of objections to this, and objections to it indeed are made. The basic objection is usually this: *are you not contributing in this way to a renewal of bureaucratic control from above, of the party over the class*, which is exactly what at least a part of the capitalist stratum demands and would like to have. That is, a control of the class through the currently existing workers' institutions, since direct control by the capitalist side over the movement of the working class as such is not possible at any point of capitalist development, much less in Italy? Are you not therefore running the risk of renewing precisely the type of control by the party over the class that you want to get away from, when you focus on the contradiction between class and party, on the workers' struggles being against the bosses and toward the party?

This objection also has some validity and intelligence to it. *But I would reject this objection*, bringing the discussion back this time as well to the real analysis of the class situation, which is always the decisive point. I would return to the discussion of that openness of the workers to struggle, of the level of working-class struggle that exists in Italy, which does not exist at other points in international capitalist development, and which leads us to forecast the greater probability of exactly the opposite resolution. In other words, it leads us to forecast that, in the moment when a channel of communication is established between party and class, between party and factory, control by the party over the class does not come into existence, but quite the opposite. That is, the possibility would be opened for workers' control over the party, which in this moment can occur only if the two levels are put back into communication, and if this communication is organized.

Given the workers' openness to struggle; given the high level of development of the class struggle; given the awareness of political problems that the working class has; given the weakness of the organizational structures of the Party, so bankrupt at precisely the level that interests us, and with *a leadership, in my opinion, barely aware of all the general development*; given the relation that still exists between the Communist Party and the capitalist political stratum (that is, the immaturity that exists on the capitalist side, unprepared for a comprehensive political initiative that would engage the Party as such and compromise it in a general, reformist operation)—for all of these reasons, it seems to us that it would be probable, or possible, to put the political relation between party and class back into play, causing this working-class pressure to flow back onto the Party, including the leadership—this pressure which is enormous when facing the boss, but which does not manage to find channels to break through when facing the Party, above all when facing the leadership of the Party. It seems that the above type of objection can be dismissed with this type of response.

But in addition to this argument, in my opinion, another fact plays in the favor of the "party in the factory." We cannot understand the need for the party in the factory as merely a moment of reckoning between class and its party: at this point, we must get back to the particular relation between the class and the capitalist stratum, between workers and bosses. To us it seems that, at this point, the existence of the party in the factory as such would produce, accumulate, and reproduce in enlarged form some working-class strength precisely in the struggle against the boss, in the struggle against the capitalist —strength that this struggle currently possesses in a very limited way, or that it possesses up to a certain point due to the lack of a political outlet, the lack of a political instrument for the workers' struggles against the boss.

All this occurs at the moment in which the organization of the struggle presents itself as long-term, before the plan and within the structures of the plan, at the moment in which the union is completely compromised within the planning of capitalist development. It will be difficult for it to free itself from this chain. The union will not be able to get out of it and we are already seeing this today. The principled affirmations being made are insufficient, and the union saying "no" to the incomes policy is not enough to prevent the incomes policy from happening in fact.[10] *The class union, the CGIL, says "no" to the incomes policy, but the incomes policy is already practically underway, and all of you know that this past year there has already been one, because there has already been a wage freeze*, because there has already been a certain capitalist control over the income from dependent labor relative to other forms of income, something that can be real without the institutionalization as such of an incomes policy.[11] To say "no" to the incomes policy, therefore, does not mean staking everything on this trade-union watchword to prevent the plan from functioning, because the plan can also work alongside this trade-union "no," because these days there are objective tools that are even able to disregard the direct institutionalization of capitalist needs. We believe the use of the trade-union channel is unlikely to emerge again in the coming years, within the structures of the plan, in a form that is alternative to capital's own plan.

Therefore, what does remain is a certain use of the Party, which is left out of capitalist planning, which is not involved in it, at least in this phase of the plan, but which could be even less involved if it were to exist once again within the structures of production. On the contrary, within the structures of production, the party in the factory is expected to become practically the only opportunity on the workers' side to escape the control exercised by the institutions and the actual policies of the capitalists and their plan, because, probably, precisely by being uninvolved in the formation of the plan, it could become a subversive element, both in particular situations and in moments of general conflict.

In short, at a time when there is a general plan for development, we must absolutely begin to identify concrete forms such that this plan does not come to function practically. We must begin to find some rocks that we can throw into the machine of the plan to prevent it from functioning. It is useless to explain how this is the alternative essentially posed today between two strategic conceptions in the workers' movement—and, I repeat, *everybody* should be *forced into open struggle* over this—namely, whether in the struggle against the capitalist plan it is necessary to present an alternative plan, one that would

10. An incomes policy refers to the government setting limits on wages and prices.

11. The CGIL is the Confederazione Generale del Lavoro, which was the largest and furthest-left of the trade union confederations.

change or begin to change the capitalist structures themselves; *or whether it is not instead a problem of preventing any planning whatsoever from functioning,* precisely because to prevent planning from functioning, at this level of capitalist development, would mean to put the capitalist structures themselves into perpetual crisis, and *to conceive a moment of permanent working-class struggle,* which clearly—at a certain point, *once the general relation between class and party has been rebuilt in the organization*—must then flow directly into a *revolutionary plan* on the workers' side.

If these are the two alternatives, they cannot be kept in the general terms that we are forced to use today: we must see concretely how they may begin to function. They can function if we find real, grassroots tools, which from the outset escape this web of capitalist planning, this possible capitalist control over the working class, and which then perpetually and practically call into question the functioning, the very existence, of the plan. This reintroduces the problem of the relation between union and party, which here we can hardly mention, because it would take us further afield. But briefly, I would say this: that when from the trade-union side it is said (and Novella has said this at various points) that the union cannot only be against the plan, but that it must also be for the plan, that is, for another plan, I truly believe that whoever says this is right.[12] Effectively, the union today cannot shy away from the opportunity and the need to oppose the capitalists' plan with a development plan that aims, above all, to defend workers' labor-power from the use capital makes of it. *The party is the one that must stand exclusively against the plan;* this is the difference between union and party. It is the party that must absolutely refuse to present an alternative to the plan of capitalist development, because the party does not have to defend the material value of workers' labor-power but only to organize the political development of the working class, which is clearly a development that is antithetical, antagonistic to the system itself. *The party does not have to suggest a different plan for development; if anything, it must suggest capitalism's own lack of development—its real contradictions, and so on.* The difference between these two moments, the trade-union and the political—it seems to me that we could bring it back to the division of labor between union and party.

I repeat that this task poses enormous difficulties, and they are problems that we must try to address in some way. Then again, the fact that we have these difficulties cannot exempt us from taking into consideration the need to do certain things.

✳ ✳ ✳

12. Agostino Novella was the secretary-general of CGIL from 1957-70.

I would conclude with a problem that returns to the conversation we were having about subjective political work, and about the experience of *Classe Operaia*, connecting this in a new way to an analysis of the objective situation, and to the tasks that this analysis poses for all of us today. The enormous difficulties that shape our work—difficulties that lead us to attach ourselves to solutions which may even turn out to be unconvincing, such as the "party in the factory"—mean that we must, practically and consciously, put back into question the value that political work can have when performed by intervention groups such as those connected to *Classe Operaia*. In other words, *at this point, given the presence of a long-term plan of capitalist development, we must reflect on the following fact: responding to this with political work carried out by a group reveals the extreme precarity of the general situation*, the extreme backwardness of the general political situation with regard to the tools of struggle.

This we must absolutely consider. We may have attained the utmost clarity about the objective situation, we may do what we too have done to seek to understand it better, but the transition to orchestrating this more precise knowledge of the class situation in such a way that favors the political development of the class itself—this is an extremely difficult problem to solve.

The relationship between capitalist planning and the work undertaken by groups tied to particular and limited experiences—those of newspapers, of magazines, of grassroots interventions, and so on—should first of all emphasize, in my opinion, *the extreme disparity that exists today between means and ends* in the work that we want to do from the workers' viewpoint and at the workers' level. Thus, work of this kind is not to be idolized, this political intervention around the general class situation which is undertaken by a group of people. It is essential that we now recognize the insurmountable limits of this type of experience, with a view toward reintroducing the issue of reorganizing this political work on a more general plane.

We may also give a positive political appraisal of the way in which our discourse has developed—and we shall, because it is correct to do so. We may then go on to argue that the grassroots political work that has been done represents, basically, a model that we will need to take up again later at different moments of capitalist development and working-class struggle. We may say all these things, but ultimately, we must absolutely advance alongside the discourse. Before now, the most positive experience connected to the newspaper *Classe Operaia* has basically been this: by means of an experience of this kind, we have produced a knowledge, a grasp of the short-term of the class struggle—something that, at bottom, we lacked. And it was lacking because our previous approach always considered the long term of the class struggle, and so it was an approach that tended by its nature toward a theoretical recapitulation of general theses, of general transitions in relations between classes. An experience such as that of a political newspaper, tied to political work, has above all has given us the opportunity to use this strategic knowledge of the long-term movements of the two classes to help our rediscovery and our grasp of short-term moments.

Analyses of the conjunctural transition—its causes, its effects, how it was and is necessary to act back upon these causes, upon these effects—are perhaps the fundamental achievement of *Classe Operaia* so far. It is an experience that we must directly tie back (and this has already been illustrated in ample detail) to the general theses which to a certain extent predated this experience, but which also were greatly enriched and deepened by the experience itself. Many fail to see, for example, how the principle of the working-class struggle *coming before* the choices made by capitalists is not only a valuable principle to guide the historical reconstruction of the working class's movements in general, but also a political thesis that must be taken up and organized in the short term, in the analysis of a conjunctural transition of the capitalist system as well. And, indeed, it is the only principle that in practice manages to provide a correct interpretation of this short term.

If we do not see the connection between these two moments, then clearly a general understanding of this experience will elude us, as the interpretation given of it would be limited. Instead, it is precisely this strategic conception of a new type—this *strategic overturning* of the knowledge and analysis of capitalist development and the working class, grasped as separate and united at the same time—which then grants this experience the right amount of *political realism*, which is not difficult to detect in the recent developments of the discourse. I believe one may also detect this in our analysis of the situation, an analysis that is much more politically realistic than that "official" realism of the parties and organizations, those historical parties of the working class so often vaunted for their ability to seize upon every concrete moment of the class struggle. This "official" realism in fact causes them to lose their handle on what the conjuncture was and what the plan probably will be: a transition for the capitalists and for the working class at the same time.

This unity between the strategic overturning and political realism seems to me to be another that we must put back together if we want to judge this experience properly. And there is a third element to be added, which is that certain amount of apprehension that research has, which seems to me to have emerged from the reconstruction that Asor Rosa made regarding the transition this discourse has undergone. In the apparent contradiction between those two moments, there is really a certain amount of continual rethinking taking place—something which perhaps appears between the lines of the newspaper itself, as well as in some of our own arguments—in which, once certain solutions have been found, we always immediately go looking for the next ones.

What we may call open, continuous research leads us today, for example, to emphasize the disparity between the tools that we are using and the ends to which we apply ourselves, to the point of calling into question the very existence of these groups which do political work and intervene in struggles *such as these groups have evolved up to now*. Personally, I believe, for objective reasons connected to the launch of the capitalist plan, and for subjective reasons tied to the growth of the discourse that we put forward, that today we find ourselves at the beginning of a process in which these groups burn out.

These groups that do political work, that intervene in the workers' struggles, which were born in Italy around 1960, orbiting a wave of very determined as well as unexpected workers' struggles—the development of these groups, which basically lasted for five years, today tends practically toward its own extinction.

And, in my opinion, if we want to treat this matter seriously, we need to organize this extinction consciously. In other words, we must conceive of the specific limits of this work, we must understand that the existence of these groups does not indicate a healthy workers' movement, or healthy relations between the working class and its movement, but a state of illness, and that as long as these groups exist, so too will the need to work in the ways in which we have been forced to work at the grassroots workers' level, and this would be proof of a real state of illness in the workers' movement, of a crisis in the relations between class and organization. When there is no longer a need for this type of work, for the existence of these groups, then we will be able to say that the workers' movement is, or is beginning to exist, in a healthy state, one which restores the possibility of a revolutionary plan for workers' struggles that is as long-term, precise, and concrete as the plan for capitalist development.

On this alternative, we do not have, and I personally do not at this point have, any answers to give. I am simply suggesting the problem that we will probably find ourselves facing in the coming months, or at least in the coming years: the need to find forms of political work, and forms of intervention in struggles, that are of a new type with respect to those that have been developed so far. The transition that absolutely must be refused, and which must be refused not only in principle, but in fact, is the easier transition, one that probably could be suggested by many people, and which indeed many suggest: the transition from an experience such as that of *Classe Operaia*, or that of other groups, to the new organization, to what is called "the new revolutionary party."

I personally do not believe in a direct transition of this type. I do not believe there is currently the possibility of organizing revolutionary vanguards of a new type inside a structure that is organized into a new party that one might call revolutionary. At this moment, there is some prior work to do, which absolutely must pass through a necessary step, one that we absolutely cannot bypass: *the crisis of the workers' movement as such—what we in fact are calling the crisis of the Communist Party.*

This necessary step is what will reintroduce, in real concrete terms, the problem of the new revolutionary organization. Before this step, any attempt to constitute a new revolutionary organization repeats the historical errors of the historical minorities of the workers' movement, which are by nature, in principle, and in fact, truly extraneous to the entire experience that we have had thus far.

A Balance Sheet of the "Intervention"

(April 1965)

These notes were written by Tronti for a conversation with the other editors of *Classe Operaia* on April 11th, following the same day's public talk on the topic of "The Party in the Factory."

In this phase of the conjunctural transition we are witnessing an ebb in the bosses' attack. It is assuming more covert forms, motivated partly by the workers' response, partly by the objective situation; in other words, by the upswing in industrial production. The capitalists even speak of this upswing in a propagandistic way (as they did previously of the unfavorable conjuncture). The capitalists intend to exit from a stage of crisis that previously they had accentuated. The upswing reveals itself, in any case, to be slow (this is demonstrated by industrial production); it will probably last for months and perhaps for years (indeed, the plan forecasts a slow rate of development over the next two years, and, even after that, the rate of development will not achieve its earlier pace). Within this phase of upswing, we must revisit direct intervention. Are our rallying cries still valid? Can the rallying cry of the mass confrontation still function? In some places, the call for the general strike remains valid (Milan); in other situations, it proves less viable (Turin). In general, the prospect of the mass confrontation must not be abandoned but organized over a longer period. Within our political discourse we must establish a rallying cry that is not only agitational; this discourse may also introduce itself step-by-step. Our appraisal of the intervention carried out in the struggles is positive. The intervention has been general and timely. Our presence in the most acute situations of the struggle has been total. In any case, there have been some limits to this work: 1) A lack of central political leadership; in certain acute situations, a political leadership and immediate judgments have been lacking. This is due also to the limit of internal circulars that communicated experiences which had already burned out. 2) *A flaw in the political approach*. The rallying cry of the struggle against the boss has not been connected to the one for the party and it has not been articulated, practiced. There is a certain reticence by groups to grasp the two faces of the workers' struggles in this moment. There is an overestimation of the workers' struggles as such; only that one moment is seen, and the others are made to disappear. The discussion of the party has passed into the background because this wave of struggles seemed sufficient by itself to keep the pressure on the party, subjectively. The intervention newspaper itself displays this flaw. The discussion of the party has not been tied to the struggles, something which is fundamental to do. There is then the fact that the wave of struggles has itself not managed to connect with the newspaper work nor with the workers' movement. Here too the groups deeply underestimate the newspaper (an essential political tool, without which political work is nothing). These two moments of work tend to be separated too much: if they are separated, the two levels both collapse.

After the Reunion in Mestre

(May 1965)

On May 16, at a rally in Mestre, a working-class district of Venice, Tronti delivered a public speech that touched on the American intervention in Vietnam, the end of the economic crisis, the upswing in capitalist planning, and the possible crisis in the relation between class and party. The editors of *Classe Operaia*, who had all attended the rally, convened the following day in nearby Padua. At this meeting, Tronti made the following remarks, after contributions from Sergio Bologna, Romolo Gobbi, Antonio Negri, Romano Alquati, and Massimo Paci. The subject of their conversation was the "party in the factory" and the relationship between political discourse and political organization.[1]

1. Thanks to Fabio Milana for clarifying these circumstances. For the other editors' comments at the Padua meeting, one can see the transcript of the conversation: "*classe operaia*: una reunione a Mestre," in *L'operaismo degli anni Sessanta*, 479–82.

The greatest difficulty is the fact that, at present, it is hardly clear, even for us, what relation there is between the class and the PCI in this particular situation. Our work has focused on analyzing the Party's policy toward the working class: it is now necessary to analyze the inverse relation, the working class's relationship to the Party, because that has not yet been done sufficiently.

If we are gathering information about the relation between workers and the PCI by counting the number of workers registered, then we can say that the relationship is broken. The foundations of our discourse took for granted that this relationship had fallen apart, and as a consequence, our work was geared toward an autonomous organization. But there have not nor can there be developments in organization.

For this reason, there was and is an urgent need to return to the discussion about the relationship between the PCI and the class from a different angle, beyond the quantitative relation. What is required, in other words, is the test that a political situation can offer, a test carried out with different instruments. The types of analyses we have done of workers' struggles, of capital—I do not understand why we could not pull these off in the case of the working class. Our work on the rallying cry of the party in the factory is an appropriate way, at the class level, to make the link to the class struggle.

It is useless to define the Party-class relation in Italy as ambiguous: this does not serve anyone. The matter instead is to eliminate the obstacle of the reformist PCI before passing to organizations of a new type. The situation is favorable for doing this; the timetable we have chosen is suitable.

Regarding organizational-tactical resolutions, it must be said that the rallying cry of the PCI in the factory need not aim toward its realization as such, *but* to the elimination of the PCI at the mass level.[2] In any case, there is no danger of opportunism, because it would also have propaganda value at the mass level if we managed to reconstruct working-class self-organization *within the Party*. There may even be particular situations in which factory organizations emerge. After all, how can the possible breakup of the PCI be realized? It cannot be done without carving out the workers' slice from the PCI.

Even if there were a concrete deployment of the PCI in the factory, a reconstruction of its cells, I do not see anything negative in that. Instead, this would be a *positive* thing, because the moment of breakup can only happen at that level! Indeed, I would say that if a level of organization cannot be established inside of the PCI, this factor would complicate rather than clarify the

2. The Italian editors had inserted a question mark in brackets following "elimination." The preceding paragraph would appear to indicate that Tronti was proposing to eliminate the "reformist PCI" and not the Party as such.

The Weapon of Organization

landscape. Some comrades instead hope that this does not come to fruition—an unfounded hope.

For us, it is a matter of establishing the theme of the Party in the factory concretely at the organizational level: at the level, that is, of cadres. It has been a matter of accepting the leadership's challenge by producing a clear argument.

The need to reconstruct the PCI in the factory proceeds by two paths: 1) either social-democratization is blocked from below; or, 2) the reformist lid must be blown off. At this point, the splitting of the PCI would be a formidable element in the reconstruction of the class party. This is the *strategy*. The difficulties derive from one of our subjective weaknesses. The causes, to my eyes, are to be found in our enormous squandering of energy, in not considering the primary importance of this political level. If we had pushed the discussion of the Party forward beginning in 1960, we would not have lost so much time in useless work at the level of the PSI, leaving the PCI so alone that it has only now begun to worry about us. If we had managed to link our discourse to the Communist cadres earlier, and if we had linked the old revolutionary cadres to the new generation of workers, thereby ensuring continuity in the leading factory cadres, such a vacuum would not have built up between them. These days, we see that the old Communist cadres are still there, and that, going forward, we will need to butt heads with them, too. These days, it is useless to go looking for cadres of a new type, because they do not exist. They were born in the postwar period and connected to the PCI, which they believed to be revolutionary.

For this reason, our work must strive to rebuild the factory cadres, trying to bind them to the discourse on the Party, which has the possibility of becoming a mass discourse. I do not believe in this division between these two levels (cadres and the social level) or that the discourse [*on the PCI*] must only be carried into places where we find Party cadres. *The discourse on the PCI must be pitched at the mass, social level, without dividing the discourse on the Party from that other one: the one about struggles against the boss.* In other words, we should aim to better unite the two discourses so that we can obtain a better relationship with a series of new factory cadres. Then, it will be necessary to put these cadres into play in the developmental process of the workers' movement, which we must constantly keep in mind, while [*conversely*] taking for granted the autonomous destiny of the working class.

Single Party or Class Party?

(June 1965)

At a June 1965 conference organized by the Roman section of *Classe Operaia* at the Teatro dei Satiri, Tronti took up the theme of the "single" or "only" party, a proposal for uniting all the parties of the left that made by Giorgio Amendola, a representative of the PCI's right wing, and which had recently achieved a certain degree of hegemony in the Party's central committee. The debate included representatives from the youth sections of the PSIUP and PCI as well as Lucio Colletti.[1]

1. See note 41 in Raffaele Sbardella, "The NEP of *Classe Operaia* (1980)," trans. Daniel Spaulding, *Viewpoint Magazine*, January 28, 2016, https://www.viewpointmag.com/2016/01/28/ the-nep-of-classe-operaia.

I believe that when initiating a debate of this kind, we must first of all guard against a temptation: that of considering the theme that today goes under the name of the "single party" to be a false problem. The temptation, then, is to eliminate it immediately and move on to talk about something else. Instead, it is worth taking another route, considering this problem to be a real problem, one that exists objectively in the class situation in Italy, and which can be traced back to the need for a general reorganization, or general organizational reconstruction, of the Italian left. A problem of this kind clearly risks gathering a broad consensus immediately. Instead, the problem is that of considering what causes this process of reorganization, what makes it necessary; this allows us, instead, to examine certain different approaches. Among the many causes that can be mentioned, I will mention just two, which to me seem to be the fundamental ones: the first is connected to the level of class struggle in Italy today. The level of class struggle, in my opinion, has grown, has risen to a decisive level, one that makes it impossible for the organized political structures of the workers' movement to fully express this level of struggle by the class itself.

In other words, it is clear that the wave of working-class struggles that have since 1960 taken on a specific feature, which we can trace back to the basic feature of open working-class struggle that has a strongly anticapitalist content—this wave of working-class struggles, which so far has grown intermittently and threatens to continue growing for at least the coming months—clearly, this wave has not found an explicit form of expression in the currently existing political organization of the workers' movement. Specifically, we have seen that the conjunctural transition has itself set off a process of further division between the working class and the political party of the working class, for the basic reason that this thrust of working-class struggle, which had endured and grown within the conjuncture, did not find a political outlet adequate to the anticapitalist charge that it possessed. In other words, practically all of us emerged from the conjuncture with the precise impression that a formidable opportunity for general political struggle had been lost. *That is, the workers' movement's ability to attack the capitalist system in Italy had fallen short right when the system was showing particular, clear, and very distinct weaknesses.*

When we ask why this political opportunity was missed, we once again bump up against the problem of the party, or of the insufficiency of the current political structure of the workers' party in Italy. The reason why this opportunity was missed was because the workers' struggles, which carried out at least two phases of rather sharp attack on the system during the conjuncture, did not practically encounter the political party at any point along their way. They did not encounter it for a reason that then became clear at the end of the conjuncture: because *a direct relation between party and class no longer existed even at the organizational level* or because it had been largely cut off by the political developments of the past several years. Clearly, we discovered that the difference between union and party cannot but ultimately be a rather traditional one: one in which the union is able, quite rightly, to articulate the struggles and do so according to tactical measurements which strive to achieve specific economic objectives for the working class (and the union's role cannot go beyond this limit, which is an objective one, by virtue of its institutional character); and that the other role, of powerfully unifying all the struggles around common political objectives, could be fulfilled only by the party. And there is no need to speak of the party in general, but rather of the encounter that did not take place, the missed encounter between the workers' struggles on the one hand and the Communist Party on the other. I would say, then, that the primary reason why the process of political reorganization of the left in Italy has become necessary derives precisely from this, that is, from a growth of class consciousness in Italy, a consciousness also at the political level of class, and its lack of organization at the level of political party. In other words, a positive cause for this problem must be found. One that, as we know, is then resolved according to characteristics that are completely negative with respect to the causes…

The second cause that I would identify, with regard to the more or less necessary process of reorganizing the Italian left, concerns instead *the level*, we might say, *of capitalist initiative*. The level of capitalist initiative also had rather precise and articulated transitions within the conjuncture. At first, there was a moment of general uncertainty—among the leading political class, among the actual entrepreneurial stratum, and within the conjuncture itself. In the second phase of the conjuncture, instead, control was recovered by these two elements having been unified—the political class, or the political government, and the actual class of capitalists—a recovery of control over the entire mechanism of capitalist development in Italy, which ultimately allowed for a rather quick and painless exit from the economic conjuncture, and even a transition from it to the proposal of planning. The transition from the conjuncture to the plan was a rather precise transition that took place along moderate lines; and, the presence of moderate lines always indicates that the dominant class has achieved control over the economic structure.

However, at this point we are seeing another element of this situation, which also turns out to be positive. Because, if we look closely, we find that the start of capitalist planning in Italy is characterized by another very precise given fact. The capitalists' control over the entire mechanism of capitalist development still has its weak spots, and this weakness concerns its direct control over the movements of the working class. One historical feature, I would say, of the transition to planning in Italy is precisely that the capitalist side attempts this kind of transition without having achieved full and direct control over the working class, through directly working-class institutions. And this is not due to some deficiency or lack of compliance on the part of the workers' institutions, be they trade-union or political, but rather it is due to the separation that is too wide: between the unions, on the one hand, and the working class at the economic level, on the other; between the party, on the one hand, and the working class and its political level, on the other. Precisely this lack of a direct relation prevents, ultimately, the capitalist side from possessing full control over the movements of the working class itself. For these reasons, the plan's own approaches, and the various uncertainties from which it still suffers, should probably also be traced back to this basic problem, to the point that we find ourselves facing contemporary situations, such as that of the start of the plan in 1966, and the forecast of a struggle such as that of the metal-workers, for example—a contractual struggle, but one that concerns the backbone of the Italian working class that still is not reliably controlled even by the capitalists. To the point that we may find ourselves facing the start of the plan and at the same time a type of working-class struggle that is capable of repeating such intense processes of generalization as those of 1962, which in fact concerned the same contractual struggle by the metal-workers and metal-mechanics. Thus, the second reason why the reconstruction of the workers' movement in Italy is necessary depends also upon the capitalist initiative, which strives to take back direct control over the movements of the working class, even by reconstituting a direct relation between historical parties or institutions of the working class and movements of the class itself.

Having examined these two causes, we maintain that, indeed, in this case and within this situation, the theme of the single party must also, without a doubt, be grasped as an opportunity for open political struggle over the issue of the party. Only open political struggle over the issue of the party is clearly capable of putting the basic line and political content of the parties' own initiatives directly back into play. We have seen—we know this somewhat from experience, and somewhat from what we are seeing lately—that as soon as the issue of the party is touched, let alone that of the party's structure, the party machine, at that point the conversation about the political line of the party itself is put back into play for the first time. In other words, the entire function of the party as such, and its direct relations with the working class, are put back into play for the first time in global terms. In other words, a mechanism for protesting an entire political perspective is put back into play. In this sense, we must identify an initial positive feature of the single-party discourse, which is precisely the fact that it offers this political opportunity to call the entire perspective into question. It must certainly be acknowledged that there is a perfect consistency between the proposal of a single party and certain political lines that predate it, including in the line of the Italian Communist Party. We must not deny this consistency, *because it is more useful to admit it, and once admitted, it must be challenged and overturned.*

It is clear that the proposal of a single generic party, in the form of a unified socialist party, has only come after a set of steps that go back to the turn of 1944, to a certain role the Party had within the antifascist revolution, as it is called. These steps even go back to a certain theorization, in Italy in particular, of the historical bloc as such.[2] Working backward, we come to the fundamental turn, which is that of the popular fronts of 1936.[3] We can without a doubt identify a consistent policy of this kind. Its latest emergence has put the entire line back into play, and indeed it should revive the discussion of this entire process, this entire path. At this point, it is a matter of overthrowing this perspective entirely, and of proposing, at the very least, a different concept of working-class political unity. Today, we can say that the political unity of the working class exists as a problem, but the problem clearly is not one that can be resolved by unifying the Communist Party and other stumps of parties that are more or less socialist. It must not be understood in this horizontal and formal way, as it traditionally has been. If there is a problem of the political unity of the working class, this is first of all a vertical relation between the party and the working class: from this vertical relation everything else can then be born. Once this relation is reconstituted, we can then move on to fighting a certain type of social-democratic unification, cordoning it off to the right and reducing it to a minority fact in Italy, even reconstituting wider formations at the formal political level. But the condition for this—for this process to radically close off the right, and thus for it to have a directly anti-social-democratic function—is that this vertical relation between party and working class would first need to be reconstituted. And it is no coincidence that the problem of the party in the factory has come back into consideration almost simultaneously. In my opinion, it should be continually placed in contradiction with everything else, because the idea of bringing the party back into the factory—after it has been recognized that the party left the factory, and that it left following some very specific incidents in Italy in recent years—the idea of bringing the

2. A reference to Togliatti and the PCI's use of Gramsci's concept; see note above on "political bloc."

3. After the seventh congress of the Comintern in 1935, Communist parties were advised to form "popular fronts" with bourgeois parties in the fight against fascism. In France and Spain in 1936, these popular fronts clearly emerged; in Italy, however, nothing of the kind materialized until 1948, when the Communists and Socialists briefly aligned. The "turn of 1944" that Tronti refers to is the so-called "Salerno turn," in which Togliatti called for partisans to abandon the goal of anti-monarchical revolution and instead to unify with all national forces that opposed fascism.

party back into the factory as a single party is clearly the greatest political illusion that can be conceived. The party can re-enter the factory only if it is reintroduced directly as a class party. That is, if the unifying point is once again discovered at the workers' level, at the mass social workers' level. There is also a problem of unity at the level of the party, but this unity can only find its unifying center in the decisive movements of the Italian working class. It is around this objective nucleus that we need, if anything, to reintroduce the theme of political unity.

It's Not Time for Social Democracy, It's Time to Fight It for the First Time from the Left

(April 1966)

From October 1965 until May 1966, *Classe Operaia* suspended publication. Tronti had already begun to question the continued relevance of political intervention carried out in small groups isolated from the network of the PCI. During this period, in addition to work around the edges of the PCI, Tronti prepared *Workers and Capital* for publication. On the eve of the newspaper's return, he delivered a speech at the conference held in Florence to inaugurate the Centro Giovanni Francovich. This conference coincided with a meeting of the editors of the newspaper, during which Tronti proposed for the first time to close *Classe Operaia*, arguing that it had exhausted its purpose. The others present, Negri and Asor Rosa most vociferously, opposed the idea, and the newspaper continued publication, albeit irregularly, for another year. This text considers the center-left proposal of a social-democratic resolution to the ongoing political crisis in Italy. Tronti explores what opportunities that situation might yet offer for militants on the left.[1]

1. Thanks to Fabio Milana for his enlightening correspondence on this subject.

Right away, I would like to single out some causes for reflection on the political situation as it presents itself to us today. Indeed, this starting point will allow us to establish a set of tasks that are practical and which simultaneously pertain to work at other levels—historical, theoretical, research-related, and so on. I mention causes for reflection on the current political situation because it seems to me that there is quite a need for this today. We find ourselves facing a political situation that is full of movement and also rather complex in terms of its internal components. For this reason we are continually forced to review, to dynamically update, certain judgments we have made, even if on appearance it might seem that nothing of importance, nothing fundamental, is stirring in the general political process.

The first finding that emerges from an inspection of today's political situation—which we always tend to see as a class situation, first of all—is the following: we find ourselves facing an entire year of workers' struggles, which have an objective continuity among them, although it is tied to a certain peculiar trait they share, which is that of being on a completely trade-union terrain, of being exclusively contractual struggles. A set of circumstances has ensured that wall-to-wall maturation has taken place this year on this trade-union contractual terrain, which is why we find ourselves before a large part—perhaps even, in quantitative terms, the majority—of the working class today in practical struggle, at the same moment, at the same time. And this could be something that is not particular to this situation, because at other moments it could turn out that various parts of the working class may, by chance, find themselves waging a certain trade-union contractual struggle at the same time.

The more interesting aspect of this situation is, instead, the direct working-class response to this total struggle. This working-class response, I would say, has one characteristic that is new compared to what took place in the past. We are witnessing, after the conjunctural transition, two political outcomes, both of which are tangible, or visible to the naked eye. We already identified the first in a previous phase of our discourse, when we said that the conjuncture, apart from its economic tendency toward crises or pre-crises at the structural level, has also resulted in a greater unity between the capitalist stratum and the Italian political stratum. A greater unity, that is, between bosses and government.

The whole arc of the conjuncture was such that, at first, it seriously put this relation into crisis, and then, in the end, its unitary growth was restored: the approval by the bosses' stratum of the center-left's organic solution in Italy is also, at bottom, an outcome—political this time—of the conjunctural transition. This is one of the outcomes of the conjuncture at the political level. The other outcome that we can see—and we are seeing it precisely in this general wave of struggles—is a new type of unity, one with political significance, which has arisen within the Italian working class. Today, there is greater unity between the various parts of the Italian working class than existed before the conjuncture. In other words, we are witnessing the phenomenon of a pronounced massification of the struggles, their totally mass result, which is why we are seeing not only that the average strike rate is more than 90 percent, not only, irrespective of the contents of individual struggles in terms of their demands, that the workers' response to the strike is always nearly total. Not only are we seeing these things, but we are also witnessing an end to the famous "islands" onto which the open struggle once did not go.

At the beginning of the metal-workers' struggle, when we found ourselves before the majority of FIAT workers for the first time, we could all see how a leap had occurred in terms of what the struggle yielded, and how this leap had definitively unified different roles that only a short time before could have been considered distinct. Even after 1962, one could have made a distinction between workers' vanguards, with their responsive logic that did not always coincide with the general logic of the working-class movement in Italy, and the rest of the mass, which also had its own logic. Today we are seeing that this difference between vanguard and mass has practically disappeared, and that there is a single logic for the whole working class, one that can be defined as the "massification" of struggles.

We clearly do not know how long the massification of struggles can last at this level: some of its symptoms could even make one think that the process cannot endure for long. The events of the metal-workers' struggle—which is clearly the central point of the entire process, the most significant, the one to which we should pay the most attention—have so far given an indication of general mass struggle, but one which, given the rather long continuation of the same struggle with too many articulations, could give rise to some blowbacks.

I believe that both the sections of the working class that are lagging furthest behind as well as those that are most advanced could be subject, for opposite reasons, to some blowbacks from the struggle, if this struggle continues to be waged as it has been up to now—in other words, entirely over the long term, with considerable intervals between one moment of generalization and the next, and so on. Indeed, some movements of the FIAT workers, above all at Mirafiori, can help us to foresee some of these blowbacks.[2]

The fact we most need to focus on, at this point, is that of the massification of the struggles. The fact is, that today, the trade-union struggle has achieved

2. Mirafiori was FIAT's largest factory complex, located in Turin.

a mass level that it had never achieved before now. It is precisely this level that must be taken as the basis for judging today's political situation, today's class situation. This new level was clearly not born of a leap in the contents of this struggle, in terms of demands, compared to preceding struggles. We cannot say that, politically speaking, there has been a leap in the trade-union demands that justifies the working-class pressure, the working-class unity that exists around these more advanced demands. This cannot be said. Yet, despite this—despite these demands not being more advanced than those which came before—the new level of working-class participation in these struggles is, without a doubt, higher than it was previously.

The basic reason for this, in my opinion, must indeed go back once again to the conjunctural transition, again to this moment of crisis in the structures of Italian capitalism, which allowed us for the first time to glimpse the possibility of subjectively and politically carrying out an operation that would rupture, this time politically, not the system in general but the structures of production, right as they were surging in Italy during the same period. Clearly, on the working-class terrain, an opportunity of this kind must be sparked, I repeat, at the mass level—in other words, the opportunity (focusing again above all on this moment of merely contractual, trade-union struggles) to keep the political stability of the system itself permanently on the table. That is to say, if it is true that the conjuncture had been provoked by a cycle of workers' struggles conducted largely at the trade-union level, then now it becomes possible for a new level, a new cycle, a new wave of workers' struggles to arise, one that reproduces the scheme of the crisis and which probably would cause a deeper crisis, to the point of having an impact on the political stability of capitalist power.

If this is the rationale for this new wave, this new level in working-class struggle, what are its effects? In my opinion, one effect at least is trade-union unity. Trade-union unity, in other words, must not be seen as what provoked this massification of struggles, but rather as the very result of this massification. That is to say, it is true that at this level, when unity is accomplished in the upper echelons, it can cause a positive reaction at the workers' level as well, in terms of the struggle being relaunched in a united way. It is also true, however, that the primary reason for the achievement of this trade-union unity lies in the fact that the workers' struggle leapt to this new level, which is a mass level, and which also prevents trade-union division in the upper echelons. I believe that, today, at the workers' level, there are some very clear ideas about trade-union unity. At the mass workers' level, it cannot be ruled out that this trade-union unity may be something positive, something which plays a real role within the struggles, as it presents the workers' front as being united, albeit formally, before that of the bosses. Hence, as a result, in this phase, trade-union unity must be used rather than combatted. Indeed, one should check to see where this is more or less true, but I believe that this is the indication that can be extracted from the general situation.

In addition to trade-union unity, we know that there is a more basic process going on today: the reappearance of the problem of the single union, that is, of organic trade-union unity. I think it is no coincidence that right now we are, once again, discussing this problem, and that we are again speaking of this perspective in a rather concrete way. Not only are all the unions, especially the Catholic one, with ACLI on its "left," disposed to work toward this prospect, but I would say that here too, perhaps at the workers' level, if this process goes forward, there is the will to let it happen.[3]

Again, we should discuss to what extent this is true. I am speaking of matters as they seem to me, although it is also possible that such things are not true. But to me it seems that even if the prospect of organic trade-union unity were clarified, were concretized, there would not then be a refusal of this prospect at the workers' level. If anything, once again, people would line themselves up at this new level to use the single trade union. We know how functional a prospect of this kind can be for capital, and that this particular prospect may receive support from the advanced capitalists anticipating control over the movements of labor-power, over the movements of the working class, which, clearly, caged in an organic trade-union unity, could be better maneuvered. If, then, we were to consider that the entire project of CISL and a part of the Catholic political stratum, to generally encage bargaining, goes hand in hand with this organic trade-union unity—a single trade union and a framework agreement are two things that go well together—then we would see how many dangers may exist in a prospect of this kind. Because it is also true that this prospect makes basic sense at the workers' level: the trade-union division is a fact that instinctually disgusts the workers, not only because they refuse any division between the organizations that are called, albeit formally, to lead the struggle, but for a deeper reason, one that is perhaps more political: because, I believe, there is a greater opportunity for the workers to gain truly direct control over the single trade union than over several unions. If in the coming period there is the need for a further use of the trade-union level, the trade-union struggles, and thus the trade-union institutions as well—if this is true, clearly it must be easier to use one than to use three.

I would add a further justification for this, which may be an even deeper one, one that is even more political: the fact that organic trade-union unity

---

3. The Catholic trade-union confederation is the Confederazione Italiana Sindacati Liberi (CISL). The Associazioni Cristiane Lavoratori Italiani (ACLI) is a conglomeration of Catholic social-welfare agencies.

could truly divide, once and for all, the tasks of the union from those of the party. Today, everyone opposes the transmission belt. I believe that even the workers at the mass level oppose the transmission belt, for a reason that is very different from that of the trade-union functionary.[4] The workers refuse the transmission belt because the party is no longer seen as capable of transmitting anything to the union. Thus, it is not due to a political prejudice, saying that these are two institutions which are formally and democratically distinct, concerns which, I believe, interest no one at the workers' level. But it is precisely for this reason: because the party-union relation today is such that there is no longer transmission of a political line from the party to the union, but instead, if anything, sometimes exactly the reverse is happening—there is a unionization of the party, which perhaps derives from the ties that still exist between union and party. A dissolution of the ties between union and party could lead each of these two institutions to their specific tasks. The situation of the trade-union institutions, which indeed we are extracting from today's level of mass struggle, can be traced back—actually, in my opinion, it must be traced back—to another level, that which is more directly political. Namely, to the entire reconstruction underway in the workers' movement, which violently shakes the historical parties of the workers in Italy.

It seems to me that the themes of trade-union unity and the single union are tightly bound to the prospects of social-democratic unification. They have also been bound together by contemporary political journalism but I believe they are connected for deeper reasons. When speaking of the reformist restructuring of the workers' movement, today there are, in my opinion, two lines at play. One starts, I believe, from a still-minority part of the Catholic movement, from CISL, from ACLI, and from the Christian-Democrat left. This one sees trade-union unity as the premise of a larger unity between the political parties; those who are focused on the single trade union are the same ones who, from there, want then also to begin to recover a greater unity, in a manner that diverges even from the current structure of the Catholic party in Italy, even from the current social-democratic solution. I believe that some Catholic forces in Italy today may have the same attitude toward their party as some forces on the left—the mistaken left—may have toward the Communist Party: that is, that the necessity of smashing the centralized, bureaucratic machine of the party is clearly the fundamental, primordial fact, the one to which all other needs must clearly be subordinated. The attempt to begin from trade-union unity to then reach a broader political unity that smashes the very structure of the Catholic party, such as it exists today—this

4. The "transmission belt" refers to the notion that the Communist Party's directives are disseminated to the masses via mediating institutions such as the trade union.

is clearly something that, I repeat, is still only imagined by limited sectors of the Catholic political stratum.

Then, there is the other line of reformism that seeks to restructure the whole workers' movement: that of social-democratic unification. Social-democratic unification apparently overturns the other process, saying: first, political unity, unity between parties, and then, on this basis, a trade-union unity that can also be attributed to these parties, a socialist trade-union unity, which then also must, by its nature, point toward an organic trade-union unity, just as social-democratic unification at the political level points toward the organic unification of all the parties of the left. This second perspective emerges today from the socialist right, from the Social Democrats, and I believe perhaps also from a minor part of the capitalist stratum, the big capitalist stratum, who see this as a long-term prospect, as a solution to the problem of political stability in Italy, which they frantically seek. The social-democratic unification must be followed with close attention; it is a game that clearly stretches much further than what the Socialists and the Social Democrats expect from the unification between their two parties, such as they present themselves today in Italy.[5] It tends toward the recovery of an organic unity at another level that would propose—it was their term, but it is also the real concept—that would propose a new alternative to the Catholic party in the management of power.

The problem that we must pose for ourselves today is this: whether for Italy the hour of social democracy has not arrived, and whether this is not beginning to become concrete for us, this prospect of a social-democratic management of the state, which then is nothing but a socialist management of capital, according to the formulae which we hold dear, even if they remain very difficult to break down and explain. Over the long term, I believe, we can consider a prospect of this kind, in Italy, to be real. There are a series of reasons that today play in its favor. The latest crisis of the government has caused a leap in maturation for this perspective, and not only because it demonstrated the remarkable fragility of the Catholic political stratum and perhaps even a certain attrition of their ability to manage power.[6] This is apparent now in

5. Tronti here refers to the merger between the PSI and PSDI, which would be officially announced in October 1966 with the creation of the PSU.

6. During negotiations to replace the fallen Moro government with a new governing coalition of the center-left, Antonio Segni, the President of the Republic and a right-wing Christian Democrat critical of the Party's alliance with the PSI, took steps toward appointing a rightist government that would sideline the PSI. Moro was able to entice the PSI to rejoin its coalition with the DC under a banner of more modest reforms than previously attempted, and the second center-left government was solidified by the end of July. In early 1967, evidence that an even deeper crisis had taken place emerged when the Italian weekly *L'Espresso* published excerpts from secret files on leftists in government amassed by Giovanni De Lorenzo, Chief of Staff of the Army, former commanding officer of the Servizio Informazioni Forze Armate (SIFAR), and former head of the Carabinieri. These files included one on the new President of the Republic, PSDI leader Giuseppe Saragat. De Lorenzo was forced to step down (although he would be elected to Parliament with the Monarchist Party and later joined the neo-fascist Movimento Sociale Italiano). Following a 1969

the internal affairs of the DC, in the differences between groups, and in the basic absence of a strategic vision, which, despite being very rigorously established at the time of the famous congress in Naples, was not then pursued with the same speed, with the same courage demanded by certain sections of the Italian capitalist stratum, those which are perhaps more influential, perhaps more advanced.[7] Clearly, there is the attrition suffered by all parties in power, by all political strata in state management who get involved in long-term solutions, and it happens also in other countries—it is enough to see how the conservatives in England used up their patrimony of technical knowledge concerning the structure of state mechanisms, concerning the very structure of society, finding themselves then unable to continue managing power at all, and needing to pass this management into other hands.[8]

The other factor that plays in social democracy's favor is the broad maturation of Italian capitalism, which can no longer afford these continually recurring crises on the formal political terrain, these crises that make capital's life difficult at the level of international relations, at the level of relations with the other parts of international capital. Today, Italian capital is integrated into the international structures of capitalism to such an extent—above all, but not only, into the European structures, with the collection of mechanisms created through the various common markets, through capitalist integration associations—that it can no longer afford (and it is continually reproached for this by international capital) to halt the general development of international capital at certain moments for its own domestic reasons, which clearly needs to be resolved within a certain period, and which international capital forces the Italian capitalists to resolve. Once again, tied to this is the problem of the rather fragile political stability of Italian capitalism, in basic contrast to its maturation at the level of the structures of production, at the level of the economic structure, a maturation which I believe proceeds with a certain speed, even in fact with a certain regularity.

The last factor, perhaps the underlying reason, which also flows in the direction of a social-democratic solution, is the need for control over the

parliamentary inquiry into the "SIFAR scandal," it emerged that in 1964, De Lorenzo had drawn up an extensive plan, called the "Solo Plan," in which the Carabinieri, in collaboration with sectors of the military under De Lorenzo's influence, would stage a coup, imprisoning prominent leftists (on whom they had ample files) on Sardinia. During the aforementioned governmental crisis of June 1964, De Lorenzo had even given orders to begin preparations for implementing the plan at a local level. At the same time, then-President Segni, also seeking a rightist solution to the government crisis, caused some alarm when he summoned De Lorenzo to the presidential palace at a moment when Moro's negotiations had broken down. Although these revelations would not have been known to Tronti, they serve to underscore the high degree of friction around the ruling bloc. See Ginsborg, *A History of Contemporary Italy*, 276-79. See also Spencer M. Di Scala, *Renewing Italian Socialism: Nenni to Craxi* (New York: Oxford University Press, 1988), 152-54; and Leonard Weinberg, "The Red Brigades," in *Democracy and Counterterrorism: Lessons from the Past*, eds. Robert J. Art and Louise Richardson (Washington, D.C.: United States Institute of Peace Press, 2007), 25-62, 45.

7. At the 1962 DC conference in Naples, Moro called for a center-left program; see note above.

8. In October 1964 the Conservative Party in Britain was defeated for the first time in thirteen years by the Labour Party, which in the March 1966 general elections increased their majority hold on government.

movements of the working-class struggles, over these continually recurring waves of struggle that are characteristic of Italian capitalism but which cannot be tolerated for long by international capitalism. Control over the workers clearly becomes much easier, much more possible, when there is a real chance of achieving a social-democratic management of power overall. This has always been one of the reasons why first the government and then the state were passed into social-democratic hands in Europe: social democracy could guarantee capital greater control over the movements of labor-power because of the institutional forms it already had in its possession, because of the type of relationship that it had with the workers through the unions and through its own party. In Italy, too, a problem of this kind may reappear: the passage of power into social-democratic hands to guarantee a process by which capital recovers stable control over the movements of labor-power and thus a stable capitalist control over the recurring waves of working-class struggles.

These are the reasons—and they are rather strong reasons—why we can, with a certain degree of probability, count on this process of social-democratization, not only of the workers' movement, but of the very political structures of the state, the capitalist political structures in Italy. At this point, in my opinion, in order to keep hold of the main thread in this process, we should distinguish between two moments in the social-democratic unification. At its outset, this process will clearly produce a further division of the workers' movement into its two classical parts: it is certainly no coincidence that the two parties, Socialist and Social-Democratic, still today exclude the Communist Party, both on principle and as a political tactic. Initially, we must expect a further division of the workers' movement, as it is being organized today: in other words, we must not imagine a rapid, complete unification, but, if anything, an immediate radicalization of the two parts into which the workers' movement is divided. This radicalization will then need to be consolidated in a broader unity; indeed, it is easy to progress from this radicalization toward a series of forms that would transcend this initial division, that would recover instead—through a series of steps that may also be actual transitions, through struggles, through crises of the state, through abrupt leaps—the need for a broader unity. Indeed, at a subsequent moment, it is also quite easy to imagine that this social-democratic unification will become a pole of attraction for a wider political unity, one that may engage the entire workers' movement, and probably the entire Communist Party.

If these forecasts are permissible, at this point I believe that it would be an error to unify these two problems: that of the initial division between these two sections of the workers' movement, and that of their possible subsequent unification. Because if we were to immediately unify these two moments and assume that, today, we already find ourselves facing a real unification of the workers' movement—and thus a social-democratic resolution of the classical type, which excludes only marginal shreds of organizations, historical minorities, revolutionary only in form and in speech, a resolution that recuperates the entire workers' movement, and thus, as such, approaches the total management of power—if we were to assume that this process was proceeding, I believe that, in the meantime, there would be empty years in terms of our political activity, that is, there would be nothing for us to do in practice. Secondly, we would be assuming this process was proceeding for the sole reason that this process has taken place via these forms in other countries, adopting a sort of political determinism that is very much alive among many people today.

Having instead glimpsed this prospect, of these two moments snapping together to form the process of social-democratic unification, I believe that, within these moments, we must find a political terrain, the grounds for taking a positive initiative. This must be done in a way that does not lock one behind the other, with the type of logic that European social democracy always had, which has brought about the situation in which the workers' movement finds itself today, in the countries of advanced capitalism: on the one hand, complete social democracy in the organized workers' movement, and on the other, historical minorities, absolutely incapable of countering the social-democratic management of power with another force, an equivalent political power. We must therefore emphasize, in our political work within the working-class left in Italy, the need for a transitional program—transitional not in the sense of the transition to socialism, because we never use these words in this traditional sense, but transitional in terms of the party struggle, in the struggle within the workers' movement for certain solutions over others.

It is possible that, indeed, at some later date, we will all need to consolidate ourselves around a certain social-democratic victory on the general plane. At that point, obviously, the necessary conclusions will be drawn; at that moment, it will come down to seeing clearly how one must act in that situation. In other words, if the social-democratic resolution were to practically and even organically unify the entire left, the complete workers' movement as such would then put itself forward as the alternative to the management of power. I believe it is useless at this point to think about political work in these hypothetical terms. It is useful at the level of theoretical discourse, of theoretical analysis, which should show us what comes after the political work of today. But on the political terrain, on the other hand, a hypothesis of this kind does not yet offer positive directions for our work.

We find positive directions instead only if we return to this initial moment of the social-democratic unification process, and if we grasp the elementary fact that today is plain for all to see: that, clearly, if the social-democratic unification is being accomplished today, it is an element of further division on the left, one that will exacerbate relations, to a perhaps still incalculable degree, between the two sections of the workers' movement in Italy. It will radicalize these two positions, and it will do so for a certain period of time. It is within this period that I would call our attention to political work: within this period, in my opinion, there is nothing to do but oppose the rightward social-democratic unification with a leftward unification, one that is already sparking in various parts of the workers' movement, and one that might be able to block the total social-democratic unification process, the integrated social-democratic resolution in Italy. This would mark the first political experience in which social democracy fails—not in the management of power, because this is a historical failure that I do not believe needs further demonstration (by "management of power," I mean the chance of the social-democratic resolution breaking the capitalist structures of production along with capital's state-political structures), but the social-democratic resolution failing even before arriving at this political management of capital, the failure of the possibility itself of the social-democratic resolution to the crisis of capital.

If we first saw this possibility, and that capitalism in Italy has an absolute need for this social-democratic resolution, and if we then managed to nip this approach to managing power in the bud, then a major crisis would be launched within Italian capitalist development—and precisely for the reasons that we outlined, due to its integration into the international capitalist structures. Right here, a major crisis would open up in capitalism in general. I believe that, if there is an immediate goal on which we should focus, today it is precisely this failure of the social-democratic resolution before it is even able to organize itself as an integrated management of power on behalf of the capitalists.

How do we nip this social-democratic solution in the bud? The overall situation of the workers in Italy, if considered in terms of the level of class struggle that we mentioned earlier, is basically quite favorable. For the first time in an advanced capitalist society, a social-democratic solution that aspires to the overall management of power is found incapable of gathering the entire workers' movement as it has been organized; it is found incapable of recovering a major part of the workers' movement, not because it has been subjectively refused—at least in the upper echelons—but because of a complex of objective contradictions. Whence is born the opportunity for a political experience of a new type in Italy. Social democracy, and a mature social democracy, which directly seeks the management of capitalist state power, does not manage to funnel into itself, institutionally, the entire organizational network of the workers' movement. For the first time, social democracy does not find itself confronted with a minority at the margins of the movement, but with a great political movement that is itself already organized. Clearly, at this point, if a wedge is driven between these two movements, within the process of integrated social-democratization, then social democracy's passage to the management of power becomes no longer possible, precisely because it fails to achieve majority control over the entire workers' movement, which is the bare minimum it requires if it actually expects to manage power. We would have before us, in other words, a long period—or perhaps not so long, perhaps even short, because, I repeat, we keep in mind that abrupt leaps in the movement can accomplish not greater division but greater unity. In any case, we can count on some sort of period like this if we grasp the development of a social-democratic position in this way, through this perspective. This is perhaps the political resolution that offers the best opportunities for concrete, practical work.

What is left, after all this? There is, once again, something that needs to be experienced historically for the first time. Grasping the development of social democracy in a country such as Italy, in which political stability could probably only be achieved at a certain point through a socialist type of management of power, means concretely keeping open a set of perspectives that are able to go beyond the opportunities the situation offers today. It means, first of all, preventing what most needs to be prevented: the political stabilization of the system over the very long term; in other words, at least in Italy, it means persistently keeping open this continual uncertainty about this possible general management of power, this possible control over the structures of production, over the movements of labor-power, and so on—it means keeping a situation open, before anything.

In other words, I would suggest a negative rather than a positive outcome for this process. I am not saying that if we prevent the social-democratic resolution and if we keep the workers' movement divided, without assuming the integrated social-democratic unification of capital—I am not saying that this opens the revolutionary process; I am saying that it does not close it. And this is quite important, because, in my opinion, at this point, the situation in Italy is such that the first problem, the immediate political objective, is no longer that of opening the process, but rather of not closing it, of ensuring that political stability in Italy is not over the long term recovered—something that was accomplished in every point of advanced capitalism in Europe, as well as outside of Europe—because this effectively would mean the end of all political work, by us or by anybody, and it would indeed mean the classical recuperation, the recuperation that is even traditional in Italy, with the workers' struggles that unfolded here during previous historical experiences.

This is because, in view of the still-negative task that we have before us, perhaps only at a later moment will we be able to take an additional step forward in organization. If rightward unification has a leftward unification as its repercussion even from the viewpoint of the workers' political organizations, then we will in the meantime achieve this first objective of not closing the process in Italy. But we will need to set off again from there to carry the problems of organization onto the most advanced terrain achieved by the struggles, to the point of making social democracy itself a minority movement within the overall workers' movement formation, and directly overturning the classical situation of the big capitalist countries. In other words, we are hypothesizing a development of the class situation in Italy that does not see social democracy on the one hand and a revolutionary historical minority on the other, but rather one that sees exactly the opposite. At its limit, it sees, on the one hand, social democracy as a minority element of the movement, itself being a historical, reformist minority, and, on the other hand, it sees the bulk of the movement organized politically. Only then, at that point, can the revolutionary process be declared open, and no longer in the negative sense, but in the positive sense, with a strategy and a tactic of open upheaval. And with this hypothesis, basically a rather optimistic one, I will close this first part of the discussion.

Within and Against

(May 1967)

At the end of October 1966, the first edition of *Workers and Capital* was published by Einaudi Editore. Shortly thereafter, Tronti decided to close *Classe Operaia*, and its final issue was released the following March. Some of the comrades reconvened in Florence from April 29 to May 1 for the "First Seminar on the Political Composition of the Class" at the Centro Giovanni Francovich, and Tronti closed the seminar with the following presentation. This text, which subsequently appeared in the autumn issue of the journal *Giovane Critica*, proposed to use an old tactic—working not only within the Communist Party but within a social-democratic movement, even within the state itself—for an end to which it had not yet been put: to smash the capitalist state machine.

I will attempt to look at the same problems that have been treated in the previous talks from a slightly different angle, trying in a certain way to advance the discourse that we have produced on these things so far, including the discourse contained in the "final issue" of *Classe Operaia*. We have said that we are preparing to situate some perspectives and working hypotheses in view of the 1970s. This entails three levels of discourse: 1) analysis of recent events in the class struggle; 2) a forecast of the coming terrain of these struggles; 3) and something that should be extracted from the latter, the elaboration of a provisional political conduct. This third one is perhaps precisely what has been missing so far in the discussion, and perhaps this is what limits the conversation and, indeed, what prevents us from seeing where this conversation can then lead. For us, provisional political conduct means, precisely because we want to grasp the scale of the 1970s, a *long-term* provisional political conduct—provisionality here applied not to the short term of the struggle, but to a term that is perhaps rather long.

Regarding the first theme, the analysis of recent events in the class struggle, we find ourselves confronted with the necessity of reconstructing twenty years of workers' struggles. This reconstruction, it must immediately be said, still remains to be done. It must be put onto the agenda according to a new measurement, indeed, an international measurement of the class struggle (and this is, at bottom, one of the novelties of this seminar, with respect to our past conversations as well): to reconstruct, in other words, the terrain of the class struggle after the Second World War. In this sense, it is also a matter of critically judging some of the attempts we made before in the newspaper. One of the limits was precisely that, in large part, its reconstruction of the two decades of class struggle focused principally, and in some cases exclusively, on Italy. This was a limit that prevented us, in our forecast, from grasping the scale of the problems beyond the narrow margins of strictly national capitalist initiatives.

There was also, however, another limit, one still greater than this, in my opinion, that consisted in relying mainly on the *immediate* application of what we have called the "strategic overturning" between the working class and capital. That is, in the reconstruction we made of the last twenty years of workers' struggles, we attempted to make this operate mechanically and immediately, this guiding hypothesis, which clearly remains a guiding hypothesis for all the research that we do: namely, the historical-theoretical-political precedence of the movements of the working class with respect to the movements of capital. We find ourselves instead, now, before the necessity of discovering some *concrete mediations* when applying this guiding criterion to the history of workers' struggles, concrete mediations that manage to grasp historically specific points and moments that are tied to a precise epoch of the class struggle and to a cycle of capital and its political initiatives. When we confront this problem more closely, we realize that only after and on the basis of these experiences of the 1960s in Italy have we truly understood something rather simple, even though the comprehension of it turns out—and it is enough just to say this in passing—to be difficult to communicate externally. The fact, in other words, that the linchpin of this whole current of workers' struggles, which grabbed hold of the entire postwar period in a practical way, which demonstrated an intuitive understanding of this period—that this current had the struggle *over* the wage, and therefore *over* profit, as its unifying center. I use these terms, specifically—*over* the wage instead of *for* the wage, *over* profit instead of *against* profit—precisely because, even before considering the subjective dimension of the struggles, it is a matter of judging the real terrain on which these struggles took place. The real terrain is exactly this: the wage on one side, profit on the other. The Italian conjuncture of 1964–65 has posed for us once again this problem of the political result of the struggles, thus representing for all of us a sort of critical summary of the conjuncture of international capital that has endured over the last twenty years. It has already been said that this enduring conjuncture hinges on the problem of the "cost of labor," which comes to the fore as a contradiction of capitalist development. It hinges, therefore, on the problems concerning so-called "cost-push" inflation, and above all the type of creeping inflation that starts from an aggravated wage dynamic.

We find ample evidence of this in the most advanced consciences of international capital. And, indeed, we can cite Carli, someone whom we regularly consult in these cases, who in some recent "Viennese Reflections of a Governor of the Central Bank," from November 1966, expressed himself in these terms: "The annual report of the International Monetary Fund affirms that the persistence of inflation derives in large measure from the inability to otherwise resolve the conflict between the demands of different social groups, each one in struggle against the others to win a greater portion of income." This leads to an initial conclusion: that the international economic situation is dominated by basic tendencies toward increasing costs and prices. Therefore, and this is verbatim, "in the two decades of 1947–66, in all the industrialized countries, the elements of rigidity within the economic system have increased."[1] At a subsequent conference, in April 1967 in Washington at the American Bankers Association, he again speaks of the price mechanism and the income mechanism as the central elements of an extremely delicate

---

1. Guido Carli was the governor of the Banca d'Italia from 1960-75. Tronti here refers to the text of a speech delivered by Carli in Vienna, published as "Riflessioni di un Governatore di Banca centrale" [Reflections of a governor of the central bank], *Bancaria: mensile dell'Associazione Bancaria Italiana* 22, no. 11 (1966): 1301-09, 1301 and 1302.

international economic situation. He denounces the failure to achieve reasonable stability on this terrain, and then, doing a modicum of historical analysis, he continues with praise for what he calls the "virtuous circle" between growing incomes and growing domestic production as one of the discoveries—perhaps the greatest discovery, from the capitalist viewpoint—of this epoch of the class struggle. In some cases, this circle is broken by the aggravation of one of the elements, the income mechanism, which then has its immediate reflection in the price mechanism. The causes are found either in a boom of investments or in what Carli calls, and what in general is correctly called, a *wage explosion*.[2] The concept of the wage explosion stands at the center of the class dynamic over the last twenty years and thus accounts for a large part of the international political-economic situation.

Another text, by De Meo concerning productivity and the distribution of income in Italy during the period of 1951–63, a text that was widely cited at that conference in Fiuggi on the incomes policy, provides the following data: analogous structural changes would have occurred in the economy of the United States during the years 1934–43 and 1949–57 (for a period of seventeen years) and in the Italian economy during the years 1951–61 (a period that covers eleven years).[3] The difference is that, in Italy, notwithstanding the shorter length of the period under consideration, the income from labor per employee, what is called the price of labor, grew more substantially, by 89.4 percent, while in the United States over the period cited, it increased by 66.8 percent. On the other hand, the income from capital-enterprise per thousand units of capital employed, what is called the price of capital, grew by 12.6 percent in Italy and by 24.2 percent in the United States. In both countries, the ratio between income per unit of capital-enterprise and income of labor experienced a sharp decline, this too being more accentuated in Italy, where it fell by 40.7 percent, as compared to the United States, where it fell by 28.7 percent. I cite these data to say, for now, something extremely simple: over the eleven years mentioned here, which are at the center of the two decades that we are evaluating, a process has taken place that is analogous to what had taken place in the United States immediately after the great crisis and the great capitalist initiative that followed the crisis.

This is an extremely delicate matter, one that must be studied in order to see, in concrete terms, what political effects it has had. What is clear to us is

2. See Guido Carli, "Monetary Policy and Economic Stability: An International View," in American Bankers Association, *Proceedings of a symposium on money, interest rates and economic activity: Thursday, April 6, 1967, Sheraton-Park Hotel, Washington, D.C.* (New York: The Association, 1967), 134-49. Carli describes the "virtuous circle" on 139 and the "wage explosion" on 141.

3. Giuseppe De Meo was an Italian statistician. The article cited here was published in English as "Productivity and the distribution of income to factors in Italy (1951-63)," *PSL Quarterly Review* 19, no. 76 (1966): 42-71. Confindustria held a conference on "incomes policy" in Fiuggi from May 20-22, 1966.

that it is a matter of finding some new causes, today, for the cyclical capitalist crises. New causes that, clearly, no longer correspond to those ancient and traditional ones, still so often cited, which date back to a period before the great crisis of U.S. capitalism, and therefore to before the general crisis of international capitalism. The truth is that the terms of the cyclical crises within capital have changed, and so the causes that have given rise to these cyclical crises have also changed. This must not lead us to excesses of economism and then to catastrophic conceptions of a new type that see in the economic contradictions of capital the fundamental impetus for its coming dissolution. We start from the principle that capital interests us as a historical system of the reproduction of the working class. We must hold firmly onto this thesis. The analysis that we are conducting of capitalism does not interest us as the analysis of capitalism but rather as a moment of the reproduction of the working class at the international level. The cyclical crisis, and therefore the conjunctural crisis, under these circumstances, becomes for us a moment of growth, or a leap, in working-class political organization. The analysis of the crisis is for us the analysis of this moment of a leap in working-class organization, and not the analysis of the crisis or its causes per se.

When we proceed, then, to inspect this new form of the capital cycle, we see that there has been precisely and only this as its basis: *a working-class choice of the wage*, a working-class choice of the wage as the terrain of struggle. This involves two movements, at once consecutive and simultaneous.

The first movement takes the great capitalist initiative at its word. It uses and intensifies the Keynesian revolution, which is above all a revolution of incomes, as it is very often and perhaps correctly called, and which coincides with the discovery of capitalist society. The revolution of incomes, the Keynesian revolution, is directly tied to the moment in which capital discovers its own society. It discovers it conceptually, theoretically, and hence presents itself with concrete possibilities for dominating it. It is precisely this type of capitalist discovery that had set the income mechanism in motion, based on its own intrinsic needs. There was a point, a moment, when capital had this material need of setting the incomes mechanism in motion again, the mechanism that had been blocked by a series of secondary contradictions in the connective, productive, and social tissue of national and international capital. And, at a certain point, it took the great crisis, and a very powerful theoretical realization by capital regarding this great crisis, to unblock it. Hence the profound insight that putting the incomes mechanism back into motion—in other words, focusing on a revolution of incomes—would resolve capital's own contradictions. So, capital's rediscovery of the wage at this point is a very important historical rediscovery and also one that is wonderful to study from the historical viewpoint. What does it mean that, at a certain point, capital rediscovers the wage? Earlier we said that the workers choose the wage. But, before this working-class choice of the wage, there had been a *capitalist rediscovery of the wage* as a dynamic moment of the total structure of capitalist society and as a possible way to achieve overall control over this social structure. The capitalist rediscovery of the wage coincides with the conscious use of social labor-power, which had been expressed in other ways during other epochs of the class struggle, and which from this moment begins to be expressed mainly in this form: the use of social labor-power as the use of the wage by capital, of the wage mechanism as incomes mechanism, which then sets not only the income from labor but also the income from capital itself moving again. Revolution of incomes means precisely that both of the fundamental incomes are put back into motion. Both are intensely invigorated and exit from the blind alley in which, up until that moment, they had been stuck. It is from this moment that the working class—that mobile engine of capitalist development, as we call it—becomes *consciously* utilized, as a matter of fact, in what now begins to take shape as the plan of capital.

There is a second movement that must be emphasized, and it is the refusal that the workers make, simultaneously or perhaps after this initiative by capital (and let us recall that when we speak of working-class movements, we are speaking of objective movements), of the general social interest, which was the ideological form in which those capitalist discoveries were clothing themselves. In other words, at the moment in which society, the social nexus, the social fabric, becomes a conscious conquest of capital, from that moment forward, an opposing mechanism is set into motion: a working-class refusal of this sociality of capital and an aggravation of the particularistic element in the working class.

At the same time, other events were happening at the institutional-political level. We are speaking of the years between 1920 and 1930. These events were fascism and antifascism, which helped to intensify, on one side, the capitalists' choice of the society, and, on the other, the working-class refusal of this sociality of capital. In this sense, a carefully prepared research project could show how, for example, the totalitarian solution at the level of the state—fascism, Nazism, etc.—served an ideological purpose in this process of the international renewal of capitalist development, before and after the great crisis.[4] All of this worked mechanically, but in an ideological sense. In other words, these major institutional events were superimposed over this fundamental discovery by capital, which was also working in its own way. Firstly, with the authoritarian solution being extraneous to the

---

4. With "great crisis" Tronti refers to the Great Depression.

new economic policy of capital. Secondly, with the capture of the workers' movement at levels that were more backward, in politico-ideological terms, than those of the past. These two processes are, at bottom, one and the same. And how can this be shown? It can be shown, for example, that this capitalist rediscovery of the wage—this reliance on the wage dynamic to put the incomes mechanism back into motion, and starting from there to reclaim control over society—was something that especially concerned capital's choice of democracy. It was blocked in those places where the choice of democracy was not made explicit, and, by contrast, it began to develop from the moment when the democratic choice was made in other places, that is, after the overthrow of the totalitarian regimes.

We have some rather telling facts on this point. From the work of Ruggero Spesso, published in *Critica Marxista*, on the dynamic of wage gains before and after the founding of the Republic, we can extract these data: for wage gains, the most significant periods (his discussion concerns only Italy) were 1920–22, 1946–47, and 1960–65. Between 1946 and '47 the wage reduction that had taken place from 1923 onward was recovered in full. In 1948, the real wage index equaled that of the 1920–22 average, while in the two years of 1944–45 the real wage index—again compared to that of the 1920–22 average—had in fact dropped by 78 percent![5] This is rather striking data. I do not have the data for Germany here, to see if the situation was the same there. Even if not in these proportions, there should be, at minimum, some general coincidence. What does this show? It shows that putting the mechanism of income from labor back into motion—in production and in society, through direct and indirect wages—coincided at the institutional political level with *capital's choice of democracy*. This is the formidable power bloc in front of which the working class finds itself in the postwar period in the capitalist West. Political democracy brought forward by capital possessed great weapons, and not only ideological weapons of propaganda but mechanisms for the overall operation of capitalist society. Capital's choice of democracy coincided with an extremely strong renewal of the wage dynamic. It opened the door to workers directly sharing in the general profits of society, with a general assimilation of the working class into society, to the point of achieving a global redistribution of income that gave the working class a direct glimpse of further possibilities, not just of struggle, but of life inside capitalist society. It must be said that this type of mechanism also served as an ideological opposite to socialism, which like totalitarianism was based on low wages. Immediately after the overthrow of fascism, this was an ideological justification that helped not

5. Ruggero Spesso, "Dinamica della conquista salariale prima e dopo la repubblica" [Dynamic of wage gains before and after the founding of the republic], *Critica Marxista*, no. 5-6 (September-December 1966).

only capital's political propaganda; it also showed how a totalitarian choice at the institutional level would coincide with wage stasis and therefore with the lowering of workers' living standards, something now presented as typical not of the fascist solution but of the socialist one.

Every power bloc clearly has some causes and some consequences directly pertaining to the workers. The factors provoking this power bloc—*democracy + a wage dynamic* in the working class's favor—must be researched much further, with historical research that should probably reach back to the 1920s, and perhaps back to the moment of the October Revolution. It lies in the great fear caused by the working class beginning in October 1917, which became explicit with its open demand for power, and which for the first time became a concrete, historically possible fact.

At this point, a question must be asked—one that may seem odd, but which, on the contrary, helps to establish the complexity of the problem. If the thesis of the strategic overturning of the working class and capital had been elaborated in the 1920s, immediately after the October Revolution and that modest revolutionary explosion that also took place in the West following the Soviet October—if this had happened, what kind of fate would the idea have had? It does not seem that Marxist theory had reached conclusions of this type at that time, yet that would seem to have been the ideal historical climate, much more ideal than the postwar period. The truth is, upon careful reflection, this impression proves inexact because the demand for power during those years was not anchored in the real contradictions of capitalist development. At bottom it reflected, in my opinion, a still low degree of political development in the working class. The violent conquest of the state machine clearly did not strike the capitalist relation of production in the heart. The working class clearly still needed this relation of production for its own growth—which would then go well beyond it—so much so that it is possible to say that 1929 and the great crisis of capital had a working-class origin only indirectly, and that perhaps searching for a direct working-class origin would, in that case, be vain.

Meanwhile, what does have a direct working-class origin, in my opinion, is the *resolution* of that crisis, in the sense that, up until that moment, capital was still barely and in a very unintentional way using the working-class engine, the mobile engine of the working class, for its own development, and perhaps it recognized only then, only within its great crisis, that the relation between capital and society, between production and the system, needs to be mediated by the working class. It requires a mediation that must be and can only be a working-class mediation: here is the other great indication of the rising consciousness in capital. And so, once again, it is on this basis that the wage, and therefore the income from waged labor, arrives as the element capable of restarting the overall income mechanism, including the income from capital. Hence all the consequences at the institutional level, with the social policy of the state, which also carries the possibility of institutional mediation by the official workers' movement, something which up until that point had not been considered possible. Again, the terrain of the class struggle shifts to this foundation, to this series of initiatives, and it is increasingly separated from the traditional political terrain, to the point that from then on, we see the traditional political terrain become increasingly less real, and the real terrain of the class struggle become increasingly less political—increasingly less "political" in the traditional sense—"traditional," in this sense, meaning the explicit demand for power, or the violent, direct assault on the state machine. Up until that moment, that had been the political terrain common to the working class and to the workers' movement. From this moment forward, that terrain becomes "formal," while the real terrain of the class struggle shifts to the ground where instead the capitalist initiative was marching forward—the terrain of the income mechanism, of the wage, of profit, etc.

Here, in my opinion, is the historical origin of the crisis in the relation between class and party. It is no longer possible to understand which is the true political terrain of the struggle and which is the false one, and thus which is the terrain of the class and which is that of the party. In the postwar period, we find ourselves unquestionably before a working-class initiative, one which must be explained and to which we must lay claim. The initiative arises, as always, on top of a need that capital has. And this need was the one we spoke of earlier, concerning the capitalist discovery of the wage, and the necessity of the wage dynamic as its own moment of development. The working-class initiative immediately relies on this. And when speaking of victories or defeats of the working class, we must pay attention to this terrain, not to the heavens of the general conquest of the state or the general crisis of capitalism. The capitalist initiative, which seemed to have avoided for good the dangers that the class struggle brought into capitalist society, which seemed to have settled for good the history of capitalist society's crises—by conceding high wages and political democracy to the working class simultaneously—this now becomes the terrain on which the new cycle of class struggle catches fire.

In this sense, I believe that the workers' successes are undeniable. As usual, the working class and capital make a stretch of road together—a very normal thing for anyone familiar with the history of capitalist society. There is always some moment when the working class and large-scale capitalism, a more advanced capitalism, find themselves making the same road, having the same needs. It is only at a certain point that these needs are overturned, either by one side or by the other, changing the relation of forces, either closing off the course of the struggle or opening it up again on new terrains. We can see that, in the postwar period, the working-class initiative overturns the capitalist initiative. It bends it to its own advantage, on this terrain, and so it creates new imbalances, new contradictions in capitalist society. Perhaps for the first time, the particular interest of the working class shows itself to be hostile toward the whole of society and, for the first time, on the terrain of the struggle around the wage and profit. In the moment when capital had chosen the overall plan of society—and on its own terrain, on the terrain of the revolution of incomes—precisely at that moment, a series of workers' struggles, accentuating and aggravating the wage dynamic, instead put the entire mechanism of the capitalist initiative back into crisis.

This process is fostered and perhaps even intensified by the separation between workers and party. The rallying cry "*more money*," which we find in recent years as a fundamental constant of all the workers' demands, of every working-class claim, is one that, on appearance, may lead us to lament the integration of the working class into the general social system of capital. But, upon deeper and more careful consideration, it proves to be a rallying cry that simultaneously gathers together two polemical objectives: on one side, the struggle against the boss; on the other, the polemic directed toward the organizations, above all toward the political organizations of the party of the working class. Once again, what is called the "dual face" of the wage comes to the fore: at once an element of costs and an element of demand, as bourgeois science teaches us. But for us, the dual face of the wage is the new form in which the twofold character of the working class presents itself—the dual character of workers' labor, which we find again in social labor-power, which we find again in the working class in general.

On the one hand, therefore, the antinomy of employment/inflation that the capitalist side constantly puts forward as a danger; on the other, the increase in productivity that has, must have, and cannot but have wage pressure as its stimulus. It is a very difficult balance. If you take the Italian Plan itself, which is hardly one of the highest moments of international capital's consciousness, but which in any case has accepted, with the modesty of a notary, some of the general needs of international capital, we see that the problem of the wage, in the overall context of capitalist society, has been posed correctly.[6] The Plan says that an increase in the income from dependent labor that significantly and regularly exceeds the average rate of increase in productivity forecasted by the program would compromise the accumulation process, in

---

6. Tronti is referring to the five-year economic plan then being put forward by the Socialist Giovanni Pieraccini, Budget Minister in Aldo Moro's government.

terms of both the volume of investments and the rate of development of income, and would jeopardize the stability of prices. It is not difficult to see how many dangers exist on this point of the wage. By contrast, an increase in the income from dependent labor that is regularly lower than that of productivity tends to slow down the increase in private consumption, and in this way it can then come to distort the development of the system that the Plan had assumed. So, the wage dynamic is on the one hand necessary but, on the other hand, it must not come to eat away at profit shares. This is a contradiction that is typical of the entire structure, of the entire movement of capitalist society; it is a contradiction that is typical of the category of capital, in which needs are always twofold and have a dual face. On the one hand, the necessity of increasing wages; on the other, the necessity of not increasing them too much. Here is the extremely difficult balance over which international capital has been fretting with all its economic policy in the postwar period.

On this basis, we think it can be said that the fundamental class contradiction of capitalist society in this cycle of the struggle has the wage on one side and profit on the other. The relation between wages and profits, in our opinion, performs a leap in the history of class struggles, because a relation between the working class, as a particular moment, facing society, as a general moment, had never before been posed with such clarity. The wages-profits relation is precisely the class-society relation. At this point, we can respond to our earlier question: why is the thesis of the strategic overturning between the working class and capital brought forward not in the 1920s but in the 1960s? Because, clearly, in the 1960s the class struggle is politically more advanced than it was in the 1920s. The demand for power in this period, in this cycle of the struggle, is not explicit, is not an open demand, and yet it works itself more thoroughly into the mechanism of capitalist production. It is more dangerous for capital than an explicit global demand for political power as such. Certainly, if the workers' political party had recognized the new terrain of the class struggle, and if it had assumed this as its area of organization, a limitless revolutionary process would now be open in the capitalist West. Everyone knows that this condition was not realized and that the entire process has remained blocked. This does not take away from the fact that the bargaining power, the trade-union strength of the workers—which in these cases can put the mechanism of capitalist production into crisis—is in certain cases stronger and more dangerous than the political-party form of the working class, which had struggled above all on the formal terrain of political struggle concerning the state. In other words, it no longer faces a capital incapable of governing the whole of society, which indeed was true of capital before the great crisis, as well as around the time of the October Revolution. It is facing instead this capital, which is incapable of achieving more important things, and above all, of *one* much more important thing: of controlling that *part* which is the working class.

Here is the difference in terms of political level: capital that fails to dominate the whole of society is stronger—even if the opposite seems true—than capital which manages to dominate the entire society, but from which the working class, that particular component of society, begins to escape. For this reason, we are saying that, at bottom, capital is weaker today than it was when the workers' demand was the demand for the "workers' state." In other words, the plan of capital, the administration of social inequalities, becomes at this point possible only on the basis of an incomes policy, only on the basis of a controlled wage-variable. Given this last condition, it is true that a new historical phase of the system, of stabilization and development at the same time, has begun. Indeed, these conditions—the incomes policy, wage controls, and control over income from labor—are precisely the fundamental conditions that one also finds in all the plans of capital, in all the long-term programs of capitalist development.

The phase in which we find ourselves today is one in which these conditions begin to exist and thus open up a new phase of stabilization and development for international capital. This, then, should not lead us to see the weakness of capital as an international pre-crisis moment for capitalism, but rather the forthcoming domination by capital over these fundamental conditions and, hence, movement toward a new phase of international stabilization—one which will also be a phase of great development for capital itself. Indeed, when we examine the strategy of international capital today, here too we find some grave and clear voices. We can mention Agnelli, here in our backyard, as one of those most aware of these international, strategic problems for capital. At the UCID congress held in March in Milan, a strategy precisely of this type emerges from Agnelli's contribution.[7] The future solution he envisions would involve the creation of an integrated economic area that would have the Atlantic as its geographical reference point. To grasp the problem on this scale without the risks, without, in other words, those imbalances in productivity, in profitability, in scale between American and European industries—those that worry all the technicians of capital today—one must look first to the markets of Eastern Europe. Hence, the idea that Eastern Europe could offer increasing opportunities for economic complementarity for the industrialized Europe of the West: an important multiplying factor of development in numerous sectors of European industry, from which the birth of

---

7. Unione Cristiana Imprenditori Dirigenti (UCID) is a Christian managers' and executives' association. Giovanni "Gianni" Agnelli, the grandson of the founder of FIAT (also named Giovanni Agnelli), assumed its presidency in 1966. The congress record from which Tronti drew these quotations could not be located.

European industry on a continental scale ought to arise, one that would see differences within Europe no longer. They are saying it explicitly: "we must no longer see the markets of the East as different from those of the West; there is no longer any reason for doing so." An industry on a continental scale could then increase its capacity for dialogue with industry across the Atlantic.

Thus, the remaining objective, of the Atlantic pole as a unifying instance of the world market, must be achieved through bargaining between the entire continent of Europe and the American colossus. Hence the greatest leap, which Agnelli expresses in this form: "probably only a well-organized, serious, Atlantic market would be able to pose the problem, with any hope of solving it, of the development of the three continents (Latin America, Asia, Africa), acquiring them as internal and no longer external zones of a single *efficient* world market." This is the international strategy of capital today—in its most advanced forms, of course, not in general. We can find thousands of contradictions to this in "low" capitalism, but then, clearly, we are keeping our eye on "high" capitalism, what we call "large-scale capitalism," which makes the history of capital's initiatives, and against which objectives and forces must always be measured. This is the ambitious, but at the same time broadly possible, capitalist project.

Faced with the impeccable historical logic of this journey, one of our ideas is, in my opinion, confirmed. It is one that basically has already been fully active in what we have said and written, and which perhaps could be repeated in simpler form: *the system of capitalist production is very young in historical terms.* We still cannot calculate the damage done to the workers' movement, to the working-class struggle in general, by all the chatter concerning international capitalism's process of decay, concerning the final phases of capital, etc. An enormous amount of damage, because it has not only blocked the theoretical development of Marxism—which no longer understands anything about the processes of capital's development—it has also blocked the workers' struggle itself, which finds itself on the one side, ideologically, struggling against a rotting "carcass," and on the other, facing a colossal capitalist initiative, one that has been making use of its every movement. The imbalance between working-class theoretical awareness and the reality of capital has been one of the most serious political impediments. This system, once we consider it in historical terms, seems to us instead to still have a disconcerting vitality with which we must courageously learn to come to terms.

Nowadays, despite this, we again find such chatter in the workers' movement to be strangely widespread. For example, there is today this great ideological polemic concerning the moment of profit, which is not a political polemic but really a polemic of an ideological character. When we open the encyclical and find the discourse on profit,[8] we see that the argumentation comes very close to what we find in the documents of the Communists in Italy, which assume the same generality, the same superficiality, the same lack of exact knowledge of the problem and therefore the same inability to judge facts such as they are. But I want to see them—and here I pose a problem of enormous scale, one that I would not even know how to solve, and which we will soon need to think about solving. I want to see them solve the problems of world hunger without the profit motive. There, I say it like this, crudely, because to me it seems a problem that must be posed in this way. The problem can also be formulated in this way: does a directly working-class solution to the economic problem of underdevelopment exist? That is, is there a practical solution to these problems that does not pass through the mediation of capitalist interests? It is a question to which I would not want to give a response, because any reply would be superficial and improvised. I pose it as a problem for reflection.

The truth is that the strategy of advanced capital, at its limit, extends to the so-called Third World the solution that once it gave to the problems internal to its own development. And the Second World, which is called the "socialist world," does not, in my opinion, have before it a road that is different from the revolution of incomes from labor and from capital, wages and profits, which, for example, hinging on the manufacturing industry's production of durable consumer goods, could ignite the spark of the general development of society and the welfare of all citizens. The problem of the countries that find themselves in the phase of industrial takeoff, to use these awful terms, is that the "virtuous circle" of which Carli spoke is difficult to stabilize, given the meagerness and sometimes the inexistence of the sector that produces investment goods, and given the frequent intervention of a crisis in the balance of payments. We are not, however, interested in this point, but rather in another, one that poses a new and serious problem: capital that can be bent to become a function of the working class for a long historical period, for an entire historical epoch. Here arises the problem of the *why* and of the *how*. Let us turn again to the incredible reconstruction of a Leninist strategy, which basically we have already offered, albeit to a limited extent, and which contains many obscure points that must be clarified. But it is clear that we too are lacking the *great discovery* here. It will come in the years ahead.

For now, we can conclude this presentation in the following way: the timeframe of the revolutionary process is growing longer. And if it is true that our theoretical apparatus, the hypothetical theoretical apparatus that we have

8. Tronti may be referring to the discussion of profit in Pope Paul VI's "*Populorum Progressio*: Encyclical on the Development of Peoples," March 26, 1967, available online: https://w2.vatican.va/content/paul-vi/en/encyclicals/documents/hf_p-vi_enc_26031967_populorum.html.

given ourselves, allows for practically unlimited political experimentation in forms of struggle and organization, then it is necessary to courageously introduce different political hypotheses. The non-subaltern character, for example, of the working class, its vocation to be the dominant class, as we often say, the possibility, that is, of its ruling over all of society from within the capitalist relation of production—all this leads to the conquest of power, to the government of the state, not in the interests of society, but in its own particular interest. In this case capital would be *consciously* managed by the working class, at certain national points, or even at certain supranational points, and for a historical period, as long as its existence does not become unnecessary for the working class itself, and therefore as long as the international conditions for its overturning mature. With two formidable conditions.

The first: a practice of class struggle and class organization conducted this time from the apex of power. The second: a theoretical-strategic view that would contain within itself, as a purely propagandistic moment, the ideology of the management of capital as the overcoming of capitalism. In this sense, we find ourselves before the two obstacles of social democracy and of realized socialism. Does the working class's tactical alliance with capitalist development, that stretch of road, as we said earlier, which is common to capital and the working class, bring with it—and this is another enormous problem that I am consciously posing in a crude way—does it bring with it a political alliance between workers and social democracy? In other words, can there be a *working-class use of social democracy*? A working-class use of the socialist management of capital? If this comes into view as the only way to control society from above, and to introduce oneself into the machine of power, to introduce, in other words, workers' power at the apex of the state, and to work there to smash the state machine, then in that case the historical error of social democracy was not that of having aspired to the management of the state and society such as they were, but of not having used that management for other ends. In that case, Lenin's error was not the violent blow brought upon capital, but to have believed it dead or moribund after this blow. In that case, Togliatti's error at Salerno was not the attempt to bring the Communist movement into the sphere of bourgeois power, but to believe that this needed to happen because the party coincided with the people and with the nation. We wish to praise duplicity, which was correctly present in the working class during that period, but which by contrast was missing in the top Communist leadership, neither in Togliatti's head nor in anyone else's.

The working class *within* and *against* capital: this is the premise from which we must begin for any type of general struggle. And so, if this is true: the party *within* and *against* the state. Once again, the error is and would be in mixing up tactics and strategy. The party in government, the popular fronts, the Salerno turn, etc.—as tactical moves these are perhaps admissible, even if each of them is debatable as a single choice. They are inadmissible, rather, as strategic designs, that is, as they were presented and brought forward by the official workers' movement. As strategic designs, they are overturned in the interests of the opposing class, only mediated by the interests of the working class. The discriminating factor therefore is the partial interest of the working class, which utilizes capital as the social interest, as the resolution of the contradictions and imbalances of society in general, to make capital resolve, in other words, some secondary contradictions of the society in general over a long historical period, and to then reintroduce the relations between the working class and capital as relations between politics and the economy. This seems to be the most correct solution to these problems.

Needless to say, this type of discourse is easy to extend to the moment that precedes all this. That is, to the moment that precedes the opening of the revolutionary process, to the moment, in other words, of the party struggle today and in the coming years. As the class is within and against capital, and as the party is within and against the state, so must one be *within* and *against* the party, such as it is. To make it explode, in other words, one must be there within it. To use it, one must be there within it. On this basis, we must definitively refuse the old maximalism that operated always and in every case from the outside. To operate tactically from the inside but in a strategically alternative way: today, this is the operative solution that presents itself to our eyes. And when I speak of the party, given the preceding considerations, clearly I am not referring to the Communist Party as such, but even to a possible, general, social-democratic solution in the organization of the workers' movement.

Power in these cases is everything. Only force—the relations of force—is decisive. Tactics rule out no solution. There is no solution that tactically could be ruled out *a priori*. Tactically, all solutions are good ones. Therefore, these solutions must not be ruled out: not in the party struggle, nor in the relations between party and class, nor in the struggle between class and society, nor in the relations between party and state. There is a sentence of Lenin's that we must get into our heads, because it coincides with our entire conception of the revolutionary process, even of the ends of the revolution. Lenin says: "Revolution is a dirty job," and "you do not make it with white gloves."[9]

9. The translation here follows the quote in Wladimir S. Woytinsky, *Stormy Passage: A Personal History Through Two Russian Revolutions to Democracy and Freedom: 1905-1960* (New York: The Vanguard Press, 1961), 121. Woytinsky had been a Russian economist and friend of Lenin, but after 1917 he left Bolshevism for Menshevism by way of the Democratic Republic of Georgia, eventually making a career in the United States as a statistician. Woytinsky's book is the earliest known source for this quote; it is possible that Tronti was familiar with it via the book's recent Italian translation, *Dalla rivoluzione russa all'economia rooseveltiana* [From the Russian Revolution to the Rooseveltian economy], trans. Elisabetta Rispoli (Milan: Il Saggiatore, 1966).

Based on the strategic analysis of all the processes that we have discerned, and based on the use of all the tactical solutions that may present themselves in the near future, it is a matter of producing what we have called the *new synthesis*. The concept of the new synthesis is not a theoretical-cultural concept; it is not a matter of arriving at a new conception of the world, of life and of culture and of man, etc. The new synthesis for us is this strategic-theoretical awareness, lucid and cold, of all the processes that take place within capital, of all the movements of the working class's struggle, and simultaneously the practical capacity of using all the opportunities that are momentarily offered to conquer positions of power, positions of strength, because only with power and strength can those strategic solutions of capital then be overturned.

The new synthesis is therefore between these two moments that are so terribly distant from one another. Up until now, capital, as the general social interest, has used the particular working-class interest. The overthrow of power is precisely, first of all, the overturning of this hierarchy between the two interests: the capitalist general one and the working-class particular one. It must be carried out such that the general social interest of capital is used by the particular working-class interest. This is a historical prospect for the development of the class struggle, which precedes the new forms of immediate destruction of capitalist power. It is probable that the confrontation between these two opposing interests, the working-class and the capitalist, the particular and the general, will be the new form in which the struggle for power will present itself in the coming years. I prefer to leave matters in this schematic form.

A Mario Tronti Bibliography, 1958–1970

Below the reader will find a chronological bibliography of known texts written by Tronti between 1958 and 1970, beginning with his first published work on Antonio Gramsci and ending with his postscript to the second edition of *Workers and Capital*. Entries begin with their English title if a translation is available and with the Italian title if a translation has yet to appear.

"Some Questions around Gramsci's Marxism (1958)." In "The Young Mario Tronti," edited and translated by Andrew Anastasi, dossier, *Viewpoint Magazine* (October 3, 2016), https://www.viewpointmag.com/2016/10/03/some-questions-around-gramscis-marxism-1958. Originally published in Italian as "Alcune questioni intorno al marxismo di Gramsci." In *Studi Gramsciani: Atti del convegno tenuto a Roma nei giorni 11–12 gennaio 1958* (Rome: Editori Riuniti - Istituto Gramsci, 1958), 305–21.

"Between Dialectical Materialism and Philosophy of Praxis: Gramsci and Labriola (1959)." In "The Young Mario Tronti," edited and translated by Andrew Anastasi, dossier, *Viewpoint Magazine* (October 3, 2016), https://www.viewpointmag.com/2016/10/03/between-dialectical-materialism-and-philosophy-of-praxis-gramsci-and-labriola-1959. Originally published in Italian as "Tra materialismo dialettico e filosofia della prassi: Gramsci e Labriola." In *La città futura: Saggi sulla figura e il pensiero di Antonio Gramsci*, edited by Alberto Caracciolo and Gianni Scalia (Milan: Feltrinelli, 1959), 139–62. Republished in Mario Tronti, *Il demone della politica: Antologia di scritti (1958–2015)*, edited by Matteo Cavalleri, Michele Filippini, and Jamila M.H. Mascat (Bologna: il Mulino, 2017), 67–94.

"On Marxism and Sociology (April 1959)." In this volume. Revised from translation published in "The Young Mario Tronti," edited and translated by Andrew Anastasi, dossier, *Viewpoint Magazine* (October 3, 2016), https://www.viewpointmag.com/2016/10/03/on-marxism-and-sociology-1959. Originally published in Italian as "Communicazione al seminario: 'Marxismo e Sociologia' (Roma, Istituto Gramsci, 13/19 Aprile 1959)." In "Quattro inediti di Mario Tronti," dossier, *Metropolis* 1, no. 2 (June 1978): 10–13. Abridged version published in Italian as "A proposito di marxismo e sociologia." In *L'operaismo degli anni Sessanta: da "Quaderni rossi" a "classe operaia,"* edited by Fabio Milana and Giuseppe Trotta (Rome: DeriveApprodi, 2008), 77–79.

"Tronti a Panzieri, Roma 28 dicembre '60" [Mario Tronti to Raniero Panzieri, Rome, December 28, 1960]. In *L'operaismo degli anni Sessanta: da "Quaderni rossi" a "classe operaia,"* edited by Fabio Milana and Giuseppe Trotta (Rome: DeriveApprodi, 2008), 107–08.

"Letter to Raniero Panzieri (June 1961)." In this volume. Originally published in Italian as "Tronti a Panzieri, Roma 30 giugno '61." In *L'operaismo degli anni Sessanta: da "Quaderni rossi" a "classe operaia,"* edited by Fabio Milana and Giuseppe Trotta (Rome: DeriveApprodi, 2008), 118–19.

"Studi recenti sulla logica del *Capitale*" [Recent studies on the logic of *Capital*]. *Società* 17, no. 6 (December 1961): 881–903.

"Marx Yesterday and Today" [January 1962]. In *Workers and Capital*, translated by David Broder (London: Verso, 2019), 3–11. Originally published in Italian as "Marx ieri e oggi." *Mondo Nuovo* 1 (January 1962): 27–28. Republished in Mario Tronti, *Operai e capitale* (Rome: DeriveApprodi, 2013 [1966]), 27–34. Alternate English translation available online: https://libcom.org/library/marx-yesterday-today.

"Intervento al seminario di S. Severa, primavera 1962" [Opening speech at the Santa Severa seminar, Spring 1962]. Authorship unknown. Attributed to Mario Tronti in "Quattro inediti di Mario Tronti" [Four unpublished works by Mario Tronti], dossier, *Metropolis* 1, no. 2 (June 1978): 14–17. Attributed to Raniero Panzieri in Fondo Panzieri, archives of the Fondazione Feltrinelli; see editorial notes in *L'operaismo degli anni sessanta: da "Quaderni rossi" a "classe operaia,"* edited by Fabio Milana and Giuseppe Trotta (Rome: DeriveApprodi, 2008), 169.

"Closing Speech at the Santa Severa Seminar (April 1962)." In this volume. Originally published in Italian as "Intervento conclusivo al seminario di San Severa." In *L'operaismo degli anni Sessanta: da "Quaderni rossi" a "classe operaia,"* edited by Fabio Milana and Giuseppe Trotta (Rome: DeriveApprodi, 2008), 162–70.

"Panzieri-Tronti Theses (June 1962)." Co-authored with Raniero Panzieri. In this volume. Originally published in Italian as "Tesi Panzieri-Tronti." In "Raniero Panzieri e i 'Quaderni rossi,'" edited by Dario Lanzardo, special issue of *aut aut* 149–50 (September–December 1975): 6–10. Republished in *L'operaismo degli anni Sessanta: da "Quaderni rossi" a "classe operaia,"* edited by Fabio Milana and Giuseppe Trotta (Rome: DeriveApprodi, 2008), 181–85. Alternate English translation available online: https://libcom.org/library/panzieri-tronti-theses.

"Factory and Society" [June 1962]. In *Workers and Capital*, translated by David Broder (London: Verso, 2019), 12–35. Originally published in Italian as "La fabbrica e la società." *Quaderni rossi* 2 (Rome: Sapere, 1978 [June 1962]): 1–31. Republished in Mario Tronti, *Operai e capitale* (Rome: DeriveApprodi, 2013 [1966]), 35–56. Also republished in Mario Tronti, *Il demone della politica: Antologia di scritti (1958–2015)*, edited by Matteo Cavalleri, Michele Filippini, and Jamila M.H. Mascat (Bologna: il Mulino, 2017), 95–122. Alternate English translation available online: https://libcom.org/library/factory-society.

"The Strike at FIAT (July 1962)." In this volume. Originally published in Italian as "Lo Sciopero alla Fiat." *Problemi del socialismo* 7–8 (July–August 1962): 649–52. Republished in *L'operaismo degli anni Sessanta: da "Quaderni rossi" a "classe operaia,"* edited by Fabio Milana and Giuseppe Trotta (Rome: DeriveApprodi, 2008), 194–97.

"Baldi, Camillo." In *Dizionario Biografico degli Italiani*, vol. 5 (1963), http://www.treccani.it/enciclopedia/camillo-baldi_%28Dizionario-Biografico%29.

"Baranzano, Redento." In *Dizionario Biografico degli Italiani*, vol. 5 (1963), http://www.treccani.it/enciclopedia/redento-baranzano_%28Dizionario-Biografico%29.

"Introduction." In *Scritti inediti di economia politica* [Unpublished writings on political economy], by Karl Marx, edited and translated by Mario Tronti (Rome: Editori Riuniti, 1963), vii–xxxvi.

"Letter to Raniero Panzieri (January 1963)." In this volume. Originally published in Italian as "Tronti a Panzieri, Roma 9 gennaio '63." In *L'operaismo degli anni Sessanta: da "Quaderni rossi" a "classe operaia,"* edited by Fabio Milana and Giuseppe Trotta (Rome: DeriveApprodi, 2008), 258–61.

"The Copernican Revolution (May 1963)." In this volume. Originally published in Italian as "[La rivoluzione copernicana]." In *L'operaismo degli anni Sessanta: da "Quaderni rossi" a "classe operaia,"* edited by Fabio Milana and Giuseppe Trotta (Rome: DeriveApprodi, 2008), 290–300. Republished in Mario Tronti, *Il demone della politica: Antologia di scritti (1958–2015),* edited by Matteo Cavalleri, Michele Filippini, and Jamila M.H. Mascat (Bologna: il Mulino, 2017), 123–36.

"The Plan of Capital" [July 1963]. In *Workers and Capital,* translated by David Broder (London: Verso, 2019*),* 36–64. Originally published in Italian as "Il piano del capitale." *Quaderni rossi* 3 (Rome: Sapere, 1978 [July 1963]): 44–73. Republished in Mario Tronti, *Operai e capitale* (Rome: DeriveApprodi, 2013 [1966]), 57–83. Alternate English translation available as "Social Capital." *Telos* 17 (Fall 1973): 98–121.

"The Two Reformisms (July 1963)." In this volume. Originally published in Italian anonymously as "I due riformismi." *Quaderni rossi – Cronache operaie* (July 15, 1963): 1 and 6. Republished and attributed to Tronti in *L'operaismo degli anni Sessanta: da "Quaderni rossi" a "classe operaia,"* edited by Fabio Milana and Giuseppe Trotta (Rome: DeriveApprodi, 2008), 306–09.

"Letter to Antonio Negri (September 1963)." In this volume. Originally published in Italian as "Tronti a Negri, Roma 19 settembre 1963." In *L'operaismo degli anni Sessanta: da "Quaderni rossi" a "classe operaia,"* edited by Fabio Milana and Giuseppe Trotta (Rome: DeriveApprodi, 2008), 323–26.

"A Replacement of Leadership (Autumn 1963)." In this volume. Originally published in Italian as "Un gruppo dirigente di ricambio." In *L'operaismo degli anni Sessanta: da "Quaderni rossi" a "classe operaia,"* edited by Fabio Milana and Giuseppe Trotta (Rome: DeriveApprodi, 2008), 343–44.

"Lenin in England" [January 1964]. In *Workers and Capital,* translated by David Broder (London: Verso, 2019), 65–72. Originally published in Italian as "Lenin in Inghilterra." *classe operaia* 1, no. 1 (January 1964): 1 and 18–20. Republished in Mario Tronti, *Operai e capitale* (Rome: DeriveApprodi, 2013 [1966]), 87–93. Also republished in Mario Tronti, *Il demone della politica: Antologia di scritti (1958–2015),* edited by Matteo Cavalleri, Michele Filippini, and Jamila M.H. Mascat (Bologna: il Mulino, 2017), 137–44. Alternate English translation available in *Working Class Autonomy and the Crisis: Italian Marxist Texts of the Theory and Practice of a Class Movement: 1964–79* (London: Red Notes, 1979), 1–6. Republished in *Autonomia: Post-Political Politics* (Los Angeles: Semiotext(e), 2007), 28–34.

"'Sì' al centro-sinistra, No al riformismo" ["Yes" to the center-left, No to reformism]. *classe operaia* 1, no. 1 (January 1964): 1. Originally published anonymously. Attributed to Mario Tronti in the bibliography of *L'operaismo degli anni Sessanta: da "Quaderni rossi" a "classe operaia,"* edited by Fabio Milana and Giuseppe Trotta (Rome: DeriveApprodi, 2008), 850.

"Che fare del sindacato?" [What to do about the union?]. *classe operaia* 1, no. 1 (January 1964): 5. Originally published anonymously. Attributed to Mario Tronti in the bibliography of *L'operaismo degli anni Sessanta: da "Quaderni rossi" a "classe operaia,"* edited by Fabio Milana and Giuseppe Trotta (Rome: DeriveApprodi, 2008), 850.

"PSIUP, P proletaria o P popolare?" [PSIUP: P for proletarian or P for people's?]. *classe operaia* 1, no. 2 (February 1964): 1. Originally published anonymously. Attributed to Mario Tronti in the bibliography of *L'operaismo degli anni Sessanta: da "Quaderni rossi" a "classe operaia,"* edited by Fabio Milana and Giuseppe Trotta (Rome: DeriveApprodi, 2008), 851.

"Critica marxista del partito" [Marxist critique of the party]. *classe operaia* 1, no. 2 (February 1964): 11 and 15. Originally published anonymously. Attributed to Mario Tronti in the bibliography of *L'operaismo degli anni Sessanta: da "Quaderni rossi" a "classe operaia,"* edited by Fabio Milana and Giuseppe Trotta (Rome: DeriveApprodi, 2008), 851.

"Tronti a Gobbini, Roma 24 marzo 1964" [Mario Tronti to Mauro Gobbini, Rome, March 24, 1964]. In *L'operaismo degli anni Sessanta: da "Quaderni rossi" a "classe operaia,"* edited by Fabio Milana and Giuseppe Trotta (Rome: DeriveApprodi, 2008), 367.

"An Old Tactic for a New Strategy" [May 1964]. In *Workers and Capital*, translated by David Broder, (London: Verso, 2019), 73–80. Originally published in Italian as "Vecchia tattica per una nuova strategia." *classe operaia* 1, no. 4–5 (May 1964). Republished in Mario Tronti, *Operai e capitale* (Rome: DeriveApprodi, 2013 [1966]), 94–100.

"Report at Piombino (May 1964)." In this volume. Originally published in Italian as "Relazione al convegno di Piombino." In *L'operaismo degli anni Sessanta: da "Quaderni rossi" a "classe operaia,"* edited by Fabio Milana and Giuseppe Trotta (Rome: DeriveApprodi, 2008), 373–86.

"Un nuovo luglio '60" [A new July 1960]. From notes by Mauro Gobbini taken July 4–5, 1964. In *L'operaismo degli anni Sessanta: da "Quaderni rossi" a "classe operaia,"* edited by Fabio Milana and Giuseppe Trotta (Rome: DeriveApprodi, 2008), 389–90.

"Contro il padrone di Stato" [Against the state boss]. *classe operaia* 1, no. 7 (July 1964): 1–2. Originally published anonymously. Attributed to Mario Tronti in the bibliography of *L'operaismo degli anni Sessanta: da "Quaderni rossi" a "classe operaia,"* edited by Fabio Milana and Giuseppe Trotta, (Rome: DeriveApprodi, 2008), 852.

"1905 in Italy" [September 1964]. In *Workers and Capital*, translated by David Broder (London: Verso, 2019), 81–8. Originally published in Italian as "1905 in Italia." *classe operaia* 1, no. 8–9 (September 1964): 1 and 15–16. Republished in Mario Tronti, *Operai e capitale* (Rome: DeriveApprodi, 2013 [1966]), 101–07. Also republished in Mario Tronti, *Il demone della politica: Antologia di scritti (1958–2015)*, edited by Matteo Cavalleri, Michele Filippini, and Jamila M.H. Mascat (Bologna: il Mulino, 2017), 145–52.

"Occhio all'Italia" [Eyes on Italy]. *classe operaia* 1, no. 8–9 (September 1964): 3–4. Originally published anonymously. Attributed to Mario Tronti in the bibliography of *L'operaismo degli anni Sessanta: da "Quaderni rossi" a "classe operaia,"* edited by Fabio Milana and Giuseppe Trotta (Rome: DeriveApprodi, 2008), 852.

"Ceto politico Borghese alla tribuna" [Bourgeois political stratum to the stand]. *classe operaia* 1, no. 8–9 (September 1964): 5–6. Originally published anonymously. Attributed to Mario Tronti in the bibliography of *L'operaismo degli anni Sessanta: da "Quaderni rossi" a "classe operaia,"* edited by Fabio Milana and Giuseppe Trotta (Rome: DeriveApprodi, 2008), 852.

"Sul partito" [On the party]. *classe operaia* 1, no. 10–12 (December 1964): 1. Originally published anonymously. Attributed to Mario Tronti in the bibliography of *L'operaismo degli anni Sessanta: da "Quaderni rossi" a "classe operaia,"* edited by Fabio Milana and Giuseppe Trotta (Rome: DeriveApprodi, 2008), 852.

"Class and Party" [December 1964]. In *Workers and Capital*, translated by David Broder (London: Verso, 2019), 89–100. Originally published in Italian as "Classe e Partito." *classe operaia* 1, no. 10–12 (December 1964): 2–6. Republished in Mario Tronti, *Operai e capitale* (Rome: DeriveApprodi, 2013 [1966]), 108–18. Alternate English translation available online: https://libcom.org/library/class-party.

"Ricordo di Raniero Panzieri" [Remembrance of Raniero Panzieri]. *classe operaia* 1, no. 10–12 (December 1964): 23–24. Originally published anonymously. Attributed to Mario Tronti in the bibliography of *L'operaismo degli anni Sessanta: da "Quaderni rossi"* a *"classe operaia,"* edited by Fabio Milana and Giuseppe Trotta (Rome: DeriveApprodi, 2008), 852.

"Tronti a Gobbini, Roma 16 febbraio '65" [Mario Tronti to Mauro Gobbini, Rome, February 16, 1965]. In *L'operaismo degli anni Sessanta: da "Quaderni rossi" a "classe operaia,"* edited by Fabio Milana and Giuseppe Trotta (Rome: DeriveApprodi, 2008), 408.

"La risposta operaia c'è" [The working-class response exists]. *classe operaia* 2, no. 1 (January–February 1965): 1–3. Originally published anonymously. Attributed to Mario Tronti in the bibliography of *L'operaismo degli anni Sessanta: da "Quaderni rossi" a "classe operaia,"* edited by Fabio Milana and Giuseppe Trotta (Rome: DeriveApprodi, 2008), 852.

"The Party in the Factory (April 1965)." In this volume. Originally published in Italian as "Conferenza sul tema: 'Il partito in fabbrica' (Torino, Teatro Gobetti, 14 [sic] Aprile 1965)." In "Quattro inediti di Mario Tronti," dossier, *Metropolis* 1, no. 2 (June 1978): 18–30. Republished as "Il partito in fabbrica (aprile '65)." In *L'operaismo degli anni Sessanta: da "Quaderni rossi" a "classe operaia,"* edited by Fabio Milana and Giuseppe Trotta (Rome: DeriveApprodi, 2008), 461–76.

"A Balance Sheet of the 'Intervention' (April 1965)." In this volume. Originally published in Italian as "Un bilancio dell' 'intervento.'" In *L'operaismo degli anni Sessanta: da "Quaderni rossi" a "classe operaia,"* edited by Fabio Milana and Giuseppe Trotta (Rome: DeriveApprodi, 2008), 427–28.

"After the Reunion in Mestre (May 1965)." In this volume. Excerpted from a longer conversation originally published in Italian as "'classe operaia,' una riunione a Mestre." In *L'operaismo degli anni Sessanta: da "Quaderni rossi" a "classe operaia,"* edited by Fabio Milana and Giuseppe Trotta (Rome: DeriveApprodi, 2008), 479–82.

"O partito unico o partito in fabbrica" [Either single party or party in the factory]. *classe operaia* 2, no. 3 (May 1965): 1–2. Originally published anonymously. Attributed to Mario Tronti in the bibliography of *L'operaismo degli anni Sessanta: da "Quaderni rossi" a "classe operaia,"* edited by Fabio Milana and Giuseppe Trotta (Rome: DeriveApprodi, 2008), 853.

"Single Party or Class Party? (June 1965)." In this volume. Originally published in Italian as "Interveno [sic] al dibattito: 'Partito unico—partito di classe' (Roma, Teatro dei Satiri, 12 Giugno 1965)" [Intervention at the debate: Single party—class party (Rome, Teatro dei Satiri, June 12, 1965]. In "Quattro inediti di Mario Tronti," dossier, *Metropolis* 1, no. 2 (June 1978): 31–33.

"Una sola unificazione tra classe e partito" [Only one unification between class and party]. *classe operaia* 2, no. 4–5 (October 1965): 1–2. Originally published anonymously. Attributed to Mario Tronti in the bibliography of *L'operaismo degli anni Sessanta: da "Quaderni rossi" a "classe operaia,"* edited by Fabio Milana and Giuseppe Trotta (Rome: DeriveApprodi, 2008), 853.

"Tronti a Gobbini, Roma 21 ottobre '65" [Mario Tronti to Mauro Gobbini, Rome, October 21, 1965]. In *L'operaismo degli anni Sessanta: da "Quaderni rossi" a "classe operaia,"* edited by Fabio Milana and Giuseppe Trotta (Rome: DeriveApprodi, 2008), 511.

"Marx, Labour-Power, Working Class" [1965]. In *Workers and Capital,* translated by David Broder (London: Verso, 2019), 103–276. Originally published in Italian as "Marx, forza-lavoro, classe operaia," in Mario Tronti, *Operai e capitale* (Rome: DeriveApprodi, 2013 [1966]), 121–266. Excerpted in Mario Tronti, *Il demone della politica: Antologia di scritti (1958–2015),* edited by Matteo Cavalleri, Michele Filippini, and Jamila M.H. Mascat (Bologna: il Mulino, 2017), 153–98. Alternate English translation of point 14 available as "The Struggle against Labor." *Radical America* 6, no. 3 (May–June 1972):

22–25. Alternate English translation of point 12 available as "The Strategy of Refusal." In *Working Class Autonomy and the Crisis: Italian Marxist Texts of the Theory and Practice of a Class Movement: 1964–79* (London: Red Notes, 1979), 234–52. Alternate English translations of points 9 and 12 available as "Selections from *Workers and Capital*." Translated by Timothy Murphy, *Genre* 43, no. 3–4 (Fall–Winter 2010): 337–52. Alternate English translation of introduction available as "Introduction to Marx, Labor-power, Working Class." https://libcom.org/library/marx-labor-power-working-class.

"Una lettera a Giulio Einaudi" [Mario Tronti to Giulio Einaudi, Rome, January 16, 1966]. https://operavivamagazine.org/una-lettera-a-giulio-einaudi.

"It's Not Time for Social-Democracy, It's Time to Fight It for the First Time from the Left (April 1966)." In this volume. Originally published in Italian as "Non è l'ora della socialdemocrazia, è l'ora di batterla per la prima volta da sinistra (Registrazione delle conferenza tenuta a Firenze il 2 aprile, al Centro 'Giovanni Fracovich' dal compagno Mario Tronti)." *classe operaia* 3, no. 1 (May 1966): 29–31.

"Fronte unico contro la socialdemocrazia" [United front against social democracy]. *classe operaia* 3, no. 1 (May 1966): 1 and 32.

"A Course of Action" [September 1966]. In *Workers and Capital*, translated by David Broder (London: Verso, 2019), xv–xxxiv. Originally published in Italian as "La linea di condotta." In Mario Tronti, *Operai e capitale* (Rome: DeriveApprodi, 2013 [1966]), 7–24. Also republished in Mario Tronti, *Il demone della politica: Antologia di scritti (1958–2015)*, edited by Matteo Cavalleri, Michele Filippini, and Jamila M.H. Mascat (Bologna: il Mulino, 2017), 199–226.

"L'alternativa alla socialdemocrazia: unificazione a sinistra" [The alternative to social democracy: unification to the left]. *classe operaia* 3, no. 2 (October 1966): 1–4. Originally published anonymously. Authorship unknown. Attributed to Mario Tronti in Michele Filippini, *Leaping Forward: Mario Tronti and the History of Political Workerism* (Maastricht: Jan van Eyck Academie, 2012), 42n150. Attributed to Pierluigi Gasparotto in the bibliography of *L'operaismo degli anni Sessanta: da "Quaderni rossi" a "classe operaia,"* edited by Fabio Milana and Giuseppe Trotta (Rome: DeriveApprodi, 2008), 854.

Workers and Capital [October 1966]. Translated by David Broder. London: Verso, 2019. Originally published in Italian as *Operai e capitale*. Turin: Einaudi Editore, 1966. Republished in enlarged 2nd edition, Turin: Einaudi Editore, 1971. Republished, Rome: DeriveApprodi, 2013.

"Classe partito classe" [Class party class]. *classe operaia* 3, no. 3 (March 1967): 1 and 28. Originally published anonymously. Attributed to Mario Tronti in the bibliography of *L'operaismo degli anni Sessanta: da "Quaderni rossi" a "classe operaia,"* edited by Fabio Milana and Giuseppe Trotta (Rome: DeriveApprodi, 2008), 854. Republished in Mario Tronti, *Il demone della politica: Antologia di scritti (1958–2015)*, edited by Matteo Cavalleri, Michele Filippini, and Jamila M.H. Mascat (Bologna: il Mulino, 2017), 221–26.

"Within and Against (May 1967)." In this volume. Originally published as "La nuova sintesi: dentro e contro" [The new synthesis: within and against]. *Giovane critica* 17 (Autumn 1967): 17–27. Republished as "Dentro e contro." In *L'operaismo degli anni Sessanta: da "Quaderni rossi" a "classe operaia,"* edited by Fabio Milana and Giuseppe Trotta (Rome: DeriveApprodi, 2008), 567–81.

"Estremismo e riformismo" [Extremism and reformism]. *Contropiano* 1, no. 1 (January–April 1968): 41–58.

"Gli anni Venti come precedente politico dell'attuale livello della lotta di classe. Intervento conclusivo al seminario sul socialismo realizzato. Mario Tronti, Bologna 31 marzo 1968" [The 1920s as political precedent to the current level of class struggle. Concluding intervention at the seminar on realized socialism. Mario Tronti, Bologna, March 31, 1968]. In *Materiali del Centro Francovich* (1968). Republished as "Un movimento operaio 'post-comunista'" [A "post-Communist" workers' movement]. In *L'operaismo degli anni Sessanta: da "Quaderni rossi" a "classe operaia,"* edited by Fabio Milana and Giuseppe Trotta (Rome: DeriveApprodi, 2008), 583–85.

"Il partito come problema" [The party as problem]. *Contropiano* 1, no. 2 (May–August 1968): 297–317.

"Internazionalismo vecchio e nuovo" [Internationalism old and new]. *Contropiano* 1, no. 3 (September–December 1968): 505–26.

"Potere politico e potere economico" [Political power and economic power]. In Ferruccio Parri et al., *Società e potere in Italia e nel mondo* (Turin: Giappichelli, 1970), 141–45.

"Classe operaia e sviluppo" [Working class and development]. *Contropiano* 3, no. 3 (September–December [November] 1970): 465–77. Republished in Mario Tronti, *Il demone della politica: Antologia di scritti (1958–2015)*, edited by Matteo Cavalleri, Michele Filippini, and Jamila M.H. Mascat (Bologna: il Mulino, 2017), 229–42.\

"Postscript of Problems" [December 1970]. In *Workers and Capital*, translated by David Broder (London: Verso, 2019), 277–326. Originally published in Italian as "Poscritto di problemi," in *Operai e capitale*, 2nd edition (Turin: Einaudi Editore: 1971), 267–311. Republished in new edition (Rome: DeriveApprodi, 2013), 269–316. Excerpted in Mario Tronti, *Il demone della politica: Antologia di scritti (1958–2015)*, edited by Matteo Cavalleri, Michele Filippini, and Jamila M.H. Mascat (Bologna: il Mulino, 2017), 243–84. Alternate English translation available as "Workers and Capital." *Telos*, no. 14 (Winter 1972): 25–62.

Bibliography of Works Cited

Accornero, Aris. *Fiat confine: storia della OSR*. Milan: Edizioni Avanti, 1959.

Althusser, Louis. "Contradiction and Overdetermination." In *For Marx*, translated by Ben Brewster, 87–128. London: Verso, 2005.

Althusser, Louis. "On the Materialist Dialectic." In *For Marx*, translated by Ben Brewster, 161–218. London: Verso, 2005.

Althusser, Louis. *On the Reproduction of Capitalism: Ideology and Ideological State Apparatuses*. Translated by G.M. Goshgarian. London: Verso, 2014.

Althusser, Louis. "The Object of *Capital*." Translated by Ben Brewster. In *Reading "Capital": The Complete Edition*, by Louis Althusser, Étienne Balibar, Roger Establet, Pierre Macherey, and Jacques Rancière, 215–355. London: Verso, 2015.

Alquati, Romano. "Co-research and Worker's Inquiry" [1994]. Edited by Matteo Polleri. In "Against the Day: Militant Inquiry, History and Possibilities," 470–78. Dossier, *South Atlantic Quarterly* 118, no. 2 (April 2019).

Alquati, Romano, ed. "Documenti sulla lotta di classe alla FIAT" [Documents on the class struggle at FIAT]. *Quaderni rossi* 1 (Rome: Sapere, 1978 [October 1964]): 198–215.

Alquati, Romano. "Relazione di Romano Alquati sulle 'forze nuove' (Convegno del PSI sulla FIAT, gennaio 1961)" [Report by Romano Alquati on the "new forces" (PSI Convention on FIAT, January 1961)]. *Quaderni rossi* 1 (Rome: Sapere, 1978 [October 1964]): 215–40.

Anastasi, Andrew. "A Living Unity in the Marxist: Introduction to Tronti's Early Writings." In "*The Young Mario Tronti*," edited and translated by Andrew Anastasi. Dossier, *Viewpoint Magazine* (October 3, 2016). https://www.viewpointmag.com/2016/10/03/a-living-unity-in-the-marxist-introduction-to-trontis-early-writings.

Aronoff, Kate, Alyssa Battistoni, Daniel Aldana Cohen, and Thea Riofrancos. *A Planet to Win: Why We Need a Green New Deal*. London: Verso, 2019.

Aronowitz, Stanley. *False Promises: The Shaping of American Working Class Consciousness*. Expanded edition. Durham: Duke University Press, 1992 [1973].

Arruzza, Cinzia. "From Women's Strikes to a New Class Movement: The Third Feminist Wave." *Viewpoint Magazine*, December 3, 2018. https://www.viewpointmag.com/2018/12/03/from-womens-strikes-to-a-new-class-movement-the-third-feminist-wave.

Arruzza, Cinzia, Tithi Bhattacharya, and Nancy Fraser. *Feminism for the 99%: A Manifesto*. London: Verso, 2019.

Balibar, Étienne. "A Point of Heresy in Western Marxism: Althusser's and Tronti's Antithetic Readings of *Capital* in the Early 1960s." In *The Concept in Crisis: "Reading Capital" Today*, edited by Nick Nesbitt, 93–112. Durham: Duke University Press, 2017.

Balbo, Laura, and Vittorio Rieser. "La sinistra e lo sviluppo della sociologia" [The left and the development of sociology]. *Problemi del socialismo* 3 (March 1962): 169–93.

Balestrini, Nanni. *We Want Everything*. Translated by Matt Holden. London: Verso, 2018.

Battle, Andy. "We Will Not Negotiate." *Commune*, February 18, 2019. https://communemag.com/we-will-not-negotiate.

Belli, G.G. "Translations from G.G. Belli." Translated by Harold Norse. *The Hudson Review* 9, no. 1 (Spring 1956): 71–85.

Bologna, Sergio. "Bologna a Tronti, 30 marzo" [Sergio Bologna to Mario Tronti, March 30, 1964]. In *L'operaismo degli anni sessanta: da "Quaderni rossi" a "classe operaia,"* edited by Fabio Milana and Giuseppe Trotta, 368–70. Rome: DeriveApprodi, 2008

Boggs, James. *The American Revolution: Pages from a Negro Worker's Notebook*. In *Pages from a Negro Worker's Notebook: A James Boggs Reader*, edited by Stephen M. Ward, 82–143. Detroit: Wayne State University Press, 2011.

Bologna, Sergio. "Class Composition and the Theory of the Party at the Origin of the Workers-Councils Movement." Translated by Bruno Ramirez. *Telos* 13 (Fall 1972): 4–27.

Carnevali, Emilio. "I fatti d'Ungheria e il dissenso degli intellettuali di sinistra. Storia del manifesto dei '101'" [The Hungarian events and left intellectuals' dissent. History of the manifesto of the "101"]. *MicroMega*, February 9, 2010. http://temi.repubblica.it/micromega-online/i-fatti-dungheria-e-il-dissenso-allinterno-del-pci-storia-del-manifes-to-dei-101.

Carli, Guido. "Monetary Policy and Economic Stability: An International View." In *Proceedings of a symposium on money, interest rates and economic activity: Thursday, April 6, 1967, Sheraton-Park Hotel, Washington, D.C.*, edited by American Bankers Association, 134–49. New York: The Association, 1967.

Carli, Guido. "Riflessioni di un governatore di banca centrale" [Reflections of a governor of the central bank]. *Bancaria: mensile dell'Associazione Bancaria Italiana* 22, no. 11 (1966): 1301–09.

Carpignano, Paolo. "U.S. Class Composition in the Sixties." *Zerowork* 1 (December 1975): 7–31.

Cavalleri, Matteo, Michele Filippini, and Jamila M.H. Mascat. Introduction to *Il demone della politica: Antologia di scritti, 1958–2015* [The demon of politics: Anthology of writings, 1958–2015], by Mario Tronti, 11–63. Edited by Matteo Cavalleri, Michele Filippini, and Jamila M.H. Mascat. Bologna: il Mulino, 2017.

"*classe operaia*: un volantino a Milano" [*classe operaia*: a flyer in Milan] [January 1964], in *L'operaismo degli anni sessanta: da "Quaderni rossi" a "classe operaia,"* edited by Fabio Milana and Giuseppe Trotta, 351–52. Rome: DeriveApprodi, 2008.

"*classe operaia*: una reunione a Mestre" [*classe operaia*: a reunion in Mestre]. In *L'operaismo degli anni Sessanta: da "Quaderni rossi" a "classe operaia,"* edited by Fabio Milana and Giuseppe Trotta, 479–82. Rome: DeriveApprodi, 2008.

Cleaver, Harry. *Reading "Capital" Politically*. Austin: University of Texas Press, 1979.

Colletti, Lucio. "Marxism as a Sociology." In *From Rousseau to Lenin: Studies in Ideology and Society*, translated by John Merrington and Judith White, 3–44. New York: Monthly Review Press, 1972.

Colletti, Lucio. "The Theory of the Crash." *Telos*, no. 13 (1972): 34–46.

"Contra la lotta articolata" [Against the articulated struggle]. *classe operaia* 2, no. 2 (March–April 1965).

Dalla Costa, Mariarosa. *Women and the Subversion of the Community: A Mariarosa Dalla Costa Reader*. Edited by Camille Barbagallo. Translated by Richard Braude. Oakland: PM Press, 2019.

Dalla Costa, Mariarosa, and Selma James. *The Power of Women and the Subversion of the Community.* Bristol: Falling Wall Press, 1972.

De Meo, Giuseppe. "Productivity and the distribution of income to factors in Italy (1951–63)." *PSL Quarterly Review* 19, no. 76 (1966): 42–71.

Di Scala, Spencer M. *Renewing Italian Socialism: Nenni to Craxi.* New York: Oxford University Press, 1988.

Dunayevskaya, Raya. *Marxism and Freedom: From 1776 until Today.* Updated edition. London: Pluto, 1975 [1958].

Estes, Nick. "A Red Deal." *Jacobin*, August 6, 2019. https://www.jacobinmag.com/2019/08/red-deal-green-new-deal-ecosocialism-decolonization-indigenous-resistance-environment.

Federici, Silvia. *Revolution at Point Zero: Housework, Reproduction, and Feminist Struggle.* Oakland: PM Press/Common Notions, 2012.

Filippini, Michele. *Leaping Forward: Mario Tronti and the History of Political Workerism.* Maastricht: Jan van Eyck Academie, 2012.

Ginsborg, Paul. *A History of Contemporary Italy: Society and Politics, 1943–1988.* London: Penguin, 1990.

Gobbini, Mauro. "Gobbini a Tronti, Bologna, 2 aprile 1964" [Mauro Gobbini to Mario Tronti, April 2, 1964], in *L'operaismo degli anni sessanta: da "Quaderni rossi" a "classe operaia,"* edited by Fabio Milana and Giuseppe Trotta, 371–73. Rome: DeriveApprodi, 2008.

Gobbini, Mauro. "Mauro Gobbini" [Interview, Rome, May 12 1998], in *L'operaismo degli anni sessanta: da "Quaderni rossi" a "classe operaia,"* edited by Fabio Milana and Giuseppe Trotta, 679–95. Rome: DeriveApprodi, 2008.

Goncharov, Ivan. *Oblomov.* Translated by Marian Schwartz. New Haven: Yale University Press, 2010.

Gramsci, Antonio. *Selections from the Prison Notebooks.* Edited and translated by Quintin Hoare and Geoffrey Nowell Smith. New York: International Publishers, 1971.

Gramsci, Antonio. "The Revolution against *Capital*." In *Selections from the Political Writings (1910–1920),* edited by Quintin Hoare, 34–37. Translated by John Mathews. London: Lawrence and Wishart, 1977.

Haider, Asad. "Crise et enquête" [Crisis and inquiry]. *Période*, March 7, 2014. http://revueperiode.net/crise-et-enquete.

Haider, Asad. "Socialists Think." *Viewpoint Magazine*, September 24, 2018. https://www.viewpointmag.com/2018/09/24/socialists-think.

Haider, Asad, and Salar Mohandesi. "Workers' Inquiry: A Genealogy." *Viewpoint Magazine* 3 (September 2013). https://www.viewpointmag.com/2013/09/27/workers-inquiry-a-genealogy.

Hardt, Michael, and Antonio Negri. *Assembly.* New York: Oxford University Press, 2019.

Harney, Stefano, and Fred Moten. *The Undercommons: Fugitive Planning & Black Study.* Wivenhoe/New York/Port Watson: Minor Compositions, 2013.

Harootunian, Harry. *Marx after Marx: History and Time in the Expansion of Capitalism.* New York: Columbia University Press, 2015.

Hoare, Quintin, and Geoffrey Nowell Smith. Introduction to *Selections from the Prison Notebooks*, by Antonio Gramsci, edited and translated by Quintin Hoare and Geoffrey Nowell Smith, xvii–xcvi. New York: International Publishers, 1971.

"Intervento politico nelle lotte" [Political intervention into the struggles]. *classe operaia* 1, no. 6 (June 1964).

James, Selma. *Sex, Race, and Class: The Perspective of Winning; A Selection of Writings, 1952–2011*. Oakland: Common Notions/PM Press, 2012.

King, Patrick. "Introduction to 'Black Power: A Scientific Concept Whose Time Has Come' by James Boggs." *e-flux* 79 (February 2017). https://www.e-flux.com/journal/79/94671/introduction-to-boggs.

King, Patrick. Introduction to "Young Patriots at the United Front Against Fascism Conference (1969)," by William "Preacherman" Fesperman. *Viewpoint Magazine*, August 10, 2015. https://www.viewpointmag.com/2015/08/10/young-patriots-at-the-united-front-against-fascism-conference.

Koivisto, Juha, and Mikko Lahtinen. "Conjuncture, Politico-Historical." Translated by Peter Thomas. *Historical Materialism* 20, no. 1 (January 2012): 267–77.

Krauss, Clifford. "Trump's Methane Rule Rollback Divides Oil and Gas Industry." *The New York Times*, August 29, 2019. https://www.nytimes.com/2019/08/29/business/energy-environment/methane-regulation-reaction.html.

La Malfa, Ugo. "Nota aggiuntiva alla Relazione generale sulla situazione economica del Paese per il 1961" [Additional note to the general report on the economic situation of the country for 1961] [May 22, 1962] (Rome: Edizione Janus, 1973). http://www.fulm.org/articoli/economia/nota-aggiuntiva-relazione-generale-situazione-economica-paese-1961.

Lassere, Davide Gallo. "La traiettoria teorica e politica di Mario Tronti" [The theoretical and political trajectory of Mario Tronti]. *Effimera*, January 11, 2018. http://effimera.org/la-traiettoria-teorica-politica-mario-tronti-davide-gallo-lassere2.

Lazare, Sarah. "We Have To Make Sure the 'Green New Deal' Doesn't Become Green Capitalism: A conversation with Kali Akuno of Cooperation Jackson." *In These Times*, December 12, 2018. http://inthesetimes.com/article/21632/green-new-deal-alexandria-ocasio-cortez-climate-cooperation-jackson-capital.

Lazarus, Sylvain. *Anthropology of the Name*. Translated by Gila Walker. New York: Seagull Books, 2015.

Lazarus, Sylvain. "Workers' Anthropology and Factory Inquiry: Inventory and Problematics (2001)." Translated by Asad Haider and Patrick King. *Viewpoint Magazine*, January 9, 2019. https://www.viewpointmag.com/2019/01/09/workers-anthropology-and-factory-inquiry-inventory-and-problematics.

Lenin, V.I. "Kommunismus." In *Collected Works*, vol. 31., 165–67. Moscow: Progress Publishers, 1965 [1920].

Lenin, V.I. *What Is To Be Done?* Translated by Lars T. Lih. In *Lenin Rediscovered: "What Is to Be Done?" in Context*, by Lars T. Lih, 673–840. Haymarket Books: Chicago, 2008.

Leogrande, Alessandro. "I prigionieri delle fabbriche" [The prisoners of the factories]. Photographs by Maila Iocovelli and Fabio Zayed. *Internazionale*, October 27, 2014. https://www.internazionale.it/reportage/maila-iacovelli/2014/10/27/reparti-confino-in-italia-9.

Licciardello, Danilo, dir. *Democrazia sconfinata*. 2010. https://vimeo.com/18307344.

Lih, Lars T. *Lenin Rediscovered: "What Is to Be Done?" in Context*. Haymarket Books: Chicago, 2008.

London Edinburgh Weekend Return Group. *In and Against the State*. 2nd edition London: Pluto, 1980.

Malgeri, Francesco. *La stagione del centrismo: Politica e società nell'Italia del secondo dopoguerra (1945–1960)* [The season of centrism: Politics and society in Italy in the postwar period (1945–1960)]. Rubbettino: Saveria Mannelli, 2002.

Mangano, Attilio. "Per una critica del trontismo e delle ideologie 'autonome'" [Toward a critique of Trontismo and of "autonomous" ideologies]. In *Autocritica e politica di classe*. Milan: Ottaviano 1978.

Marx, Karl. *Capital: A Critique of Political Economy*. Vol. 1. Translated by Ben Fowkes. London: Penguin, 1976.

Marx, Karl. *Grundrisse: Foundations of the Critique of Political Economy (Rough Draft)*. Translated by Martin Nicolaus. New York: Penguin, 1993.

Medina, Daniel A. "The grassroots coalition that took on Amazon...and won." *The Guardian*, March 24, 2019. https://www.theguardian.com/technology/2019/mar/23/the-grassroots-coalition-that-took-on-amazon-and-won.

Meriggi, Maria Grazia. "Rileggendo 'Operai e capitale': dall'autonomia operaia all'autonomia del politico" [Re-reading *Workers and Capital*: from workers' autonomy to the autonomy of the political]. *aut aut* 147 (May–June 1975): 47–65.

Meriggi, Maria Grazia. *Composizione di classe e teoria del partito: sul marxismo degli anni '60* [Class composition and theory of the party: on the Marxism of the '60s]. Bari: Dedalo, 1978.

Milana, Fabio, and Giuseppe Trotta, eds. *L'operaismo degli anni sessanta: da "Quaderni rossi" a "classe operaia* [The workerism of the 1960s: from *Quaderni Rossi* to *Classe Operaia*]. Rome: DeriveApprodi, 2008.

Milanesi, Franco. *Nel Novecento: storia, teoria, politica nel pensiero di Mario Tronti* [In the twentieth century: history, theory, politics in the thought of Mario Tronti]. Milan: Mimesis, 2014.

Mohandesi, Salar. "All Tomorrow's Parties: A Reply to Critics." *Viewpoint Magazine*, May 23, 2012. https://www.viewpointmag.com/2012/05/23/all-tomorrows-parties-a-reply-to-critics.

Mohandesi, Salar. "Class Consciousness or Class Composition?" *Science & Society* 77, no. 1 (January 2013): 72–97.

Mohandesi, Salar, and Emma Teitelman. "Without Reserves." In *Social Reproduction Theory: Remapping Class, Recentering Oppression*, edited by Tithi Bhattacharya, 37–67. London: Pluto, 2017.

Negri, Antonio. *Factory of Strategy: Thirty-Three Lessons on Lenin*. Translated by Arianna Bove. New York: Columbia University Press, 2014.

Negri, Antonio. *Marx Beyond Marx: Lessons on the Grundrisse*. Translated by Harry Cleaver, Michael Ryan, and Maurizio Viano. Edited by Jim Fleming. South Hadley, Mass.: Bergin & Garvey, 1984.

Negri, Antonio. "What to Do Today with *What is to Be Done?*, or Rather: The Body of the General Intellect." Translated by Graeme Thomson. In *Lenin Reloaded: Toward a Politics of Truth*, eds. Sebastian Budgen, Stathis Kouvelakis, and Slavoj Žižek, 297–307. Durham: Duke University Press, 2007.

"O partito unico o partito in fabbrica" [Either single party or party in the factory]. *classe operaia* 2, no. 3 (May 1965).

Palazzo, David P. "The 'Social Factory' in Postwar Italian Radical Thought from *Operaismo* to *Autonomia*." PhD diss., City University of New York Graduate Center, 2014.

Panzieri, Raniero. *La crisi del movimento operaio: Scritti interventi lettere, 1956-60* [The crisis of the workers' movement: Writings, interventions, letters, 1956–60]. Edited by Dario Lanzardo and Giovanni Pirelli. Milan: Lampugnani Nigri Editore, 1973.

Panizeri, Raniero. "Panzieri a Asor Rosa, 10 maggio 1962" [Raniero Panzieri to Alberto Asor Rosa, May 10, 1962]. In *L'operaismo degli anni sessanta: da "Quaderni rossi" a "classe operaia,"* edited by Fabio Milana and Giuseppe Trotta, 177–81. Rome: DeriveApprodi, 2008.

Panizeri, Raniero. "Separare le strade" [Separating the roads] [August 31, 1963]. In *L'operaismo degli anni sessanta: da "Quaderni rossi" a "classe operaia,"* edited by Fabio Milana and Giuseppe Trotta, 312–314. Rome: DeriveApprodi, 2008.

Panizeri, Raniero, and Mario Tronti. "Tesi Panzieri-Tronti." In "Raniero Panizeri e i 'Quaderni rossi,'" edited by Dario Lanzardo, 6–10. Special issue of *aut aut* 149–50 (September–December 1975).

Partito Comunista Italiano. *X Congresso del partito comunista italiano, Atti e risoluzioni* [10th Congress of the Italian Communist Party: acts and resolutions]. Rome: Editori Riuniti, 1963.

"Per la terza conferenza dei comunisti nelle fabbriche" [For the third conference of the Communists in the factories]. Special supplement to *classe operaia* 2, no. 2 (March–April 1965).

Pizzolato, Nicola. *Challenging Global Capitalism: Labor Migration, Radical Struggle, and Urban Change in Detroit and Turin.* New York: Palgrave Macmillan, 2013.

Pope Paul VI. "*Populorum Progressio*: Encyclical on the Development of Peoples." March 26, 1967. https://w2.vatican.va/content/paul-vi/en/encyclicals/documents/hf_p-vi_enc_26031967_populorum.html.

Poulantzas, Nicos. "Preliminaries to the Study of the State." Translated by Gregory Elliott. In *The Poulantzas Reader: Marxism, Law and the State*, edited by James Martin, 74–120. London: Verso, 2008.

Poulantzas, Nicos. "The Problem of the Capitalist State." In *The Poulantzas Reader: Marxism, Law and the State*, edited by James Martin, 172–85. London: Verso, 2008.

Poulantzas, Nicos. "Towards a Democratic Socialism." Translated by Patrick Camiller. In *The Poulantzas Reader: Marxism, Law and the State*, edited by James Martin, 361–75. London: Verso, 2008.

Quaderni rossi 1. Rome: Sapere, 1978 [October 1961].

Revelli, Marco. "Defeat at Fiat." Translated by Red Notes. *Capital & Class* 6, no. 1 (February 1982): 95–109.

Rieser, Vittorio. "Interview with Vittorio Rieser" [October 3, 2001]. Translated by generation-online. *generation-online*, October 2006. http://www.generation-online.org/t/vittorio.htm.

Rieser, Vittorio. "Sociologia e marxismo" [Sociology and Marxism]. In *L'operaismo degli anni sessanta: da "Quaderni rossi" a "classe operaia,"* edited by Fabio Milana and Giuseppe Trotta, 160–62. Rome: DeriveApprodi, 2008.

Roediger, David R., and Elizabeth D. Esch. *The Production of Difference: Race and the Management of Labor in U.S. History.* New York: Oxford University Press, 2014.

Roggero, Gigi. "Notes on framing and re-inventing co-research." *ephemera: theory & politics in organization* 14, no. 3 (2014): 515–23.

Sassoon, Donald. *Contemporary Italy: Economy, Society and Politics since 1945.* London: Routledge, 2013.

Sbardella, Raffaele. "The NEP of *Classe Operaia* (1980)." Translated by Daniel Spaulding. *Viewpoint Magazine*, January 28, 2016. https://www.viewpointmag.com/2016/01/28/the-nep-of-classe-operaia.

Sciascia, Leonardo. *The Moro Affair*. Translated by Sacha Rabinovitch. New York: New York Review of Books, 2004 [1978].

Sonnie, Amy, and James Tracy. *Hillbilly Nationalists, Urban Race Rebels, and Black Power: Community Organizing in Radical Times*. Brooklyn: Melville House, 2011.

Spesso, Ruggero. "Dinamica della conquista salariale prima e dopo la repubblica" [Dynamic of wage gains before and after the founding of the republic]. *Critica Marxista*, no. 5–6 (September–December 1966).

Sweezy, Paul. *The Theory of Capitalist Development: Principles of Marxian Political Economy*. London: Dennis Dobson, 1962 [1942].

Taylor, Christopher. "The Refusal of Work: From the Postemancipation Caribbean to Post-Fordist Empire." *small axe* 18, no. 2 (July 2014): 1–17.

Taylor, Keeanga-Yamahtta. "Five Years Later, Do Black Lives Matter?" *Jacobin*, September 30, 2019. https://www.jacobinmag.com/2019/09/black-lives-matter-laquan-mcdonald-mike-brown-eric-garner.

Thomas, Peter D. *The Gramscian Moment: Philosophy, Hegemony and Marxism*. Leiden: Brill, 2009.

Togliatti, Palmiro. "La voce di Gramsci in Parlamento" [The voice of Gramsci in Parliament]. Now in *La politica nel pensiero e nell'azione: Scritti e discorsi, 1917–1964* [Politics in thought and action: Writings and speeches, 1917–1964], edited by Michele Ciliberto and Giuseppe Vacca, 2759–73. Milan: Bompiani, 2014. iBooks digital edition.

Tronti, Mario. "1905 in Italy" [1964]. In *Workers and Capital*, translated by David Broder, 81–88. London: Verso, 2019.

Tronti, Mario. *Arbeiter und Kapital*. Translated by Karin Monte and Wolfgang Rieland. Frankfurt: Neue Kritik, 1974.

Tronti, Mario. "Autobiografia Filosofica" [Philosophical autobiography]. In *Dall'estremo possibile* [From the extreme possible], edited by Pasquale Serra, 234–42. Rome: Ediesse, 2011. https://www.centroriformastato.it/wp-content/uploads/autobiografia_filosofica.pdf.

Tronti, Mario. "Between Dialectical Materialism and Philosophy of Praxis: Gramsci and Labriola (1959)." In "The Young Mario Tronti," edited and translated by Andrew Anastasi. Dossier, *Viewpoint Magazine* (October 3, 2016). https://www.viewpointmag.com/2016/10/03/between-dialectical-materialism-and-philosophy-of-praxis-gramsci-and-labriola-1959.

Tronti, Mario. "Class and Party" [1964]. In *Workers and Capital*, translated by David Broder, 89–100. London: Verso, 2019.

Tronti, Mario. "Classe partito classe" [Class party class]. *Classe Operaia* 3, no. 3 (March 1967): 1 and 28.

Tronti, Mario. "A Course of Action" [1966]. In *Workers and Capital*, translated by David Broder, xv–xxxiv. London: Verso, 2019.

Tronti, Mario. "Estremismo e riformismo" [Extremism and reformism]. *Contropiano* 1, no. 1 (January–April 1968): 41–58.

Tronti, Mario. "Factory and Society" [1962]. In *Workers and Capital*, translated by David Broder, 12–35. London: Verso, 2019.

Tronti, Mario. "Internazionalismo vecchio e nuovo" [Internationalism old and new]. *Contropiano* 1, no. 3 (September–December 1968): 505–26.

Tronti, Mario. "Intervento al seminario di S. Severa, primavera 1962" [Opening speech at the Santa Severa seminar, Spring 1962]. In "Quattro inediti di Mario Tronti" [Four unpublished works of Mario Tronti], 14–17. Dossier, *Metropolis* 1, no. 2 (June 1978).

Tronti, Mario. "Intervista a Mario Tronti – 8 agosto 2000" [Interview with Mario Tronti – August 8, 2000]. In CD-ROM supplement to Guido Borio, Francesco Pozzi, and Gigi Roggero, *Futuro Anteriore: Dai "Quaderni Rossi" ai movimenti globali: richezze e limiti dell'operaismo italiano* [Future Perfect: From *Quaderni Rossi* to the global movements: the riches and limits of Italian workerism]. Rome: DeriveApprodi, 2002. https://www.autistici.org/operaismo/tronti/index_1.htm.

Tronti, Mario. "Lenin in England." In *Working Class Autonomy and the Crisis: Italian Marxist Texts of the Theory and Practice of a Class Movement: 1964–79*, 1–6. London: Red Notes, 1979.

Tronti, Mario. "Lenin in England." In *Autonomia: Post-Political Politics*, 28–34. Los Angeles: Semiotext(e), 2007.

Tronti, Mario. "Lenin in England" [1964]. In *Workers and Capital*, translated by David Broder, 65–72. London: Verso, 2019.

Tronti, Mario. "Mario Tronti" [Interview]. In *Gli operaisti: Autobiografie di cattivi maestri* [The workerists: Autobiographies of wicked teachers], edited by Guido Borio, Francesca Pozzi, and Gigi Roggero, 289–307. Rome: DeriveApprodi, 2005.

Tronti, Mario. "Mario Tronti" [Interview, Rome, January 12 and April 2, 1998]. In *L'operaismo degli anni sessanta: da "Quaderni rossi" a "classe operaia,"* edited by Fabio Milana and Giuseppe Trotta, 589–612. Rome: DeriveApprodi, 2008.

Tronti, Mario. "Marx, Labour-Power, Working Class" [1965]. In *Workers and Capital*, translated by David Broder, 103–276. London: Verso, 2019.

Tronti, Mario. "Noi operaisti" [We workerists]. In *L'operaismo degli anni sessanta: da "Quaderni rossi" a "classe operaia,"* edited by Fabio Milana and Giuseppe Trotta, 5–58. Rome: DeriveApprodi, 2008.

Tronti, Mario. "An Old Tactic for a New Strategy" [1964]. In *Workers and Capital*, translated by David Broder, 73–80. London: Verso, 2019.

Tronti, Mario. "On Marxism and Sociology (1959)." In "The Young Mario Tronti," edited and translated by Andrew Anastasi. Dossier, *Viewpoint Magazine* (October 3, 2016). https://www.viewpointmag.com/2016/10/03/on-marxism-and-sociology-1959.

Tronti, Mario. *Operai e capitale* [Workers and capital]. Turin: Einaudi Editore, 1966.

Tronti, Mario. *Operai e capitale*. 2nd edition. Turin: Einaudi Editore, 1971.

Tronti, Mario. *Operai e capitale*. Rome: DeriveApprodi, 2013.

Tronti, Mario. "Our *Operaismo*." Translated by Eleanor Chiari. In *Workers and Capital*, translated by David Broder, 327–48. London: Verso, 2019.

Tronti, Mario. *Ouvriers et capital*. Translated by Yann Moulier-Boutang and Giuseppe Bezza. Paris: Entremonde, 2016 [1977].

Tronti, Mario. "Il partito come problema" [The party as problem]. *Contropiano* 1, no. 2 (May–August 1968): 297–317.

Tronti, Mario. "The Plan of Capital" [1963]. In *Workers and Capital*, translated by David Broder, 36–64. London: Verso, 2019.

Tronti, Mario. "Postscript of Problems" [1970]. In *Workers and Capital*, translated by David Broder, 277–326. London: Verso, 2019.

Tronti, Mario. "Selections from *Workers and Capital*." Translated by Timothy Murphy. *Genre* 43, no. 3–4 (Fall–Winter 2010): 337–52.

Tronti, Mario. "Social Capital." *Telos* 17 (Fall 1973): 98–121.

Tronti, Mario. "Some Questions around Gramsci's Marxism (1958)." In "The Young Mario Tronti," edited and translated by Andrew Anastasi. Dossier, *Viewpoint Magazine*

(October 3, 2016). https://www.viewpointmag.com/2016/10/03/some-questions-around-gramscis-marxism-1958.

Tronti, Mario. "The Strategy of Refusal." In *Working Class Autonomy and the Crisis: Italian Marxist Texts of the Theory and Practice of a Class Movement: 1964–79*, 234–52. London: Red Notes, 1979.

Tronti, Mario. "The Struggle against Labor." *Radical America* 6, no. 3 (May–June 1972): 22–25.

Tronti, Mario. "Tronti a Gobbini, Roma 24 marzo 1964" [Mario Tronti to Mauro Gobbini, Rome, March 24, 1964], in *L'operaismo degli anni sessanta: da "Quaderni rossi" a "classe operaia,"* edited by Fabio Milana and Giuseppe Trotta, 367. Rome: DeriveApprodi, 2008.

Tronti, Mario. "Workers and Capital." *Telos*, no. 14 (Winter 1972): 25–62.

Tronti, Mario. *Workers and Capital*. Translated by David Broder. London: Verso, 2019.

Viewpoint Magazine. "The Border Crossing Us." *Viewpoint Magazine*, November 7, 2018. https://www.viewpointmag.com/2018/11/07/from-what-shore-does-socialism-arrive.

Weeks, Kathi. *The Problem with Work: Feminism, Marxism, Antiwork Politics, and Postwork Imaginaries*. Durham: Duke University Press, 2011.

Weinberg, Leonard. "The Red Brigades." In *Democracy and Counterterrorism: Lessons from the Past*, edited by Robert J. Art and Louise Richardson, 25–62. Washington, D.C.: United States Institute of Peace Press, 2007.

Williams, Evan Calder. "Invisible Organization: Reading Romano Alquati." *Viewpoint Magazine* 3 (September 2013). https://www.viewpointmag.com/2013/09/26/invisible-organization-reading-romano-alquati.

Woytinsky, Wladimir S. *Stormy Passage: A Personal History Through Two Russian Revolutions to Democracy and Freedom: 1905–1960*. New York: The Vanguard Press, 1961.

Woytinsky, Wladimir S. *Dalla rivoluzione russa all'economia rooseveltiana* [From the Russian Revolution to the Rooseveltian economy]. Translated by Elisabetta Rispoli. Milan: Il Saggiatore, 1966.

Wright, Steve. Foreword to *Workers and Capital*, by Mario Tronti, xii–xiv. Translated by David Broder. London: Verso, 2019.

Wright, Steve. *Storming Heaven: Class Composition and Struggle in Italian Autonomist Marxism*. 2nd edition. London: Pluto, 2017.

Wright, Steve. *The Weight of the Printed Word: Text, Context and Militancy in "Operaismo."* Unpublished draft manuscript, last modified December 21, 2018. PDF.

Index

of working class from traditional
organizations, see: self-organization
of working-class strategy, 21
political autonomy current within PSI, 24
self-management by workers of
revolutionary movement, 18, 36
sustained through organization, 73, 95
territorial autonomy, xiii
working class as autonomous political force,
viii, 10, 90

B

balance
balancing of social conflict, 96
balancing of workers' collaboration within
capitalist development, 14, 71, 73, 99
imbalance
organizing working class as imbalance,
19, 73
between working-class theoretical
awareness and reality of capital, 185
of payments, 186
of wages and productivity, 183–84
state planning to balance capitalist
development, 18, 36, 59, 71n6, 73, 99
Banca d'Italia [Bank of Italy], 24, 175, 175n1
bargaining (trade-union), ix, 15, 19, 23, 61, 71,
73, 73n9, 163, 183, 185, see also: articulation
Barro, Gianni, 49, 49n7
Belli, Giuseppe Gioachino (G.G.), 52, 52n1
Black Lives Matter, xn14
bloc
historical, 6n23, 70, 157
of employers/bosses, 70, 72
power, xiii, 96, 96n1, 97, 99, 179–80
ruling, 165–66n6
Boggs, Grace Lee, see: Lee, Grace
Boggs, James, viiin7, ixn11, 8n28
Bolsheviks (Bolshevism), 23n90, 37, 107, 110,
188n9
bourgeoisie, 21, 86, 88
Brunatto, Monica, 81, 81n6

C

cadre
editorial network of cadre tied to *Classe
Operaia*, 22, 25, 109, 114n10, 118–23
of the PCI, 25, 28, 79, 136, 151
of a new type, 25, 151
Capital (by Karl Marx), xvn30, 2, 4, 6, 8–12,

17, 50, 55–56, 64
capital
capitalist class, xiii, 5, 9, 19, 20, 28, 88–89,
129–131, 133–34
capitalist society, vii, xi–xii, xiv, 2–4, 8,
11–15, 18, 32, 39, 45, 56–57, 59, 65, 67, 71,
84–86, 89, 169, 177–79, 181–83
collective capitalist, 13–14, 56–59, 61, 71
"high" capitalism, 185
international capital, 40, 166, 175, 177,
182–84
large-scale capitalism, 181, 185
"low" capitalism, 185
social capital, xii, 10, 11, 14–15, 20, 72n7, 79
Carli, Guido, 175–76, 175n1, 176n2, 186
catastrophe, 12
catastrophic crisis, 20, 33, 52, 53, 177
catastrophism, xiii, 40, 51, 52, see also:
collapse, crash, crisis
center-left (governments, initiatives), 18, 23,
26, 28, 36, 62, 71, 71n4, 71n6, 72n7, 97, 98n3,
109, 130n5, 131, 159–60, 165n6, 166n7
Centro Francovich (Giovanni Francovich),
35–36, 39, 58n4, 159, 173
Centro Gobetti (Piero Gobetti), 80, 80n3
channel
channeling workers' struggles, xi, 19, 23,
29, 97
of communication between working class
and its organizational forms, 2, 28, 111–12,
132, 135–40
Chicago Teachers Union, ix
choice
made by the capitalists, of democracy, 40, 60,
143, 178–80
made by the party, 188
made by the working-class, of the wage,
177–78
the role of choice in capitalist planning, 60,
71, 143
Cicogna, Furio. 130, 130n5
circle, virtuous, 176, 176n2, 186
circular (publication), 148, see also: flyer
Classe Operaia [Working Class] (newspaper),
xiv, xivn27, xivn28, xvn30, 3n10, 8n28, 10,
14, 23–25, 28–31, 31n133, 34, 35, 35n154, 39,
39n172, 58n4, 83, 93n4, 101, 105, 106, 109,
109n2, 109n4, 114n10, 116, 117n11, 123n12,
127, 127n2, 132n6, 133n7, 142–44, 147, 149,
149n1, 153, 153n1, 159, 173, 174
newspaper as tool for unifying political
practice and theory, 25, 103, 122, 148
see also: cadre
Coldagelli, Umberto, 81, 81n7

collapse
economic collapse of capitalist system, xiii, 5, 7, 33, 33n141, 40, 52–53, 53n3
government collapse, 26
ideology of, 53
vertical collapse of organizations, 24, 106
Zusammenbruch, 33, 33n141
see also: catastrophe, crash, crisis
Colletti, Lucio, xvn30, 4n16, 6, 7n26, 17, 17n59, 45–50, 84n3, 153
Communist International (Comintern), 157n3
communism, xiii, 5, 30, 48n4
comportment, 129, 129n4, 135
composition
decomposition, viiin6, 5, 56
political, of the working class, ix, ixn8, ixn9, xii, 22–23, 39, 99, 112, 173
recomposition, xii, 23–24, 56, 72–73, 97–98, 102, 107
technical, of the working class, ixn8, viii, 13
theoretical, 60
Confederazione Generale Italiana del Lavoro (CGIL) [Italian General Confederation of Labor], 19, 140, 140n10, 141n11
Confederazione Italiana Sindacati Liberi (CISL) [Italian Confederation of Free Unions], 163–64, 163n3
Confindustria, 130n5, 176n3
conferences
factory conferences, 133, 133n7, 136
in which Tronti was involved, 6, 45, 109, 109n2, 121, 153, 159
confrontation (between classes), 27, 62, 72, 94, 96, 133–36, 148, 189
conjuncture, 26, 29, 33, 39, 128, 128n3, 129–31, 133–34, 143, 148, 154–55, 160–62, 175
consciousness
as subjective moment of working-class organization, 16, 27, 64, 155
class composition as alternative to class consciousness, ix, 9
representatives of capital's advanced, 20, 129, 180
Cooperation Jackson, xiii, xivn24
Copernican revolution (Tronti's work as) 1, 1n3, 5, 8, 30, 39, 83–94
Conservative Party (UK), 166, 166n8
corporation (trade-union form), 70–71, 70n3, 102
co-research, 66, 66n3
crash (economic), 7, 9, 128n3, see also: catastrophe, collapse, crisis
crisis

conjunctural, 128, 128n3, 149, 160, 177
cultural (intellectual), 65, 79
economic, of capitalism, 21, 26, 29–30, 33, 36, 40, 52, 60, 72, 90–91, 95, 128, 134–35, 148, 162, 181–84
of reformism, 97
of the capitalist state, 26, 28, 60, 62, 72, 95, 162
of the government, 27–28, 62, 95, 165, 165–66n6
of the PCI, 7, 24, 27, 30, 62, 78, 106, 138, 144–45, 181
political, 20, 23–24, 33, 60, 90, 95, 159
social democracy as solution to, 169
the great (Great Depression), 176–78, 180, 183
working-class struggles within, 129, 141
see also: catastrophe, collapse, crash
Cronache dei Quaderni Rossi [Chronicles of the Red Notebooks], 63, 79, 79n1
Cronache Operaie [Workers' Chronicles], 22, 79n1, 95, 101, 102n1

D

Dalla Costa, Mariarosa, viiin7, 3, 3n11
De Caro, Gaspare, 81, 81n7
De Lorenzo, Giovanni, 165–66n6
Della Volpe, Galvano, xvn30, 6, 6n20, 17, 17n59, 45, 45n1, 49n6, 84n3
De Meo, Giuseppe, 176, 176n3
Democratic Party (U.S.), xii–xiii
Democrazia Cristiana (DC) [Christian Democrats], 18, 20, 61n7, 96n1, 98n3, 131, 164, 165n6, 184n7
Department of Homeland Security (DHS), x
despotism
of the boss, 72
of the state, 96
determinate abstraction, 17, 49, 56, 66, see also: method
determinism
objectivist, 90
political, 36
dictatorship
of the Italian Communist Party, 29
of the proletariat, 65, 67
political dictatorship of capital, 15, 97
Di Leo, Rita, 53, 53n5
division (between class and organization), see: unity
Dunayevskaya, Raya, 8n28
duplicity (dual nature), xi, 25, 107, 137, 187

particular, of the workers, 182, 187–89
public, 130
workers, all born with the same, viii, 92
integration
  failure of, with regard to workers, 72, 73n8, 95
  of Italy into international capitalism, 36, 166, 169
  of struggles, xii, 14–16, 18, 20, 62, 95
  refusal of integration through political power, see: refusal
  seeming, of workers in postwar Italian development, 7, 182
  see also: corporative
International Women's Strike, x
Istituto Gramsci (Antonio), 45
Istituto Morandi (Rodolfo), 80, 80n2
Italian Marxism, 4–5

J

James, CLR, 8n28
James, Selma, viiin7, 3

K

Kennedy, John Fitzgerald, 71n4

L

labor-power, see: workers
Labour Party (UK), 3, 166n8
La Malfa, Ugo, 71, 71n6
Lanzardo, Liliana, 55
law
  law of value, 32
  laws of development of the working class, 21, 29, 86–87
legislation, 11–14
leadership, of the PCI, 28–29, 31, 38, 70n2, 105–07, 139, 151, 187–88
leaflet, 22, 109, 112
leap, 18, 21, 24, 36, 60–61, 70, 71, 72, 80, 83, 87, 89, 93, 102, 106, 114, 120, 161, 162, 165, 167, 170, 177, 183, 185
Lee, Grace, 8n28
Lenin, V.I., xiiin21, xiv, 3, 4, 6, 33, 37, 50, 94, 128n3, 187
Leninism, 2, 16, 17, 38, 59, 87, 94, 110, 137, 186
Lih, Lars T., 137n8
liquidation, xii, 116–17
Longo, Luigi, 30
Luxemburg, Rosa, 94

M

Machiavelli, Niccolò, 128n3
machinery, 2, 11–12
  state machine, 13, 40, 67, 173, 187
Marx, Karl, vii–viii, xivn28, xv, 1–4, 6, 8–14, 17, 27, 31, 32, 47, 49–50, 55, 56, 59, 84n3, 85–86, 93–94
  Marxism, xiv, 1, 4–6, 17, 33, 40, 41, 45–50, 65, 84n3, 185
massification
  of workers, 91
  of workers' struggles, 36, 161–62
materialism
  dialectical, 45–49
  historical, 45–49
  vulgar, 64
McDonnell, John, 3
maximalism, 53, 53n3, 114, 188
mediation
  between capitalists, 92, 186
  political, 13, 39–40, 95, 122, 174, 180–81
  theoretical, 81n5
methodology, 5, 11, 14, 17, 17n59, 21, 45, 49n6, 56, 64, 116–19, see also: determinate abstraction, science
Milan, 7, 21, 80, 80n2, 81, 81n4, 81n6, 83, 84, 84n2, 102, 102n1, 104, 109n2, 148, 184
militancy, ix–x, xvi, 2, 5, 23, 25, 29, 34–35, 41, 66n3, 70n2, 77, 101, 102n2, 109, 122, 159
Mirafiori (FIAT factory), 69, 161, 161n2
Moro, Aldo, 24, 26, 61, 61n7, 98n3, 165–66n6, 166n7, 182n6
Moten, Fred, 3

N

Naples, 98n3, 166,
Negri, Antonio, viiin3, 3, 22–24, 83, 98n2, 101–04, 129n4, 149, 159
neocapitalism, 14
New Left, 78
newspaper, see: *Classe Operaia*
nonprofit organizations, see: apparatus
Novella, Agostino, 141, 141n11

O

Oblomov, 52
objectivity, 33
October Revolution, see: revolution
Olivetti, 55
one-sidedness, 33, 56

T

tendency, 33–34, 48, 119, 160

theory, vii, xiv, 3, 5, 6, 8, 16, 17, 24, 25, 33–35, 37, 39, 48–50, 53, 59, 64, 66, 67, 78, 79, 90, 95, 107, 110, 180

thrust (of workers), 18–19, 29, 72, 134, 137–38, 154

Togliatto, Palmiro, viiin2, 26–27, 30, 48n4, 70n2, 96n1, 128n3, 157n2, 157n3, 187

transmission belt, 164, 164n4

Trontismo, viii, viiin2

Trump, Donald, xiii

Turin, 7, 17–19, 20n71, 27–28, 30, 58n4, 69–70, 77, 80, 80n3, 81, 84n2, 94, 98n2, 104, 111, 111n7, 127, 148, 161n2

U

Unione Cristiana Imprenditori Dirigenti (UCID) [Christian Union of Managers and Executives], 184, 184n7

Unione Italiana del Lavoro (UIL) [Italian Labor Union], 19, 98n2

United Kingdom (England, Great Britain), 3, 27, 78, 166

United States of America, viii, ixn8, xi, xiii–xiv, 3, 176, 188n9

unity

contradictory unity of strategy and tactics, 25, 31

living unity in person of the Marxist, 6, 29, 33, 34, 45, 50

party unity, 36, 157, 164–65

power bloc as unity, 96n1

trade-union unity, 36, 162–65

unity among militants, 78, 81, 109n4

unity-distinction between politics and theory, 24, 31, 107, 113–15

unity of capitalist production, 56, 59

unity of class and class organization (working class and party; capitalist class and state), 5, 15, 27–28, 31, 56, 59, 73, 98–99, 127, 130–31, 133–34, 157–58, 160, 167, 170

unity of political discourse and economic analysis, 58, 64

unity of the heterogeneous (as opposed to identity), 4, 31, 49–50

working-class unity as process of composition and decomposition, viii, ixn9, xiv, 4, 19, 22, 72–73, 92, 161–62, 167

V

Valletta, Vittorio, 18, 71, 71n4

vanguard, 30, 36, 145, 161,

Vegezzi, Augusto, 93, 93n4

Venice, 103, 149

Vietnam, 149

violence, 23, 24, 66, 70, 98, 102

vitality, of capitalism, 2, 40, 185

voluntarism, 91

W

wage

wage dynamic, 175, 179–183

wage explosion, 176

wage gains (growth), 18–19, 27, 40, 179

Weimar Republic, 94

welfare, ixn8, 70, 163, 186

Western Europe, 40, 179–80, 183–85

will, 27, 33, 96, 163

within and against, xi, xii, 3, 32, 37, 39, 41, 187–88

workers

collective worker, 10, 31, 55–58, 64–65, 79, 84

distinction between labor-power and working class, 33, 86

distinction between proletariat and working class, 88

workers' control, xii, 2, 18, 29, 30, 72, 139

workers in the plural, 10, 31, 91

workers' openness to struggle, 28, 132–39

working-class struggle as engine of capitalist development, 2, 8, 12, 35, 178, 180

Workers and Capital, vii, xiv, xivn28, xv, 1, 3, 5, 31, 37, 159, 173

working day, x, 8–14, 26

About the Author

Mario Tronti is a philosopher and politician. In the 1960s he was among the founders of *operaismo* (Italian "workerism"), a heterodox school of Marxist thought, and later he played a leading role in the Italian Communist Party. He has been a newspaper editor, university professor, president of the Centro per la Riforma dello Stato, and Senator of the Italian Republic. He is the author of *Workers and Capital* and many anthologized essays as well as other books in Italian.

About the Editor and Translator

Andrew Anastasi is a member of the *Viewpoint Magazine* editorial collective and a doctoral candidate in Sociology and Critical Theory at the Graduate Center, City University of New York. He is the translator of numerous works from Italian as well as the editor of *The Young Mario Tronti* (Viewpoint, 2016), a dossier on the early philosophical and political development of one of the founders of Italian *operaismo* (workerism). His doctoral research investigates relations between New Left movement organizations and the U.S. capitalist state during the 1960s and 1970s, focusing on the War on Poverty and its afterlives. Anastasi has worked in public high schools and colleges for the past decade and currently teaches courses in political sociology, social movements, and social theory at Queens College, City University of New York.

About Common Notions

Common Notions is a publishing house and programming platform that advances new formulations of liberation and living autonomy.

Our books provide timely reflections, clear critiques, and inspiring strategies that amplify movements for social justice.

By any media necessary, we seek to nourish the imagination and generalize common notions about the creation of other worlds beyond state and capital. Our publications trace a constellation of critical and visionary meditations on the organization of freedom. Inspired by various traditions of autonomism and liberation—in the U.S. and internationally, historically and emerging from contemporary movements—our publications provide resources for a collective reading of struggles past, present, and to come.

Become a Monthly Sustainer

These are decisive times, ripe with challenges and possibility, heartache and beautiful inspiration. More than ever, we are in need of timely reflections, clear critiques, and inspiring strategies that can help movements for social justice grow and transform society. Help us amplify those necessary words, deeds, and dreams that our liberation movements and our worlds so need.

Movements are sustained by people like you, whose fugitive words, deeds, and dreams bend against the world of domination and exploitation.

For collective imagination, dedicated practices of love and study, and organized acts of freedom.

By any media necessary.

With your love and support.

Monthly sustainers start at $5, $10, and $25.

At $10 monthly, we will mail you a copy of every new book hot off the press in heartfelt appreciation of your love and support.

At $25, we will mail you a copy of every new book hot off the press alongside special edition posters and 50% discounts on previous publications at our web store.

Join us at commonnotions.org/sustain.

More From Common Notions

Hope Against Hope:
Writings on Ecological Crisis
Out of the Woods Collective

978-1-942173-20-5
$20.00
272 pages

Climate disaster is here. Capitalism can't fix it, not even with a Green New Deal. Our only hope against hope is disaster communism.

We are told we are living in the middle of a climate crisis of unprecedented proportions. As doomsday scenarios mount, hope collapses. Even as more and more people around the planet experience climate disaster as immediate and urgent as ever, our imagination and programs for transformation lag. The disasters are already here, and the crises, longstanding, are ongoing.

In *Hope Against Hope*, the Out of the Woods collective investigates the critical relation between climate change and capitalism and calls for the expansion of our conceptual toolbox to organize within and against ecological crisis characterized by deepening inequality, rising far-right movements, and—relatedly—more frequent and devastating disasters. While much of environmentalist and leftist discourse in this political moment remain oriented toward horizons that repeat and renew racist, anti-migrant, nationalist, and capitalist assumptions, Out of the Woods charts a revolutionary course adequate to our times.

More From Common Notions

Organizing for Autonomy:
History, Theory, and Strategy
for Collective Liberation
CounterPower

978-1-942173-21-2
$20.00
208 pages

Organizing for Autonomy takes on the urgent task of critically clarifying and contextualizing a multitude of possibilities, spaces, and opportunities to resist capitalism, climate catastrophe, heteropatriarchy, white supremacy, workers' exploitation, and a range of other oppressive structures. Delineating the mechanisms of these violent institutions paired with a historical account of revolutionary movements from around the world, and ending with a radical reimagining of contemporary life, CounterPower offers a brazen and determined articulation of a world that centers community, love, and justice.

With unparalleled breadth and synthesizing innumerable sources of revolutionary thought and history into a single vision, *Organizing for Autonomy* is the result of years of struggle and resistance that acts as both an introduction to revolutionary theory and a practical prompt to the burning questions of how we get free. Bold, fearless, and radically original, *Organizing for Autonomy* imagines a decolonized, communist, alternative world order that is free from oppressive structures, state violence, and racial capitalism.

More From Common Notions

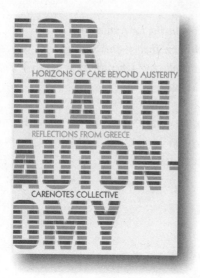

For Health Autonomy:
Horizons of Care Beyond Autonomy—
Reflections From Greece
CareNotes Collective

978-1-942173-14-4
$15.00
144 pages

The present way of life is a war against our bodies. Nearly everywhere, we are caught in a crumbling health system that furthers our misery and subordination to the structural violence of capital and a state that only intensifies our general precarity. Can we build the capacity and necessary infrastructure to heal ourselves and transform the societal conditions that continue to mentally and physically harm us?

Amidst the perpetual crises of capitalism is a careful resistance—organized by medical professionals and community members, students and workers, citizens and migrants. *For Health Autonomy: Horizons of Care Beyond Austerity—Reflections from Greece* explores the landscape of care spaces coordinated by autonomous collectives in Greece. These projects operate in fierce resistance to austerity, state violence and abandonment, and the neoliberal structure of the healthcare industry that are failing people.

For Health Autonomy is a powerful collection of first-hand accounts of those who join together to build new possibilities of care and develop concrete alternatives based on the collective ability of communities and care workers to replace our dependency on police and prisons.

More From Common Notions

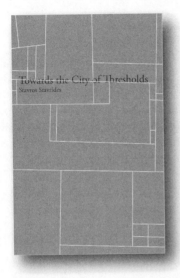

Towards the City of Thresholds
Stavros Stavrides

978-1-942173-09-0
$20.00
272 pages

In recent years, urban uprisings, insurrections, riots, and occupations have been an expression of the rage and desperation of our time. So too have they expressed the joy of reclaiming collective life and a different way of composing a common world. At the root of these rebellious moments lies thresholds—the spaces to be crossed from cities of domination and exploitation to a common world of liberation.

Towards the City of Thresholds is a pioneering and ingenious study of these new forms of socialization and uses of space—self-managed and communal—that passionately reveals cities as the sites of manifest social antagonism as well as spatialities of emancipation. Activist and architect Stavros Stavrides describes the powerful reinvention of politics and social relations stirring everywhere in our urban world and analyzes the theoretical underpinnings present in these metropolitan spaces and how they might be bridged to expand the commons.

What is the emancipatory potential of the city in a time of crisis? What thresholds must be crossed for us to realize this potential? To answer these questions, Stavrides draws penetrating insight from the critical philosophies of Walter Benjamin, Michel Foucault, and Henri Lefebvre—among others—to challenge the despotism of the political and urban crises of our times and reveal the heterotopias immanent within them.

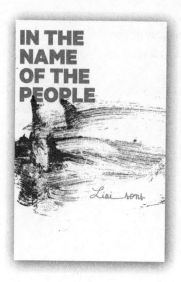

In the Name of the People
Liaisons

978-1-942173-07-6
$18.00
208 pages

In the Name of the People is an analysis and reflection on the global populist surge, written from the local forms it takes in the places we inhabit: the United States, Catalonia, France, Italy, Japan, Korea, Lebanon, Mexico, Quebec, Russia, and Ukraine. The upheaval and polarizations caused by populist policies around the world indicates above all the urgency to develop a series of planetary revolutionary interpretations, and to make the necessary connections in order to understand and act in the world.

The ghost of the People has returned to the world stage, claiming to be the only force capable of correcting or taking charge of the excesses of the time. The relationship between the collapse of certain orders, the multiplication of civil wars, and the incessant appeal to the People is clear: as the liberal mode of governance experiences a global legitimation crisis, different forms of right and left populism gain strength within the fractures of ever expanding ruins.

How do we distinguish the new from the old? What are their limits and potentials? What is the nature of the affective flows that characterize their relations? How do we address the indeterminacy inherent in mass movements and mobilizations, as well as their confusions, fears, and hesitancies?

Wages for Students | Sueldo para estudiantes | Des salaires pour les étudiants
George Caffentzis, Monty Neill, and John Willshire-Carrera (Introduction)
Jakob Jakobsen, María Berríos, and Malav Kanuga (editors)

978-1-942173-02-1
$13.95
224 pages

Wages for Students was published anonymously by three activists in the fall of 1975. It was written as "a pamphlet in the form of a blue book" by activists linked to the journal *Zerowork* during student strikes in Massachusetts and New York.

Deeply influenced by the Wages for Housework Campaign's analysis of capitalism, and relating to struggles such as Black Power, anticolonial resistance, and the antiwar movements, the authors fought against the role of universities as conceived by capital and its state. The pamphlet debates the strategies of the student movement at the time and denounces the regime of forced unpaid work imposed every day upon millions of students. Wages for Students was an affront to and a campaign against the neoliberalization of the university, at a time when this process was just beginning. Forty years later, the highly profitable business of education not only continues to exploit the unpaid labor of students, but now also makes them pay for it. Today, when the student debt situation has us all up to our necks, and when students around the world are refusing to continue this collaborationism, we again make this booklet available "for education against education."

More From Common Notions

Family, Welfare, and the State: Between Progressivism and the New Deal
Mariarosa Dalla Costa

978-1-942173-01-4
$15.95
128 pages

Over twenty years ago, President Clinton signed legislation to end "welfare as we know it." But did we ever really know it?

Mariarosa Dalla Costa's *Family, Welfare and the State* powerfully reminds us that the welfare system can only be understood through the dynamics of resistance and struggle, and women have been at the center of it. The attack on welfare was and is an attack on our class autonomy, structured to maintain a patriarchal and racist order, drive divisions and disrupt our ability to collectively refuse capital's exploitation and the state's discipline.

Dalla Costa reflects on the history of struggles around the New Deal in which workers' initiatives forced a new relationship with the state on the terrain of social reproduction. Were the New Deal and the institutions of the welfare state the saviors of the working class, or were they the destroyers of its self-reproducing capacity?

Family, Welfare and the State offers a comprehensive reading of the welfare system through the dynamics of women's resistance and class struggle, their willingness and reluctance to work inside and outside the home, and the relationship with the relief structures that women expressed in the United States during the Great Depression.